I GO WITH CUSTER

The Life and Death
of
Reporter MARK KELLOGG

By SANDY BARNARD

For Mal,
all my best, +
good reading!

Sandy Barnard
6/21/96

To
LEONARD F. KELLOGG,
who always believed in the
Mark Kellogg story.

THE BISMARCK TRIBUNE
707 E. Front Ave. • Bismarck, North Dakota 58504

Cover design and maps by STACE GOODING, THE BISMARCK TRIBUNE

Production and layout by LINAE WEIGEL AND GARY ARNTZ, THE BISMARCK TRIBUNE

Table of Contents

Acknowledgments

As a youngster in the 1950s, I probably became aware of Mark Kellogg in two ways: through the Walt Disney movie, "Tonka," and the novel by Loring MacKaye, *The Great Scoop*. Both offer highly fictionalized treatments of the Little Big Horn story, but each in its own way was fun to watch or read back then. However, I paid little attention to Kellogg until July 29, 1980, when I made my first visit to then-Custer Battlefield National Monument. On that hot summer day, my wife Betty and son Michael, then 4 years old, were little inclined to walk the battlefield with me. So at the battlefield's visitors center, I bought several books, including Robert Utley's, *Custer and the Great Controversy*, which featured a number of references to Kellogg and the role of newspapers in the campaign and its aftermath. As a journalism professor, I found the subject of Kellogg intriguing enough to begin researching his life.

Many people have contributed to whatever success I have enjoyed. First, Bob Utley pointed me toward the late John M. Carroll, who, in turn, referred me to the late Leonard F. Kellogg. Leonard turned out to be not only my most significant source of "Kelloggiana" but also a great friend. During my time researching Kellogg's life, a number of people at Custer Battlefield National Monument, now Little Bighorn Battlefield National Monument, have been helpful. Several people stand out among the many friends I have made at the battlefield over the years. Through the kindness of former Supt. Jim Court, I spent several weeks on two occasions living at the battlefield while working in a media advisory role for the National Park Service. That afforded me many opportunities for research in the archives and on the field itself. Jim's successors, including current Supt. Gerard Baker, have been equally kind. Two former chief historians, Neil Mangum and Doug McChristian, patiently answered my questions, offered their interpretations and provided me with access to the collections.

A number of permanent and seasonal rangers also have helped me. They include Dan Martinez, Doug Keller, John Doerner, Michael Moore and Michael Donahue. Battlefield Archivist Kitty Belle Deernose and her predecessor Mark Nelson never complained, no matter how many times I asked for yet one more file or photo. In addition, archeologists Douglas Scott of the National Park Service and Richard Fox of the University of South Dakota provided great assistance in interpreting historical events, both while I worked with them during the formal projects at the battlefield in the 1980s and more informally since then.

A number of other private researchers provided substantial assistance and advice across the years. They included Brian Pohanka, C. Lee Noyes, William Huntzicker of the University of Minnesota, Ron Nichols and James Brust. Ed Hill of the Area Research Center at the University of Wisconsin at La Crosse offered superb help countless times with information about Kellogg's years in that area. Numerous other research centers and libraries also aided my search for information about Kellogg. Foremost among these would be the La Crosse, Wis., Public Library, the Council Bluffs, Iowa, Public Library, the Wisconsin Historical Society, the Minnesota Historical Society, the State Historical Society of North Dakota, the Montana Historical Society and the University of Wyoming American Heritage Center. Closer to home, the reference and interlibrary loan departments of the Vigo County Public Library, Terre Haute, Ind., and the Indiana State University Cunningham Library frequently obtained microfilm and other research materials for me. The Indiana State University Faculty Research Committee twice provided me with grants to support my Kellogg research. Dan P. Millar, former chairman of the Department of Communication, offered considerable encouragement to pursue and publish my research. My journalism colleagues in the department, Mike Buchholz and Dave Bennett, have patiently listened to my tales of Custer and Kellogg over the years and offered writing and research hints. My other journalism colleague, Paul Hightower, has processed and printed countless rolls of film of the various sites I visited associated with Kellogg's and Custer's lives.

Over the years, many other people, whose names I lack the space to mention here, contributed in small but significant ways by providing clippings, tips or advice. For their help, I am grateful. A special mention must go to Joe Sills, who never failed to ask me, "How is Kellogg coming?"

SANDY BARNARD

Finally, projects like this are impossible to complete without the understanding and support of my best friend, my wife Betty. She willingly listens to my thoughts, understands my need to travel to faraway places to gather information, and often accompanies me in searching out information. No man could be more lucky. Likewise, my son Michael deserves special thanks for asking me the best question I heard during all my time researching Kellogg. In 1987, while accompanying me to the battlefield, he asked, "Dad, are we really going to spend seven days here?"

Preface

Lt. Col. George A. Custer, dressed in a blue shirt and a fringed buckskin jacket, turns to his assembled staff officers and company commanders of the 7th U.S. Cavalry. Gesturing with his right hand toward a small man wearing a dark tan civilian jacket and a gray vest seated at the rear of the headquarters tent, Custer says, "Mark Kellogg, Gentlemen, newspaperman from Bismarck. He's here for a story, and I think we can give him one."

Kellogg raises his right hand and with his open fingers touches the brim of his gray hat in a wordless salute.

The scene is from the 1958 Walt Disney film, "Tonka," one of the many movies that have featured the story of Custer's last battle against the Sioux and Northern Cheyenne on June 25, 1876, as an essential plot element. The film focuses on an Indian boy, played by Sal Mineo, and his love for a horse he calls Tonka; the animal ends up as Comanche, the mount ridden by cavalry Capt. Myles Keogh at the Battle of Little Big Horn.

Other Custer/Little Big Horn films may have had reporters appearing as characters, but "Tonka" is the only one to present a character by the name of Mark Kellogg, an actual reporter for the *Bismarck (Dakota Territory) Tribune*. The movie features a second reference to Kellogg, the only accredited journalist accompanying the 7th Cavalry. Custer, played by actor Britt Lomond, is about to order his command to chase an Indian war party near the Little Big Horn River. He turns again to Kellogg and tells the reporter, "You'll get a story today, Mr. Kellogg. You'll write history."

Kellogg responds with another wave and open-fingered touch of his hat brim. The actor, who went unnamed in the movie's credits, purses his lips, a non-verbal gesture suggesting Kellogg was uncertain that he would write history that day. The real Kellogg, in his last dispatch to his editor, Col. Clement A. Lounsberry, had written: "We leave the Rosebud tomor row, and by the time this reaches you we will have met and fought the red devils, with what result remains to be seen. I go with Custer and will be at the death."[1] An experienced newsman, he never wrote words more true. Army relief parties found his body on the main field of battle with Custer and the other 208 soldier casualties. As a result, he never wrote his story of Custer's clash with the Plains Indians that day.

Kellogg's untimely death deprived him of his greatest news story and his last opportunity to realize significant success in his otherwise modest life. Instead, Kellogg, 43 at his death, slipped into obscurity, a footnote in the Custer story. If so, why focus on Kellogg as the subject of this book? His life interests us for three reasons:

• For any number of reasons, the 1876 battle in which Custer died and which gave the Indians a final moment of glory intrigues many people even today. Given the scope of the fighting and its relatively small number of participants, it's easy to focus on the life of a single individual, white or Indian, and to speculate about that person's actions during the battle. A civilian, Kellogg participated in the battle and paid with his life.

• In the aftermath of the battle, Kellogg's friends failed to assure that his sacrifice of life would receive proper recognition from history. Instead, later researchers came to misread the Kellogg persona. If the facts of his life weren't readily known to them, they concluded it had to be because of some flaw in the "mysterious" Kellogg himself. However, Kellogg was far from mysterious.

• Historian Oliver Knight criticized Kellogg's journalistic coverage of the 1876 military campaign, suggesting his "stories had a trained-seal quality" because of his favorable coverage of Custer himself.[2] In assessing Kellogg's career, Knight and other researchers focused too narrowly on his Little Big Horn role. They too often overlooked Kellogg's significant body of work for the *St. Paul Pioneer* and other newspapers that marks him as an outstanding example of the frontier reporter. As historian Oliver Gramling suggested, Kellogg was "one of news gathering's first part-time, or 'string,' correspondents."[3] If anything, Kellogg's campaign writings may well capture a more authentic Custer as seen by people of his era than many today are willing to accept.

After a visit to then-Custer Battlefield National Monument in July 1980, I found myself intrigued by reporter Kellogg and wanted to learn more. My initial review of the voluminous body of Little Big Horn literature failed to satisfy my curiosity. Inevitably, Kellogg received brief mention

SANDY BARNARD

as the correspondent who substituted for his editor Lounsberry, only to be killed during the battle. Few details about his life were provided. I set out to discover Kellogg, and through the assistance of historian Robert M. Utley and the late Custer researcher John M. Carroll, I made the acquaintance of Leonard F. Kellogg, a retired forestry professor at Iowa State University at Ames and a collateral descendant of the reporter. For some 15 years, he had ferreted out genealogical details of Kellogg's life. At first, Leonard offered just tantalizing clues as he expected me to develop my own image of Mark Kellogg. Gradually, as my research proved more enlightening, our relationship changed to co-partners in a quest to unravel the mysteries of Mark Kellogg. For nearly 10 years, we exchanged letters, and numerous times I visited him at his home, where we engaged in endless hours of chatting about Kellogg, Custer and the Little Big Horn. Sadly, Leonard died at age 90 in 1990.

In our sessions, Leonard and I rehashed the efforts of previous researchers. All of them seemed to latch onto an image of Kellogg as "mysterious." For example, after a lengthy, but less than exhaustive inquiry into Kellogg's background, John Hixon felt compelled to label him as "Custer's 'Mysterious' Mr. Kellogg" in a 1950 article.[4] For a 1960 article, "The Mark H. Kellogg Story," J.W. Vaughn conducted a more extensive inquiry into the facts of Kellogg's life, only to conclude, "There is still some mystery surrounding" the man and his family.[5] Finally, in 1978, historian Lewis O. Saum wrote an excellent article, "Colonel Custer's Copperhead: The Mysterious Mark Kellogg," that summarized Kellogg's likely Copperhead political tendencies during the Civil War years and immediately after.[6]

Over the years, countless other newspaper and magazine writers have relied on other negative adjectives, such as "bitter" or "ineffectual," to describe a man who wrote for at least five newspapers in Wisconsin, Iowa, Minnesota and North Dakota. At his death in 1876, Kellogg also was claimed as a correspondent by such major papers as the *New York Herald* and *St. Paul Pioneer*. A much more positive image of Kellogg emerges from a study of his pre-Little Big Horn writings, including a series of letters that appeared principally in the *St. Paul Pioneer* between 1871 and 1876 under the *nom de plume* "Frontier." In addition, review of newspapers and other historical sources in the places where Kellogg lived has disclosed substantial information about the no longer, quite so mysterious Mr. Kellogg. Instead of the bitter, ineffectual, aloof, perhaps even angry, figure that Hixon, Vaughn and Saum found, Kellogg actually comes forth as a cheery, friendly, neighborly, honest and upbeat guy. He was well-liked, held strong standards of personal conduct and immersed himself in the social and political life of his community wherever he lived for extended periods. In his political and business ventures, it is true he usually fell short of success. Indeed, at the moment of his greatest opportunity in journalism — reporting Custer's encounter with the Indians on the Little Big Horn — Kellogg found not success, but death. Instead of lasting renown, he gained historical obscurity.

In La Crosse, Wis., his home between 1851 and 1867, he initially ran the town's telegraphy office and then launched his journalism career on the *La Crosse Daily Democrat*. At another point, he ran a feed and grain store, joined the Masons, led, perhaps heroically, the volunteer fire company, and even played shortstop on a town baseball team. Under the pen name of "Jentleman Jerks," he wrote with humor about his experiences. Alas, his baseball team was routed in its big game, his store burned and he was defeated in an election bid for city clerk.

According to the *Brainerd, Minn., Tribune* — published in the town where he lived in the early 1870s — he was called on to write the constitution and bylaws for both the city's new fire department and militia company, and he edited a newspaper, the *Brainerd Daily Greeley Wave*, in the fall of 1872.[7] The *Brainerd Daily Dispatch* listed him as a charter member of the community's Masonic lodge in 1872.[8] However, depressing economic conditions forced him from the town. His newspaper's candidate for president, Horace Greeley, was routed by incumbent Ulysses S. Grant, and Kellogg himself was defeated in another election, this time for state representative. Just before he left town in the spring of 1873, the Masonic fraternity expelled him for reasons that remain unclear.

Kellogg performed admirably as the string correspondent "Frontier," writing often lengthy, information-packed news letters. Between 1871 and 1876, he wrote at least 51 columns under that pen name: two from Duluth, Minn., four from Aitkin, Minn., 20 from Brainerd and 25 from Bismarck. A brief editorial page mention published by the St. Paul paper shortly after Kellogg's death confirmed his identity:

"Mr. Mark H. Kellogg, reported among the killed of General Custer's command, was a former correspondent of this paper, writing under the *nom de plume* of 'Frontier.' He was an army correspondent in the war for the Union, and subsequently an editor in La Crosse, and for some time telegraphic operator during the construction of the Northern Pacific, fol lowing the line as it progressed from Duluth to Bismarck. He was a bold, adventurous spirit, and greatly fascinated with frontier life."[9]

From the note, some writers have concluded Kellogg served in the army, but he was neither a soldier nor a war correspondent during the Civil War. Anything but a mystery man in life, Mark Kellogg draws our attention through the tragedy of his untimely death in an event at a place that still fascinates many people. Among the white victims who unsuccessfully challenged the Indians during the two-day battle, his body was probably the last to be found. Two days after the fighting ended at Custer Ridge, troops under Brig. Gen. Alfred H. Terry and Col. John Gibbon relieved the 7th Cavalry's survivors under Maj. Marcus A. Reno and Capt. Frederick W. Benteen, who had fought four miles away on another set of bluffs. A few days later, as Gibbon made his way from the valley floor toward the site where Custer himself had fallen, he came across the dead correspondent. Fortunately for Kellogg's identification and for history, he was still clothed, an unusual circumstance among the dead whites at the Little Big Horn.

In the substantial literature about the Little Big Horn battle, the death of the reporter has been relegated to secondary consideration and even the actual site of his killing remains an historical puzzle.[10] In 1942, the *New York Herald* and the *Bismarck Tribune* paid for a new marker for Kellogg at the traditional site of his "grave" on the east side of battle ridge. A few hundred yards from Custer Hill, it replaced a stone memorial raised for the reporter in 1896, but today few believe it represents Kellogg's actual death or burial site. Instead, his death almost certainly occurred three quarters of a mile to the west on the flats close to the river, as traditional accounts, such as Gibbon's, suggest.

In the last decade, a new group of researchers has gone beyond traditional accounts of the battle. They have reinterpreted the clash of cultures on the Little Big Horn in light of archeological findings at the battlefield in the 1980s as well as their close study of long-neglected Indian accounts. Through their work, new insights have been gained into the flow of combat on June 25-26, 1876. Now historians and battle buffs alike can theorize more thoughtfully about Kellogg's role in the Little Big Horn fight and what his death may reveal about the disaster that overtook Custer's column late on the afternoon of June 25. Based on the considerable research into his life as reported in this book, 120 years after his death Mark H. Kellogg no longer needs to be classified as the mystery man of the Little Big Horn or of frontier journalism.

Prologue

Sometime before midnight of July 5, 1876, Indiana native John Piatt Dunn heard a voice through the open screen door of his rough home in Bismarck, Dakota Territory. "Doc," it called several times.

"The next words I heard were, 'Custer and his whole command has been massacred, to a man!' I was stunned, for a moment, absolutely," recalled Dunn, the town's first druggist and an early political leader. "It seemed incredible."[11]

That night the steamer *Far West* had returned to the young pioneer settlement on the Missouri River with its sorrowful news about the June 25-26 Battle of the Little Big Horn. "It was a moonlight [sic] night, a fall harvest moon, and very warm," Dunn remembered.

Venturing outside his home, Dunn found Bismarck's streets filled. "The excitement was intense and the gloom and grief when the news was confirmed, and when the wounded and attendants were brought off the boat, cannot be understood now — one must have been here to realize the feeling which existed," Dunn said.[12]

Custer's battle with the Plains Indians occurred on ridges above the Little Big Horn River in southeastern Montana Territory, about 400 miles west of Bismarck, which in 1889 would become the capital of the new state of North Dakota. But in 1876 the town stood at the edge of the frontier, only four years after its founding when the Northern Pacific Railroad extended its tracks to the Missouri River Crossing. It was small enough that many of its citizens knew one another well. Many also knew Custer, a Civil War hero, and they were familiar with his 7th U.S. Cavalry, stationed across the Missouri at Fort Abraham Lincoln.

The year 1876 was important for the United States, a young country whose leadership role on the world stage remained ill-defined. The early July observance of its Centennial amounted to a gala birthday celebration as it sought to put the disaster of the Civil War of the previous decade behind it. The war had devastated the country's sense of purpose. Now, with the unpopular post-war Reconstruction era nearing a close, the de feated Southern states would soon be granted full rights of participation in the country's life once again.

As a whole, the United States had high expectation for future prosperity in the regions still officially classified as territories. This was especially true on the Northern Plains, where discovery of gold in 1874 in the Black Hills had whetted the hopes of the nation's business interests for new riches. In Dakota Territory, expansionist-oriented boomers, such as newspaper publisher-editor Lounsberry of the *Bismarck Tribune*, strongly urged the federal government to open the Black Hills to white settlement and development. But in Washington, D.C., officials fretted. The 1868 Treaty of Fort Laramie had promised the Sioux and Northern Cheyenne they could continue their traditional nomadic ways in a huge arena. It encompassed about 120,000 square miles, covering much of present-day east-central Wyoming, southeastern Montana, northeastern Nebraska and western South Dakota. The Indians were little inclined to follow the solution the bureaucrats favored: Surrender their rights, move onto the Great Sioux Reservation in western Dakota Territory, adopt the living style of the dominant white culture and live peacefully there.

Undoubtedly, some government officials found themselves anchored in the midst of a moral dilemma — how to continue to recognize the Indians' treaty rights amid the increasingly shrill calls of miners, ranchers, hunters and railroads that urged expansion, no matter what the cost to another of the country's minority groups. But by late fall of 1875, decisions had been framed that would profoundly influence the country's future, yet at a frightful cost in lives. Pressure from the many whites who shared Lounsberry's expansionist views to open the Black Hills had had a telling effect on Washington, where officials were ready to acquiesce to their wishes. The crucial question: how best to force the Sioux and Northern Cheyenne to surrender their treaty-guaranteed lands?[13] Wresting the north country from the Indians would be difficult. It likely would require dispatching the Army against recalcitrant bands, including those under Sitting Bull, who roamed in the unceded area in Montana and Wyoming territories.

Sensitive to public perception of their decision, officials at least attempted to make the military campaign appear to reflect a civilian request to round up "hostile" Indians who had refused to obey a government directive to move onto the reservations. Early in December, runners were dispatched to the Indians, already in far-flung winter camps, ordering their return to the reservations by Jan. 31, 1876. If the Indians failed to comply, the Army would enforce the directive.

2   SANDY BARNARD

The wintering Indians paid little heed to the deadline. On Feb. 1, 1876, the Interior Department passed the enforcement responsibility to the War Department and the Army began preparing for campaigning. Experienced in directing military operations on the plains, Lt. Gen. Philip Sheridan, who commanded the Army's Division of the Missouri, wanted his soldiers to hit the Indian camps while winter still immobilized their residents. In the spring, the Indians would regain their mobility and put more cumbersome Army columns at a disadvantage. Sheridan immediately ordered Brig. Gen. George Crook to lead a column from Fort Fetterman, Wyoming Territory, to attack Indians in winter camps along the Powder River, but he enjoyed little success. On March 17, Crook's subordinate, Col. Joseph J. Reynolds, failed to sustain an attack against a Cheyenne village and was repulsed. Crook's overall command was forced to retreat, leaving the winter campaign, such as it had been, a failure. Moreover, the attack alerted the Indians to the Army's aggressive nature and assured that war, not peace, would arrive with spring.

For the spring renewal of his campaign, Sheridan ordered three converging columns into the field. One column under Crook would travel north again from Fort Fetterman. Col. John Gibbon's column, comprised of infantry and cavalry from Fort Shaw and Fort Ellis in western Montana Territory, would move east. The third column, marching from Fort Lincoln in Dakota Territory under Brig. Gen. Alfred H. Terry, would include all 12 companies of Custer's regiment, the 7th U.S. Cavalry, the first time since the Civil War that a unit of that size had campaigned together.[14]

By late September, the summer-long military effort limped to a close. For its part, the Army had suffered stunning rebukes in Montana Territory. On June 17, the Sioux and Cheyenne had done the completely unexpected, riding far from their villages to ambush Crook's well-armed column. Having bloodied him, they again compelled his retreat into Wyoming Territory. Their success against Crook emboldened them for other clashes and Custer appeared the next week. In defeating Custer, the Indians had decimated fully 40 percent of one of the Army's prized regiments. Despite its lack of success on the battlefield, the Army's effort pushed the Indians closer to accepting reality: Their nomadic ways were at an end. Many Indians took up permanent residence on the reservations that summer and fall. Those who remained in the field would soon be forced to the reservations by other Army units. Sitting Bull and a small group of followers went to Canada where they remained until 1881.

Since March 1876, Lounsberry had promised *Bismarck Tribune* readers they would read all the news of the military campaign first in his newspaper. In July, he delivered on that promise but in a way none of his readers or he could ever have imagined. On July 6, 1876, he published a "Tribune Extra," a special edition of his weekly newspaper that provided the first extensive report of the Indians' defeat of Custer's troops and the death of Lounsberry's reporter Kellogg.

That fall, when the remnants of Custer's 7th Cavalry reached Bismarck and Fort Lincoln, the *Tribune* reported its arrival at length. Lounsberry took special pride in noting General Terry's "handsome tribute" to his dead reporter:

"The General says he was peculiarly adapted to his work and gained the affections and esteem of all with whom he came in contact. Being a man well informed and practical, he always comprehended the situation while his social qualities were such as to commend him to everybody. He was candid and straightforward under all circumstances and therefore to be relied upon. The General says he solicited Kellogg to go with him rather than with Custer, on the March to the Little Horn, but he was so thorough a newspaper man, and so familiar with Custer that he knew there would be, as he expressed it, 'a fight or a foot race,' and he desired to be there, but he sleeps with the slain, filling like Custer and his men, a hero's grave."[15]

Not surprisingly, Custer's defeat stunned people in Bismarck and across the nation in the midst of its Centennial celebration. Among the dead buried hurriedly on the Montana battlefield was Dunn's close friend, newspaperman Kellogg, an itinerant string correspondent greatly enamored of frontier life. After his death, Kellogg's black satchel was brought back to Bismarck on the steamer *Far West* and given to Dunn. Along with his personal effects, it contained his campaign diary, written in pencil on loose sheets of paper and providing notes of six weeks on the trail with Custer to the Little Big Horn. Dunn's next actions led to what remains one of the more puzzling aspects of the story of Mark Kellogg. The druggist claimed he was unable to locate any survivors of his friend.[16] Although he was asked to return Kellogg's belongings, he kept the satchel, its contents and the diary. Supporting Dunn in this surprising claim was Lounsberry, born March 27, 1843, in Wilmington Township, DeKalb County, Ind. If Dunn and Lounsberry had done more to preserve the memory of their friend, Kellogg's sacrifice of his life while working as a journalist might be better appreciated today. Yet Kellogg had two daughters, just approaching their teen years, who had lived with their grandparents for many years in La Crosse, Wis. Kellogg's wife, Martha, had died in 1867. Unlike Dunn and Lounsberry, Bismarck telegrapher John M. Carnahan knew where the girls were. After he had transmitted the news of Custer's defeat to the world on July 6, he sent a wire to La Crosse, notifying the Kellogg girls of their father's death.

SANDY BARNARD

Chapter 1
Tracing the Kelloggs

Tracing the Kellogg family prior to its arrival in 1851 in the pioneer town of La Crosse, Wis., is not easy. What is known about the family's genealogy rests almost solely on the impressive 1903 work of Timothy Hopkins, *The Kelloggs in the Old World and the New.*[17] Even J.W. Vaughn's 1960 article, "The Mark H. Kellogg Story," relied heavily on Hopkins.[18] Prior to 1851, the Kellogg family simply wasn't prominent enough to have its activities recorded in local histories issued in a succession of small American and Canadian towns where, according to Hopkins, they had lived. Few of the towns had newspapers. Even though Mark Kellogg's father, Simeon, was active in those communities, at least as a hotel operator, his business and other doings went unrecorded. Also, no family records, letters or diaries that might reveal more about those years are known to exist.

Mark Kellogg was born March 31, 1833, and was named Marcus Henry by his parents, Simeon and Lorenda Kellogg. The family was living in Brighton, Canada, a resort town on Lake Ontario's north shore. The elder Kelloggs were native New Englanders, and so, at birth Mark Kellogg was an American citizen. Some later census records list either him or his parents as Canadians. Technically, he was Canadian by birth, but no evidence indicates he ever thought much about his dual citizenship.

Not much is known about the line of Kellogg's mother. Lorenda was born Jan. 13, 1806, in Manchester, Vt., the daughter of Philip Whelpley and Almira Eaton. Philip was still in his teens, having been born in Manchester in 1790. Almira, born in Windham, Vt., in 1784, apparently was six years older than her young husband. Neither Hopkins nor Vaughn traced Lorenda's parents beyond the fact of her birth.

Vaughn notes the Kellogg family's line can be traced to Phillippe Kellogg of Great Leighs and Braintree, England, in 1585. Vaughn also states, "The family had a long history of military service."[19] Simeon was born Feb. 28, 1800, in Brookfield, Vt.[20] Simeon's father, Enos (1761-?), served in the American Revolution and Hopkins reported that Enos witnessed the execution of Major John André, the British army officer hanged as a spy in the American Revolution for conspiring with Benedict Arnold.[21]

Hopkins records that Kellogg's parents were married Jan. 5, 1829, in Kingston, Ontario. The couple eventually had 10 children, but not all lived to adulthood. Their first child, Alson Whelpley, was born Oct. 15, 1829, in Belleville, Canada, but died April 17, 1833. The second child was Almira Ann, who was born Jan. 12, 1831, in Brighton, Canada. Mark followed her on March 31, 1833, in Brighton. Number four — and the third to be born in Brighton — was Mary Eliza on March 15, 1835.

According to the family's birth records, Simeon soon moved the family to Toronto, where the fifth child, Phebe Helen, was born April 11, 1837. However, she died six years later, April 10, 1843. Number 6, Coralinn Maria, was born on March 9, 1839, in Watertown, N.Y. Mark possibly may have had a special relationship with Coralinn, as he would name his older daughter Cora Sue, perhaps after her. The seventh child, Lorenda Dorcas, was born April 26, 1841, in Watertown, N.Y., but died two years later, May 20, 1843, in Syracuse, N.Y. That she died just about a month after her sister Phebe suggests some epidemic claimed the youngsters. At some point the Kelloggs moved to Bowmainville, Canada, where Ecton, the eighth child, was born Feb. 20, 1844. The ninth, Helen Pamela, was born May 20, 1848, in Marengo, Ill., but died Jan. 21, 1850. Three months later, the 10th child, Ella May, was born, April 20, 1850, in Waukegan, Ill.

Vaughn concluded his review of Kellogg genealogy by noting, "Here [Waukegan] Simeon owned a hotel, while young Mark was learning the new occupation of telegraph operator in nearby Kenosha, Wis."[22] Not much is known about his telegraphy lessons. As for Simeon's hotel, the *Waukegan Weekly Gazette* of Oct. 19, 1850, carried a front page business card that stated simply:

EXCHANGE HOTEL,

By S. Kellogg, • Waukegan, Ill.

General Stage Office • Passengers taken to and from boats free[23]

The hotel was started in 1840 but no record reveals when it came into Simeon's hands.[24] Only three other references to the Kellogg family's stay in Waukegan are known, two of which appeared after Mark Kellogg's death. The 1850 census, which was taken Oct. 17, 1850, for Lake County, Ill., gave no address for the family or its hotel. The dwelling was listed as No. 426 and the family as No. 450. The hotel was listed as worth $600. Another point of significance: Seventeen-year-old Mark's occupation was given as "clerk." Here is how the family was listed:

NAME	AGE	SEX	OCCUPATION	BIRTHPLACE
Simeon	50	M	Landlord	Vt.
Lorinda(sic)	44	F	blank	Vt.
Almira A.	19	F	blank	Canada
Marcus H.	17	M	Clerk	Canada
Mary E.	15	F	blank	Canada
Carolinn M. [sic]	11	F	blank	N. Y.
Ecton	6	M	blank	Canada
Ella	1/2	F	blank	Ill.

Twenty-one other residents, 18 of them men, were recorded as living at the hotel. Their varied working class occupations included barkeeper, merchant, laborer, tailor, engineer and stage driver.

On July 8, 1876, the *Waukegan Weekly Gazette* added to its telegraph report of the Little Big Horn battle, noting that "Mark Kellogg, a correspondent of the *Bismarck Tribune* and the *New York Herald*, and formerly a Waukegan boy, accompanied the expedition and was killed. He was in citizen's dress and, strangely enough, his body escaped the mutilation accorded the dead soldiers."[25] Kellogg's boyhood in Waukegan can be glimpsed through the following unsigned personal item the local paper republished July 15, 1876, from the *Dubuque (Iowa) Times*:

"Mark Kellogg, the *New York Herald* correspondent who was slain in the Custer massacre, will be known to many who have had occasion to travel on the river. His father many years ago kept a hotel near the Landing at La Crosse where Mark made himself obliging and useful to the many guests that stopped with the old gentleman. The writer of this knew him many years ago in Waukegan, Ill., going to the same school when boys together. His first newspaper experience was with Brick Pomeroy when the *La Crosse Democrat* was at the zenith of its fame. Afterward he went to Brainerd, Minn., then to Bismarck, Dakota, and was one of the most companionable of men, overflowing with wit, good nature and kindly feeling — a pleasant fellow in every sense of the word. We hope he has a good place where he has gone for he was certainly fully deserving of it. The *New York Herald* says he was 46 years old. He was nearer 43, but still kept his youthful looks."[26]

When did Simeon relocate his family to La Crosse? Likely the move occurred between the mid-spring and mid-summer of 1851. All newspaper ads for his Waukegan hotel had ceased by May 24, 1851. Property records in La Crosse indicate he was there no later than July of that year.

SANDY BARNARD

Chapter 2
The La Crosse Years — 1851-1860

The Territory of Wisconsin had been created April 20, 1836, out of the old Northwest Territory. Rapid settlement followed as the population grew from about 22,000 to more than 250,000. On May 29, 1848, President James K. Polk signed legislation admitting Wisconsin as the nation's 30th state. But much of the state remained rugged and challenging for settlers. In western Wisconsin, northwest of Madison and on the prairie astride the Mississippi River, sat the settlement of La Crosse. It had been founded on a site used for centuries by traders and Indians, often referred to as Prairie La Crosse. Reportedly, the Winnebago Indians and earlier at the site the Sioux played a game familiar to the French as lacrosse.[27] The town's establishment dates to Nov. 9, 1841, when 18-year-old Nathan Myrick, an adventurous lad from Westport, N.Y., and his partner, Eban Weld, landed with goods to set up a trading post, first on an island in the river and then on the mainland itself. Others settled near his trading post and by 1843 Myrick had been named the settlement's postmaster.

More important for his influence on the lives of the Kellogg family was John M. Levy, who arrived in La Crosse in 1845 to begin his trading business. He built a story-and-a-half log cabin for his wife and himself on what later would become the northeast corner of Front and Pearl streets. The year the Kellogg family settled in La Crosse, 1851, apparently was crucial for the pioneer town, as it was the first that suggested it would survive its status as a frontier outpost and grow. According to the *History of La Crosse County, 1881*, "The list of residents known to have been here during the years 1851 compared with that of the beginning of 1854 showed conclusively that during the years 1852 and 1853 all went lovely, as the number of families rose from about half a dozen to about half a hundred, besides about 35 single men and women."[28]

Simeon Kellogg was named on that 1851 list, but Mark, who would have been only 17 or 18, was omitted. His father appeared to be a man of some prominence in the community. Lorenzo L. Lewis, the superintendent of schools, issued a notice in July calling for "every qualified voter" to attend the school district's first meeting. Time, date and place: Aug. 2, 1851, "at the house of Simeon Kellogg."[29] Meeting-goers at Simeon's place voted a tax of $75 to pay the teacher's wages and another $5 to procure books for the school's and district's records. The district clerk's annual report, dated Sept. 1, 1852, showed Simeon had been elected a director of the school district and he apparently was its chief officer. Two other officers were listed: S.T. Smith, treasurer, and John M. Levy, clerk. Levy's house was temporarily engaged for six months at the rate of $75 per year for the school, "Mr. Levy to furnish a stove." Later, residents voted a tax of $300 on personal property to build the schoolhouse.[30]

Simeon was active in other ways, being appointed postmaster July 28, 1851.[31] The *History of La Crosse County* also lists Simeon as opening in 1851 one of the town's first two hotels. His was the Western Enterprise, corner of Pearl and Front streets.[32] *A History of La Crosse* says John Levy sold his log house to Simeon Kellogg after he built a new structure on the next lot north. "Kellogg used the former house as a tavern under the name 'Western Enterprises'."[33] Some confusion does arise over Simeon's hotel. According to a study of his hotel business, *The Kellogg House*, Simeon actually managed the Western Enterprise, owned by John Levy at Front and Pearl streets. Later, he would own his own place at Second and Pearl streets.[34] On July 9, 1851, he reportedly bought several lots at Second and Pearl in the original part of the town from founder Nathan Myrick and others, but these apparently were not used immediately for business purposes. The study concluded Simeon managed the Western Enterprise, although the building was owned by Levy. Still, it came to be known as Kellogg's, and his son Mark assisted his father closely in its operation.

In the summer of 1853, "Simeon Kellogg completed a three-story building to the rear of the Western Enterprise Hotel, corner of Second and Pearl streets."[35] Another account reported: "…amongst the evidences of enterprise and prosperity the erection by Mr. S. Kellogg of the 'large fine looking three-story building on the corner of Pearl and Second streets,' and says 'it is a decided improvement to that part of town'."[36] Another description of the hotel noted the building's "steep gable roof and general form were colonial, with southern characteristics in the three-storied open porch across the front and the low first story, which was level with the street and served the purpose of the basement."[37] Vaughn described the Kellogg House as "a two-story building with a basement housing the office and bar."[38]

On the first Sunday of October 1851, the first Sabbath school in La Crosse was organized. "All the white children in the village attended," including Mary and Cora Kellogg. For Sunday school purposes, Mark apparently was too old to attend. The *La Crosse Chronicle* recalled the event in a story headlined "Baptist Anniversary," suggesting that at least Mark's sisters were Protestant churchgoers.[39]

Mark's later writings make clear that he always enjoyed hunting and a good party, which suggests he may not have shared his sisters' Baptist leanings. The *History of La Crosse County* says that on Christmas Day 1851, he attended a turkey shoot on the Mississippi River opposite the village, which was widely attended.[40] The turkey shoot was followed by a Christmas ball attended by Mark and his sisters. "In the evening occurred the first grand ball that varied pioneer life in the present city. It, too, was a state occasion and generally attended. Among those who were present to pirouette, chassez and dance the 'monnaie mask' were...Mary and Alvira (sic) Kellogg...Mark Kellogg...."[41] The music consisted of a violin and those attending "recall it as one of the happiest experiences of their days of frontier life...the dance was continued until midnight, when an intermission was indulged to afford the guests an opportunity to partake of refreshments furnished by the ladies of La Crosse and served by Simeon Kellogg, at that time landlord of the Western Enterprise Hotel, which had been vacated a short time previously by Mr. Levy to move into his house adjoining, when the dance was resumed and kept up until daylight."[42]

The year 1852 was no less eventful for the Kelloggs. Simeon continued as postmaster. The town's population grew to 700, but life remained hard, as 21 people, including 11 children, died. The town boasted five hotels, including Simeon's, although his was not the largest. That honor went to the new Tallmadge House at State and Third streets. "It was 64 feet by 30, four stories high, and was capable of accommodating 150."[43] Simeon was doing well, catering, as he had done in Waukegan, to visitors who arrived by water. "The Western Enterprise, an old favorite, kept by Simeon Kellogg, and the New England, opened the spring of 1853 by G.H. Wilson, both being on Front Street near the steamboat landing...travel was then brisk, every boat that arrived being crowded with Eastern and

Southern people seeking homes in the West, and considerable rivalry was produced between the hotels."[44]

Despite their early popularity, the three hotels were doomed. The Tallmadge House "after passing through a checkered experience...went up in smoke." The New England House burned in the fire of 1857. As noted, the Western Enterprise would evolve into the Kellogg House, only to be sold in 1863 by Simeon and renamed the Albion House. It too would burn — in 1870.[45] The *Kellogg House* study says the older Kellogg actually sold his hotel to Mons Anderson and Ole Hansen on Sept. 9, 1865.[46]

The year 1853 brought growth to the town, as a census of Dec. 31, 1853, showed a population of 745. Both of Mark's parents were listed, but at age 20 he was not. Only "single gentlemen of over 21" were included, along with "single ladies over 18." The latter included his sister Mary.[47] Postmaster Simeon Kellogg was then in the midst of his term of office. According to the *La Crosse Republican-Leader*, "The measure of our progress may be inferred from the official statements of postal business."[48] The newspaper noted receipts for the two years ending August 1852 amounted to $7.50. The first "eastern weekly mail made up by Simeon contained only eight letters. In July 1854, when he resigned, his last mail contained 887 letters."

In the mid-1850s, Masonic involvement played an important role in the life of the community, and Simeon and Mark were active Masons. Frontier Lodge No. 45 was granted a dispensation Oct. 8, 1852, and chartered the following June, although none of the Kelloggs signed the charter. However, Simeon served as lodge treasurer from 1855 until 1859. He also served as treasurer for Smith Chapter No. 13, R.A.M., from 1857 until 1861. In 1866, Mark was listed as a second-degree mason. His brother-in-law, J.W. Robinson, was a first-degree Mason at the time.

As active residents, the Kelloggs became involved in local politics. By 1856, the community had 3,000 residents and incorporation as a city became a reality that January. The charter divided the city into three wards, each the first year electing three alderman who held staggered terms of one, two and three years respectively. A mayor and city clerk were among the usual array of local political offices established. On March 14, 1856, the Democrats nominated John M. Levy as mayor. Apparently problems arose with the nominations because a second "Citizens' Nominations" slate was picked the next day. On that ticket for Second Ward assessor was Simeon Kellogg. The *History of La Crosse County* noted, "The campaign, though brief, was spirited and not altogether devoid of the features which characterize similar undertakings of the present day."[49] Among the defeated: Simeon Kellogg.

Sometime during the 1850s, Mark received training as a telegrapher, the new magical instrument of communication. Where he received his training remains unknown. Some accounts suggest he learned telegraphy at Kenosha, but no evidence confirms that. By 1859, he was working for the Wisconsin State Telegraph Co. as the town's second telegrapher.[50] In that role he became the town's first telegrapher to take wire service-like news dispatches for the La Crosse newspapers, thereby stepping into journalism as it was practiced in those days. His name also surfaced occasionally in the news pages. For example, on Oct. 24, 1859, the *La Crosse Daily Union* noted, "Mr. Kellogg, the gentlemanly operator, gives us the following which came by express."[51] Several news stories then followed in the column below the brief reference to him.

A month later, Dec. 17, 1859, the *Union* again noted Kellogg's official assistance. "We learn by a telegraph dispatch…handed us by Mark Kellogg, telegraph operator…." The paper's editor was F.A. Moore, a friend of Mark's. The day before, Dec. 16, the editor thanked Kellogg for providing information of a different type: "FROM PIKE'S PEAK — We are indebted to MARK KELLOGG, for a sight at a letter from our old friend, SID CLINTON, who, with several others, are in the Pike's Peak country." Clinton was Kellogg's brother-in-law, having married Coralinn Kellogg.

The Kellogg family enjoyed community social events and often the family's hotel became the center for such activities. On Nov. 11, 1859, the local German community celebrated the centennial anniversary of Friedrich Von Schiller's birthday at "Kellogg Hall."[52] A month later, Dec. 20, the *La Crosse Union and Daily Democrat* published a front page advertisement for what was billed as a "Grand Military Ball," the first for the La Crosse Light Guard.[53] Scheduled for Monday evening, Dec. 26, the event revealed Mark Kellogg's increasingly well-placed ties in his community. First, "Corp'l M.H. Kellogg" was listed as one of four floor managers. The quartermaster and a member of the reception committee was his brother-in-law, J.W. Robinson. On the list of honorary managers were a number of local political figures, such as Levy, and several newspapermen, including F.A. Moore, William C. Rogers and A.P. Swineford. Kellogg probably knew the latter trio from his position as the town's telegrapher. Such contacts would prove helpful later as he moved into a journalism career.

On Dec. 25, the paper took note of the next day's ball: "No pains or cost has been spared by the managers to render it the most brilliant party in all its appointments ever attempted in our city. The hall will be put in the most splendid military array." The article also mentioned Kellogg and the other floor managers would be distinguished by a white badge.[54] How important was this ball? The *Union and Democrat* published a 17-inch story Dec. 28, reporting, "In every respect, it was a most gratifying success."[55]

Kellogg had an even larger role in mid-January 1860 at a printer's festival to celebrate the Jan. 17 birthday of Benjamin Franklin. The Light Guard Band entertained, and "Two hours and a half were delightfully passed away in Quadrilles, Polkas, Waltzes and other dances until supper...The large dining room of the Harrington House was ornamented with those well spread and luxuriously loaded tables, extending the entire length of the room." A number of toasts were raised, including one by Mark Kellogg: "Fifth regular toast — Mighty Telegraph. To which Mark Kellogg responded in an edifying little speech. Mark done himself and the telegraph great credit. He was unexpectedly called out in the absence of the person who was designated, and we are warranted by saying that Kellogg in his explanation of the 'swift' gave immense satisfaction to the audience." [56]

Despite their spirited competition in those days, the gentlemen of the press respected one another. An item in the *La Crosse Union and Democrat*, whose publishers were C.P. Sykes, A.P. Swineford and F.A. Moore, noted the sale of the *La Crosse Republican* by William C. Rogers to Leonard Lottridge. The writer found the change of ownership a sad occasion, especially because ill health forced Rogers to sell. He continued, "William and we have been pummeling and pounding away in our respective positions. During the periods of nearly six years, it may be proper to add, though there may have appeared 'bad scratching' in our papers, there has never been the slightest break in our personal intercourse and relations of friendship."

Which of the three men wrote that is unclear, although Sykes was reported elsewhere as out of town in Madison. However, the note reflects the personal civility with which frontier editors often treated one another, despite real political differences.[57]

SANDY BARNARD

Chapter 3
La Crosse in the 1860s

The Kellogg family's involvement in the La Crosse community would continue for much of the 1860s. Initially, Mark Kellogg and his father were Republicans. In March 1860, Simeon's name was included among seven Republicans under consideration for mayor, according to the *La Crosse Union and Democrat*: "We consider it of just as much value to be talked about for mayor as to be elected! As only one from the above list can be chosen mayor, the balance may severally consider themselves elected for a dish of oysters."[58] By March 15, Wilson Colwell had been nominated by the Republicans, but he would be defeated on April 3 by John Levy, the survivor among eight Democrats. Why Simeon Kellogg was not selected was never explained by the newspapers.

Partisanship apparently could be put aside for some community positions. About that time the newspaper reported a group of lawyers and other citizens had a signed a petition urging A.P. Blakeslee to run for police justice. Simeon's name was among those on the bipartisan request.[59]

Mark himself continued to grow in prominence in his community. For example, the *La Crosse Union and Democrat* remarked that he was among 150 couples "from all the important points on the La Crosse Railroad [who] attended the great Railroad Ball at the Portage Depot" March 8. His date for the evening was unmentioned, but Kellogg was referred to as a telegraph operator. According to the newspaper's account, it must have been some party: "The dancing was kept up unremittingly from 7 1/2 in the evening until 6 in the morning. It was the unanimous opinion of all that a more elegant, orderly enjoyable party had never been held in Wisconsin."[60]

Telegraphy may not have been the only new technology to have interested Kellogg in the early 1860s. On April 16, 1860, the *La Crosse Union and Democrat* reported that "[Actress] Marie Mignonette was in town Sunday. Mark Kellogg secured a very excellent ambrotype before her departure on Monday."[61] Inasmuch as it's the only known reference to Kellogg as a photographer, Ed Hill, research archivist for the Murphy Library at the University of Wisconsin at La Crosse, believes Kellogg might have worked at least as an amateur photographer and obtained a photo of the woman while she was visiting the town.[62]

While Kellogg's given names were Marcus Henry, virtually all references cite him as Mark. However, the *La Crosse Union and Democrat* might have referred to him when it reported "Hank Kellogg" was among men taking part in a successful two-day trout expedition May 3 and 4, 1860.[63]

By this time a man who would greatly influence Mark Kellogg's life for several years, Marcus M. "Brick" Pomeroy, arrived in La Crosse as associate editor for the *Union and Democrat*. Born in New York state in 1833, he learned the printing trade as a youth. After moving to Wisconsin in 1854, he edited the *Horicon Argus*. Reportedly one of his editorials caused a Louisville, Ky., editor to say that Pomeroy must be a "Brick," a nickname that stuck with him. On Feb. 19, 1862, in his newspaper, Pomeroy printed a notice from the *Chatfield (Minn.) Democrat*, whose editor had visited him recently. It included a description of Pomeroy himself: "He is rather a small man physically, with but a slight covering of hair upon his head, and that very similar in color to a Milwaukee 'Brick' — a clean shaved boyish face — a bright blue eye...his nose and mouth are unremarkable, but his tongue is 'hung in the middle' and never says a silly thing. His body, we would judge to be a composition of whip crackers and steel wire."[64]

Once in town, Pomeroy bought out the interest of C.P. Sykes in the newspaper and began making political mischief, although it would be a while before he could wrest complete control of the newspaper from its other owners, senior editor A.P. Swineford and locals editor F.A. Moore. Saum quotes a writer who labeled Pomeroy as unmatched in "malignity and malevolence."[65] In mid-May, while Swineford was out of town, a Pomeroy editorial urged the nomination of Democrat Stephen A. Douglas as president, a position Swineford did not share. On Swineford's return the two men clashed. In another editorial, Pomeroy, noting "the tone of this paper has been changed," asserted his right to say what he pleased in his columns and defended his endorsement of Douglas. In the Personals

Column, Moore made fun of the dispute between his partners, the two senior editors:

"Mr. Swineford went to Milwaukee. Mr. Pomeroy didn't, but edited the inside as usual. Mr. Swineford returned — saw something he liked not. He cometh out over his own sig. The two editors retire to a room! They divest themselves of garments! They strike an attitude! One — two — down! God protect the fatherless! There is a smell of blood coming from the other room, but as we are newly married, we gooth [sic] not in! Yes but tomorrow will bring out another card, it will be read — indeed it will!"[66]

In the May 25 edition, the erstwhile partners announced their separation, resulting from what Swineford called the "irrepressible conflict, which ought never to have begun." Unable to buy out his partner, Swineford sold his interest to Pomeroy, giving him outright control of the paper. According to a local history, "He became popular and his paper prospered during the Civil War. During the Reconstruction period the *Democrat* was violently opposed to the policy of Congress and its weekly edition had many subscribers in the South. Its circulation was reported to be 100,000 in 1868."[67]

As 1860 began, amid talk of secession and civil war on the national level, politics grew ever more controversial. In turn, through men like Pomeroy, national issues inflamed the political scene of La Crosse. But Pomeroy also was practical. He renamed his paper the *Tri-Weekly Union and Democrat* after entering into an agreement with the owners of the *Republican* to issue both papers three times a week but on alternate days — the *Democrat* on Mondays, Wednesdays and Fridays and the *Republican* on Tuesdays, Thursdays and Saturdays. As Pomeroy explained to his readers, "Many of our citizens have expressed a desire to patronize both papers, but feel unable to incur the expense of taking two, when either one will furnish the latest news of the day. This city requires a daily paper, and to meet the demand, the two English papers here will be issued on alternate days."[68] In addition, a weekly paper would be published.

As the local wire service telegrapher, Mark Kellogg got to know Pomeroy more closely, and he also retained his high visibility in the community during this period. On June 27, 1860, the *La Crosse Tri-Weekly Union and Democrat* noted a "Republican ratification meeting" would take place at Caledonia the following Saturday. Among the speakers would be "Charles Seymour, editor of the *La Crosse Republican* and other of *equal* ability!" Entertaining, the paper advised readers, would be the "La Crosse Glee Club," whose members included Kellogg. The group "will be in attendance and enliven the meeting with some of their champagne melodies."[69]

In October, two lengthy lists of "citizens and tax payers" petitioned the City Council to approve $300 for the Board of Trade to advance the interests of La Crosse. The matter was referred by the committee on the judiciary to the committee of the whole, but no final action is indicated. Petitioners included Kellogg.

Kellogg's telegraphy kept him busy as the *Democrat's* locals editor F.A. Moore noted Oct. 24: "OUR FRIEND KELLOGG, who runs that very popular institution, the Telegraph, has his hands full these times. All the messages designed for the northwest have to be recopied and dispatched, making no little work. In pleasant weather it is intended to connect the Southern and St. Paul machines, but in foul weather, the work has to be repeated here. Mark bears all the extra labor with a Christian fortitude, and we cannot see that his countenance alongates [sic], or the freshly drawn smile 'like an infant sweetly sleeping,' is at all interfered with."[70]

That Republican Kellogg was highly involved in supporting Abraham Lincoln for president that fall was evident from a satirical column published by the irrepressible Pomeroy in November.[71] He positioned the newly elected Lincoln and his supporters on an excursion boat up the Salt River. A grand opera would be followed by a "tempting bill of fare." Each local Republican was responsible for bringing a menu item. As a young Wide Awake [Republican], Kellogg was assigned to bring pecans. Apparently, the event was more than a Pomeroy flight of fantasy, as local Republicans did celebrate their national victory with a river boat excursion.

In late November, Pomeroy assumed full control of the *Union and Democrat*. In his farewell, after six years in the newspaper business, F.A. Moore wrote, "The prime and immediate cause of our withdrawal…is the want of sufficient pecuniary inducement to remain. The business of the office for the time being cannot support two 'able editors!' with a sufficient margin to fall back on. The time has been when the 'pecuniary' were less an object with us; but advancing years and added responsibilities admonish us to 'strike out' for more promising labors."

He pointed out that he was leaving the office solely in Brick's hands, adding that Pomeroy was "ample, single-handed for all the requirements of the position." Up to now, Brick hasn't had "a fair chance and has but

SANDY BARNARD

just now got the office in paying condition." Old debts and recent political cross currents have made "Democratic headway impossible. Those who are readiest to complain of newspaper pilots might not have done any better themselves."[72]

In the same issue, Pomeroy said he parted "with regret" from Moore, whom he praised as a friend and "true-hearted generous brother." He suggested the two had clashed over politics and business matters: "Besides one man can always consult himself easier than another, and with a single proprietor there can be no clashing of interests, or hesitating over an important move." He added, "We came here last spring to engage in the printing and publishing business, and then determined to make this office *the best* in this section."

In early December, under a column headed "The Last Change," Pomeroy announced the newspaper's final name change. Henceforth, it would be the *La Crosse Democrat.* The longer original had been adopted when several men operated the paper, but the primary reason for the switch stemmed from politics: "The Union part of it has been a curse to the party; no credit to the city; a sort of swindle on all who trusted it; and a nuisance to all who have had to do with it." Next, he lambasted former partner A.P. Swineford as "a liar, a villain and a scoundrel."

All the paper's problems, including its debts, Pomeroy blamed on Swineford. "Wishing to make the paper respectable, we suspend the first half of the name subject to our own order, with about the feeling of relief and satisfaction as is experienced by a man who has just recovered from a severe attack of small pox, and in honor of the event burns or buries his old rags, and dressed in a new suit, goes singing on his way, without fear of infecting or being infected."

He concluded the column: "For the future we have no fears."[73]

With editor Pomeroy such a fervent Democrat and telegrapher Kellogg having supported Republican Lincoln's election, it might seem surprising for them to end up working together. But in another column in the Dec. 3 paper, Pomeroy explained such close relationships, puzzling as they might seem, among the newspaper fraternity of the day. While he was out of town on business, Swineford and other men had conspired "to break up our business." But looking out for Pomeroy's fortunes was none other than Leonard Lottridge, editor of the *La Crosse Republican*, who, Pomeroy said, "politely informed those who were trying to injure us, that if this office went to sale in our absence, he should buy it for us. He said we were a competitor in business — a political enemy, but he should not stand still and see us imposed upon...For this noble, manly act, Mr. Lottridge has our deep and heartfelt thanks."[74]

A year that would see the country come ablaze in civil war opened with Mark Kellogg still the operator of the Wisconsin Telegraph Co. The *History of La Crosse County* listed him as the operator under its Businesses in 1861 section.[75] The *Democrat* also listed a "W.H. Kellogg" who was called for jury duty, beginning Jan. 21, according to a note on Friday, Jan. 11, 1861. W.H. presumably was M.H. Kellogg, a designation that Kellogg often went by throughout his life.[76]

On Jan. 17, the town observed a Benjamin Franklin Festival at the Harrington House. "Party and dancing ensued," the *Democrat* observed. "The assembled throng was one of the most fashionable ever congregated in this city." At midnight a grand supper was held. Later, a series of toasts was read, beginning with one by Pomeroy on Franklin. Eventually, Kellogg delivered one on the "Magnetic Telegraph," although his remarks went unreported.[77]

Kellogg's increasingly close ties to the journalistic fraternity of La Crosse were demonstrated again by a report in the *Democrat* March 4, 1861. Two nights before, a group of friends, including Kellogg, Pomeroy, Moore and Lottridge, honored the newly married C.P. Sykes, a businessman and former newspaper editor about to depart for Pike's Peak. The event took place in Pomeroy's "private room."[78]

Pomeroy stood apart from the town's mainline Democrats throughout his years in La Crosse. He frequently perceived actions of others as attempts to undercut his newspaper and himself, such as in March 1861. A new Democratic newspaper, the *Appeal*, was launched by A.P. Blakeslee, who had earlier published the *Union and Democrat*. Pomeroy claimed the new paper was started "to harmonize the Democracy of La Crosse city and county! Its real mission is to bolster up a clique and run us out of town, both of which jobs the Publisher for the Proprietors will have a good time in accomplishing."[79] In a lengthy column, Pomeroy predicted his paper would survive. Even though the *Republican* controlled all the city, county and state political advertising, he boasted the *Democrat* had the best commercial advertising patronage of any paper in the state.

Also that month, the newspaper reported the La Crosse & Milwaukee Railroad would auction unclaimed freight, including some belonging to Mark's father Simeon. No reason was given about why a lumber wagon, a neck yoke and "one set of Eaveners" had not been claimed by the elder Kellogg.[80] On March 14, Mark's younger brother Ecton narrowly escaped drowning, according to the next day's *Democrat*: "While on the ice he fell through into the water. This ice is a practical affair, and its dangers are to be learned only be experience."[81]

With the firing on Fort Sumter at Charleston, S.C., marking the start of the Civil War, the people of La Crosse convened at Leiderkranz Garden "for the purpose of obtaining an expression of opinion in reference to the condition of the country," according to the *History of La Crosse County*. With Pomeroy as secretary, a series of resolutions "expressive of the views of the assembly" was reported by a committee. Pomeroy and others made speeches, and $3,451 was subscribed "to protect the families and property of the gallant men who are volunteering into the service of the Republic," the *Democrat* reported April 24.[82] Simeon Kellogg donated $25 and Pomeroy $50. Pomeroy, who later opposed the war, published a call for 214 men to form a "horse Zouaves" unit to be called the Wisconsin Tigers.[83]

Kellogg's thoughts about all the war talk in town went unrecorded. At the same time his personal life was proving more adventurous. He was preparing for marriage, the announcement of which appeared in the newspaper of May 20, 1861:

"MARRIED

"In this city, on Sunday evening May 19th 1861 by Rev. Mr. Willett, Mr. MARK H. KELLOGG to Miss MATTIE L. ROBINSON, all of this city.

"The happy couple left this morning for an eastern tour, from which we wish them a safe return. — Friend MARK, as is well known, is the efficient Telegraph Manager here, although he can manage lightning and be safe while it may be darting around, this event shows that the glances from one of the Belles of La Crosse was too much for him. — May the fair bride's MARK last her through the Book of life, and never be out of place."[84]

Hundreds of miles east at West Point, N.Y., George A. Custer was nearing the end of his schooling and soon would be commissioned as a second lieutenant in the cavalry. In the four years of war that would follow, he would rise to the temporary rank of brevet major general and gain heroic stature across the country. Where in the east the newly married Kelloggs traveled is unknown, but certainly their path never crossed Custer's. Although some accounts after his death said Kellogg served in the Union Army, it is clear he remained in La Crosse during the war. Earlier, he had served in the La Crosse Light Guards, a local militia unit, but he never went to war with it.[85]

In late summer, a mischievous Kellogg appeared in what may have been one of his first recorded ventures into journalism. A letter addressed to Pomeroy lamenting the steady beating of drums near the telegraph office appears in the Aug. 26 paper under the pen name of "Telegraph:" "I appeal to you whether or no (sic) a snare drum continually beaten directly opposite a person's place of business…that it makes it impossible to do business with its emotional 'rub-a-dub-dub,' is not a *slight* detriment to the nerves and temper of a telegrapher? Its 'soul stirring notes' on a parade ground or battle field is well, because in its proper sphere, and creates the same excitement and 'pleasing emotion' with me as with other men; but I do protest against the present arrangement of allowing 'Tom, Dick and Harry' pounding away as for dear life. The drum must change its quarters, stop its music, or the good people do without.

Very respectfully yours,

TELEGRAPH

SOUNE. — The hammering away at a drum all day is a nuisance, when it can be dispensed with."

By September whatever feeling of good will that existed between Pomeroy of the *Democrat* and Lottridge of the *Republican* appears to have been lost. The *Republican* had criticized Wisconsin's Gov. A.W. Randall for decisions affecting the state's military forces. A letter to Randall was printed in the *Democrat* of Sept. 6, 1861, denouncing the *Republican's* attacks and expressing confidence in the governor. The letter, signed by "leading Republicans," included M.H. Kellogg. How political the letter actually was may be argued. An editor's note, pointing out four military depots existed in eastern Wisconsin and none in western, suggested the letter may have had a more economic than political purpose. Obviously, a military base would enhance the town's economy.

On Dec. 20, 1861, the *Democrat* listed the town's leading businesses. One of the 14 hotels listed was the "Kellogg House, corner Pearl and 2d St.; S. Kellogg, proprietor; accommodations 45 guests; trade increasing."[86] Under telegraph office it noted Kellogg was the operator of the office at

SANDY BARNARD

Main and Front streets. Early in 1862, Kellogg was still employed as a telegrapher. The *Democrat* reported, "We learn from M.H. Kellogg, Esq., that he has an assistant telegraph operator, who will no doubt be considerable company for himself and wife!" It was his daughter Cora, who was born Feb. 5.[87]

Even with the telegraph, newspapers of the era relied on exchanges for much of their news. So it is not surprising that Cora's birth announcement caught the attention of the *Durand Mirror*, which chided Pomeroy for his "fancy way...of telling anything. He don't (sic) tell what his name is, his age or how long he has operated (most of us know nothing about 'operating') or how he operates. We should think Mr. Kellogg would object to any one keeping company with his wife." Pomeroy, requiring the final word, added, "People don't generally name children in this country till they are, at least older than our item was."[88]

In April, Simeon Kellogg began running an ad for the Kellogg House, which noted "This house is prepared to accommodate all custum (sic) with which it may be favored. Omnibuses carry passengers to and from the cars and steamboats. Good stabling attached."[89] The paper also referred at times to Kellogg's father-in-law, Charles Robinson. On May 21, 1862, it stated, "Mr. Chas. Robinson on State St. is manufacturing an excellent article of Fanning Mill. He does all his own work by hand and uses none but the best materials, selects his own lumber and does work as it used to be done in old times, upon honor. All mills warranted."[90]

An Aug. 19, 1862, story about a new house for the Robinsons also revealed how the war was affecting the local economy: "Among the many fine residences being erected this season in our growing city is now one being commenced on the corner of Fifth and Main Sts., by Mr. Chas. Robinson. It will add much to the appearance of that vicinity. War seems to be but little felt as yet with us. Business of every branch is good and on the increase. Buildings go up rapidly, improvement follows improvement with great rapidity."[91]

Not only was the town prospering, the *La Crosse Democrat* was as well. On Sept. 9, 1862, Pomeroy claimed, "We receive the latest news by telegraph from all parts up to the hour of going to press — half past 4 in the afternoon. Readers of the *DEMOCRAT* will get their news from it from 10 to 18 hours in advance of Chicago or Milwaukee papers."[92] Two weeks later, he stepped up his news reporting, telling his readers the *Democrat's* morning edition "will furnish the news by telegraph up to 8 o'clock a. m. This will give the night report 12 hours in advance of Milwaukee papers, and the morning news 14 hours in advance of any other publication which can reach this city."

Doing so wouldn't be cheap, he added: "To do this requires a heavy expense, which we trust the business men of this city will not throw back on us entirely. We are anxious to make the *DEMOCRAT* a newspaper which shall be an honor to La Crosse, but it cannot be done without an effort on our part, and a support on the part of those who are interested in receiving the news, and in the prosperity of the city." This new morning edition would be sold on the streets. "Our regular evening edition will be furnished to subscribers as usual, but at an earlier hour."[93]

At some point that year Kellogg left his telegraphy post and joined Pomeroy's staff. Likely it occurred by the time Pomeroy expanded his paper in the fall of 1862. The newspaper itself revealed Kellogg's ongoing transformation from a Wide Awake Lincoln Republican to a fellow traveler of Pomeroy, an anti-war stance labeled as Copperheadism as the war years progressed. Copperheads were Northern Democrats who either sympathized with the South's war aims or opposed the war itself. That may explain why Kellogg never served in the army. Saum credited Kellogg with a significant infection of Copperheadism, but at best Kellogg was more of an opportunist through his ties to Pomeroy than a true believer. In any case, the paper reported the results of the First Ward's caucus of Sept. 25. Among elected delegates to the County Union Convention was none other than Kellogg. Pomeroy was elected as a member of the ward committee.[94]

According to the convention's proceedings of Sept. 29, Kellogg was one of three men appointed to the committee on credentials. During the convention he was one of nine people elected to the senatorial convention to be held Oct. 8 in La Crosse. He moved up the political ladder quickly, no doubt thanks to Pomeroy's influence.[95] Yet Kellogg also was listed among a large group of Republicans who signed a letter attesting to the nomination of T.B. Stoddard as the Union candidate for Congress. Politics in La Crosse were in turmoil. Pomeroy, for now, was flourishing. Evidently carried along with him as a dabbler in politics was Kellogg.

At the county convention Oct. 13, Kellogg moved for an informal ballot on a nominee for assembly candidate. As no senatorial candidate was nominated, the convention adjourned until Oct. 16. Kellogg was appointed secretary for the convention[96] An Oct. 21, 1862, column in the

SANDY BARNARD

Democrat explained the political goings-on. According to the newspaper, certain Democrats were actually secessionists. A party leader, Theodore Rodolf, was dismissed this way: "Not one word of sympathy for the union in its struggle for life has ever fell from his lips...No wonder democracy has become a byword when such men manage pocket conventions. No wonder honest men are driven into the Republican Party. If we had a son who ever gave sign of ever parsing Democracy as these men parse it, or who could ever train in such company, we'd cut his throat at once.... Working men, there are the honest men who do the heavy headwork for you. Douglas Democrats, there are the noble statesmen who claim to be the Democratic Party."[97]

The newspaper continued, calling such men "traitors at heart, corrupt in every vein." It criticized them for having no sympathy with the people and for offering "nothing but curses for the [military] volunteers — nothing but abuse for the government." The newspaper concluded: "The country, thank God, looks upon them as the traitors they are."

Other stories about local Democratic meetings noted Pomeroy's reluctance to support Democratic candidates, unless they agreed with his own line. Pomeroy responded that he still considered himself a Democrat, but that circumstances dictated a union approach to politics. He also did not view the Democrats' own convention as representative of that party. Asked by the Democrats whether he would support their candidates, Pomeroy wrote: "You may consider me or my paper Democratic or not. This is my position, stated fairly and freely. I believe I am right and shall go ahead."[98]

Even as far north as La Crosse, deep divisions over the war were evident among the people and the partisan press. In a column published under his own name Oct. 28, Kellogg responded to criticism the previous day by the *La Crosse Republican* of his relationship with Pomeroy and his "double shuffling" by offering allegiance to both political parties. He wrote: "We confess the 'soft impeachment' of having burned oil, and did vote for 'Abraham [Lincoln],' and still support him, but the course the *Republican* has pursued, we cannot and will not support. We heard a prominent Republican of this city state publicly last spring that he considered the course the *Republican* had been and then was pursuing injured the Republican element in this section more than 40 Republicans could benefit it. We thought so some time before we heard the remarks, and believe now that if its tone and character is not changed soon, that its influence will kill what's left of the party in this county, entirely."[99]

His closing confirmed that by October he was working for Pomeroy and was no longer running the telegraph office in the city: "As far as Mr. Pomeroy and myself are concerned — so long as I do his work satisfactorily to him, I take it, it is no business of any other parties to interfere or to intrude upon the business association which concerns us."

Soon the political season would end for 1862 in La Crosse. The Tuesday Nov. 4 *Democrat* noted that "Glorious Victory — Unionism ahead." Union candidates enjoyed large majorities in the election. In a particular example of nastiness, a subhead, entitled, "Likeness of Its [*Republican*] Editor," was accompanied by a cartoon image of a frog.

While journalists fought furiously in their newspaper pages, when one of their number was sick or died, his competitors still wished him well, as this example shows: "PERSONAL. — Mr. Seymour of the *Republican* has been confined to his bed for several days, by a severe attack of the Quinsy [acute tonsillitis]. We are happy to know that he is at present recovering his wonted health."[100]

Early in 1863, a directory of local businesses in the *Democrat* underscored the respectability of the Kellogg family's hotel. Under hotels, this notice appeared: "Kellogg House, corner Second and Pearl streets. S. Kellogg proprietor. Accommodates 50 guests, Good stables attached."[101] The largest hotel appeared to be the Harrington House, capable of serving 200 at State and Third streets. The Westcott House, Second and State streets, and Clifton House, Second and Pearl streets, accommodated about 100 each. Of the 15 listed, the Kellogg House ranked fifth in size. The directory's entry for the telegraph office listed Kellogg's successor: "Geo. Shape, Operator, corner Main and Front streets, over Lloyd and Supple's."

In March, however, a notice revealed the changing personal fortunes of the Kellogg family: "REMEMBER — The sale of household stuff at the Kellogg House on Wednesday at 11 o'clock a.m. Many valuable articles will be offered."[102] Evidently, as a result of an unspecified illness of Simeon, the family sold first the furnishing and then the hotel. The ad for the Kellogg House continued its usual content until May 5, when it was dropped. A new ad for the Albion House, Pearl and Second streets, began June 2, pointing out that J. and G. Williams were the new proprietors. "This house has of late been refitted and refurnished. Situated in the central part of the city. Bus to and from cars and boats."[103]

Through much of this period, Pomeroy was away. According to an item of March 31, 1863, he had returned after a three-month "sojourn in the south."[104] A week later, Pomeroy said he was resuming publication of the *Daily Democrat* in place of the Tri-Weekly version. He promised to support the area and its people, but not politics, except to protect against jealous political opponents.[105]

The April 20 issue provides insight into Pomeroy's developing Copperheadism. Two front page columns could be termed a Copperhead's lament. One column asked, "What Shall We Do to Be Saved?" The "We" is Democrats, who are called traitors for their failure to support the government's war policy. "If we do not believe that Abraham is King — the people his throne, and the negro his subjects, we are all classed as copperheads and even butchery is too good for us. What shall we do to be saved? To become Republicans will kill us. To remain Democrats is to court abuse and assassination."[106]

Another column asked "Is This Cause for Hanging?" and repeated Pomeroy's concern that Democrats were automatically classified as Copperheads and traitors. Pomeroy viewed things differently: "We may be called traitors — may be Peace Democrats — Copperheads, or whatever a fanatical pack of hounds may see fit to call us as a political body, but here is what we are not.... We are not the men who became dissatisfied with the best government ever conceived, and systematically worked for its overthrow.

"We are not the men who directly or indirectly brought on the war.

"We are not the men who were willing to lose a country to save an idea — to tear down the proud temple of the nation in spite, not to make war upon eight millions of white folks for four million of blacks.

"We did not for years argue on stump, in paper, and from pulpit that the south was a race of cowards who dare not fight, and if they dare, one northern man could whip five of them.

"We did not open this feast of blood by telling people that the war was a pastime, and no one would be hurt.

"We have not suspended the writ of habeas corpus...

"We are not the authors of the 'Conscription bill' which exempts office holders and rich men, but has no mercy than hell itself for a poor man whose labor will barely support himself and his family...

"We are not the men who uniform black men and make them into soldiers thus placing them on a par with the Anglo Saxon..."[107]

Poor Brick. Politically, he was without a home during the war years. Fortunately, the summer of 1863 did find his friendship with Mark Kellogg warming. Here's what Kellogg, who was the same age as Pomeroy, wrote about Brick in the newspaper's July 3 issue:

"A VALUABLE GIFT. — at the hands of M.M. Pomeroy, we are the recipient of a valuable gift in the shape of a solid silver Tobacco Box, gold lined. It is most elegantly designed and beautifully chased. On it is engraved as follows:

"Brick" Pomeroy.

to

Mark H. Kellogg.

'A good friend is better than riches.'

Democrat Office, 1863.

"The gift sprung from the generosity of a heart that is as true as steel, and one, too, that appreciates and admires true friendship. In that spirit we receive it.

"In Mr. Pomeroy we have always found those requisites that go to make up a true man. Generous to a fault; kind, noble and large-hearted. In him we have a friend in *practice*, not in theory; and as such we feel that words are inadequate to express our true feeling. For this demonstration of friendship we can only say 'thank you,' not in the mere words but with all our heart.

"'Friendship above all ties does bind the heart;

"And faith in friendship is the noblest part'."[108]

Later that month, Kellogg again put his writing talents to work as a secretary for a political party meeting, this time the Democrats. The county convention was held July 24, 1863, to elect delegates to a state party convention Aug. 5 in Madison. Kellogg, one of the representatives from the city's First Ward, was elected secretary. The county convention also elected Pomeroy as one of three delegates.[109] Just a few weeks later, on Aug. 7, the local Democratic Club elected Kellogg as treasurer, proving that he obviously ranked among party stalwarts that summer.

August of 1863 was a month of great joy for Kellogg and his wife, Martha, or Mattie, who gave birth Aug. 20 to a second daughter. She was named Mattie Grace.[110]

In the summer of 1863, Kellogg was popular with more than just the politicians. In late September, the local Sportsmen's Club planned a "game supper." Club members appointed Kellogg chairman of a committee to arrange the club insignia in the supper hall at the Westcott House. In addition, members were assigned to procure different kinds of game. Kellogg was one of two men responsible for obtaining ducks.[111]

A newspaper story about the supper labeled the event, attended by 40 men, as "the gamiest supper ever set down to in the Upper Mississippi." No specific mention of Kellogg occurred, but his success in fulfilling his duties was evident. Among the game served was mallard duck, teal duck, canvass back duck, wood duck and brown shell drake, plus a black duck with tartar sauce and a French duck in olive sauce. The writer noted, "The hall was finely decorated with the insignia of the club."[112]

On Nov. 17, 1863, the *Democrat* published a lengthy letter from a writer who signed himself as "K." Written the previous Tuesday from Milwaukee, it reflected the ring of boosterism that Kellogg's later writings on the frontier displayed. Businesses familiar to the writer had all doubled since the year before, and old friends and patrons inquired often about Pomeroy himself. Milwaukee was praised as "fortunate in having so many men of such caliber and qualities. Milwaukee stands today a head and shoulders in advance of the position she held a year ago. Her citizens may well feel proud of the rapid strides she is making — of the bright future which is in store for her — of the city of the west — of the metropolis of Wisconsin." [113]

Milwaukee was so prosperous that some men feared that it would soon end. The writer, probably Kellogg, reassured them: "We can tell them — never, so long as the great Northwest exists; never so long as men can till the soil and reap the golden harvest." Kellogg also spoke reassuringly of the way La Crosse was viewed by Milwaukeans: "It is recognized as a point whose future is certain — that future — the second city in size in the state, the only city able to cope with the Metropolis...La Crosse commands today more attention than all the other points on the Upper Mississippi, and ere long, through the energy of her citizens, she will be able to stand side by side and cope with any city in the west."

A notice in the *Daily Democrat* of Nov. 16 underscored Kellogg's devotion to his home town and his knack at being tapped for positions of responsibility in his community:

"Attention Pioneer.

"There will be a meeting of the Pioneer Engine Co. at their Engine House this evening at 7 o'clock. Members are requested to be on hand promptly as business of importance is to be transacted."[114]

The brief was signed by "M.H. Kellogg, Foreman."

The same edition carried a list of 70 names of La Crosse men who had been drafted into the Army. The *Democrat* pointed out that six of its 14 employees were eligible for the draft but none had his number called in what it called "the distribution of 'national prizes'." It stated that since the war began, seven of its employees had been drafted or enlisted, but none had been hurt or killed. Several had risen into the officers' ranks. "We firmly believe that not one who enlisted from this office will be killed and that when the war is over we shall meet with them all in the office, and at the same table celebrate their return. This office is surely a bower of luck."[115]

Whether at war's end that remained true is unknown. For Kellogg the newspaper's prediction certainly did not extend to post-war Indian engagements.

A man who was drafted could buy his way out of service by paying another as a substitute to take his place. The day after the local draft the newspaper congratulated its six employees on their narrow escape and called on local businessmen to assist local firemen in avoiding war service: "We trust the business men of this city will see that the members of the fire department who were drafted are not obliged to go to war if they do not wish to. We have 50 or a hundred dollars at the disposal of the 'boys' to help them in their hour of need. It seems too bad for a poor man to be obliged to leave his family to the charity of the world and engage in that [the war] he has no heart in. If businessmen cannot afford to go, how much harder it is for the poor man."[116] Two weeks later, the Nov. 30 paper carried a brief resolution of thanks from the fire department's members for assistance received in paying the "exemption fee" of drafted firemen.

Kellogg received one more mention in 1863 in the pages of his employer. The *Democrat's* "Local and other Intelligence" column for Dec. 4 included this item: "The best thing of the season was the other day when a stout farmer came into our counting room, and without so much as a 'by your leave' commenced to thresh Kellogg, our cashier. In just four minutes the man had more than he wanted. He got in the wrong room — was after Bliss the surveyor, whose office is in the same building, and did not discover his error till well threshed. This concern is not intended for such pranks, and is always ready in all departments."[117]

The new year of 1864 found Kellogg vitally involved with one of the local volunteer fire companies. An annual directory listing of Jan. 26 listed him as foreman for Pioneer Engine Co. No. 1.[118] But by June, the fire department was making news as its very existence was threatened. The city council had disbanded the two fire companies for economic reasons to create, as the *Democrat* phrased it, "a better fire department."[119] The newspaper's editorial expressed its outrage: "If there should break out a fire in this city today or tonight, we are at the mercy of the elements, unless God should see fit to send a shower of rain." Of the two companies in the city of 8,000, "One of them is in good order — the other is broken.... Meanwhile the city is at the mercy of the flames. The action of the council was a deliberate insult to the Fire Department, a wrong to the city, and if we were a member of either company we'd see the council damned before we'd ever touch a brake or don a uniform to be thus fooled and insulted without cause."

Was Kellogg the angry writer? That is not known, but the writer, whomever he was, lacked objectivity on the issue: "We congratulate the firemen on being at last relieved from their self-imposed obligations and the city of La Crosse on the liberality, energy and farsightedness of its city officers! The *DEMOCRAT* is the official paper of the city. The council meets — no one knows where or when. It has no hall. It has a city clerk but he is too busy to furnish us late proceedings of the meeting and so our citizens live along in blissful ignorance of passing events till at last they leak out and waste away in the sand."

The members of Kellogg's Pioneer Company reformed themselves into an independent organization under the name, Live Oak Co. No. 1. A few days later, Kellogg, described as "the efficient foreman" of the disbanded Pioneer Company, was honored by his men with a gift of a fireman's hat and belt "costing in New York 45 dollars."[120] Here's what firefighter T.J. McCarty had to say about Kellogg:

"Words cannot express the gratification it affords us to know that the intrinsic value of them are nothing compared to the pride we take in you as a leader of our company. This present was gotten up on our part exclusively as a testimonial of your efforts to sustain and aid in the welfare of the company. At all times you have been the first to resent any insult offered us."

McCarty referred to the disbanding of their Pioneer Company as the greatest insult, and noted the exchange of charges between the two newspapers. *Republican* editor Seymour was criticized for his printed abuse of the company, especially of Kellogg who did not escape "his scurrilous reproaches." But McCarty optimistically predicted that if the people provide another engine and base of operation, "We will endeavor to show the firemen of Wisconsin that Live Oak No. 1, the Pioneer of La Crosse, can compete with any fire organization in the state."

He theorized the council, playing politics, closed the company because of its success. "Notwithstanding the abuse heaped upon us, we believe, with our present organization, with you [Kellogg] as its leader, that we may be able to procure sufficient means to have, in a short time, as good and efficient fire apparatus, and as well manned as any company in the state, and one that we may well feel proud of."

According to the article, Kellogg responded with impromptu remarks, but his exact words were not printed by the *Democrat* — [He] "from a full heart thanked the gentlemen not more for the gift than for the sentiments...He has always been a true and faithful officer and the present is well deserved and will be sacredly honored or we greatly mistake the man."[121]

The rest of the newspaper's column severely criticized the council for leaving the city without fire coverage. If the council would not provide for a company, the newspaper recommended, "sell the old engines and let us trust to lick altogether." As for Kellogg's fire hat and belt, the newspaper stated they were manufactured by "Messrs & Jones of New York City, the well-known hatters. They are beauties in every sense of the world."

Kellogg remained in Pomeroy's employ, according to a notice published July 5, 1864, that was addressed to "M.H. Kellogg, cashier, *La Crosse Daily Democrat.*" In it, Pomeroy told Kellogg to advance the *Republican's* Seymour $100 to assist the latter in resuming publication after a fire burned him out: "You will extend to Mr. Seymour the full accommodations of the *Democrat* office if he wishes to keep up his publication, and also give toward re-establishing his office $100 on call."[122] Clearly, past political and personal attacks did not keep the men of La Crosse journalism from aiding one another in times of need.

The July 12 issue of the newspaper provided insight into Pomeroy's anti-war feelings, as he published a memorial notice for his brother, Sgt. Chauncey Pomeroy, "shot dead through the heart on the field of battle in front of Richmond" the month before.[123] Thus, it is not surprising that by August 1864 the *Democrat's* columns reflect increasingly more angry anti-Lincoln feeling. The president was called a traitor, a buffoon, a pet of officeholders and a tyrant.

SANDY BARNARD

By October, Pomeroy's owns columns had become emotional binges. On Oct. 17, for example, he asked, "Where are the noble volunteers who rallied to defend the constitution and save the Union?" He provides his own answer: "Dead! Killed! Starved or starving in prison! Murdered by Abraham Lincoln!"

Later he refers to the president as "Lincoln the widow maker."[124]

Pomeroy ended that diatribe with a question: "When, in God's name, will an abused, insulted and oppressed people wake up to the presence of the robber at [the] bedside and resolve to put a stop to this niggerized waste of the blood and wealth of the nation?"

Earlier, Pomeroy showed he would attack Lincoln another way — at the ballot box. September's newspapers make clear he had reconciled with the Democrats who rallied as the McClellan Invincibles to support George B. McClellan, the former Union Army commander running against Lincoln. Kellogg stood once again in Brick's shadow, as corresponding secretary for the Democrats.[125] In the November election, Lincoln was re-elected.

Kellogg did not appear again in the paper until March 20, 1865, when an exchange of correspondence between Pomeroy and a Green Bay banker about currency is published. Pomeroy's portion is signed off for him "Per Kellogg," confirming he was still in Pomeroy's employment at that time.[126] In late March, Kellogg's name appeared on a long list of prominent citizens who signed a letter to Hugh Cameron urging him to become a candidate for county judge.[127] Cameron's March 23 affirmative response appeared below the list of names.[128]

In April, Lincoln's assassination must have caused moments of serious worry for Pomeroy, and his journalistic opposition on the *La Crosse Republican* took advantage of his discomfort. "There is no doubt these assassinations are part and parcel of the conspiracy that was thwarted by the discovery of the New York and Chicago incendiaries [sic] .... These assassins and their friends are here in our midst. — Loyal citizens feed and warm them. — Their organ in this city expressed the hope that in the event of the re-election of President Lincoln, there might be one man left in the country, with sufficient moral courage to drive a dagger to his heart."[129]

The opposition paper quoted fiery language from Pomeroy's Oct. 24, 1864, column: "A succeeding revolution may develop the instrumentality which may rid the country of its destroyer, equal in guilt and atrocity, though sudden and unexpected, to anyone whose death ever became the cause of public rejoicing." The *Republican* sarcastically observed that "today a bulletin was issued from the Democrat office saying — A NATION WEEPS'."

Pomeroy must have been seriously concerned the government's investigation into the Lincoln conspiracy might reach as far as La Crosse to ensnare him. The *Democrat* immediately expressed sorrow over the president's death: "We mourn with the people, for a great man has fallen. President Lincoln was not a Napoleon — was not a Jackson — was not a Webster — was not a Douglas. But we believe was a man of genius — a lover of his country — an honest man — a statesman…We mourn with the nation more than ever, for now came the hour when a kind heart like his was better than wealth untold for the nation…. Lincoln was the president of a great Republic. He was acting as he believed to be right, and his wisdom was rapidly being substantiated and proven…."[130]

History, however, gives no indication that the La Crosse editor, despite his apparent call for physical action against Lincoln, was ever considered part of the conspiracy that led to the president's killing.

In June 1865, the *Democrat* newspaper moved from the Juneau block, corner of Main and Front streets, to a brick building on Second Street, the first door south of the Westcott House. The counting room and business office, where Kellogg undoubtedly worked, were on the first floor. "The public will find us as accommodating as ever, and not a bit stuck up over the fact of having the finest place of business in the city."[131] A week later, the newspaper noted that J.W. Robinson & Co. had become "in two years the leading grocery trade of the city." Located in the Fay's block on Main Street, the store was owned by Kellogg's brother-in-law.[132]

On Sept. 11, 1865, the newspaper carried a notice that several members of the old La Crosse Light Guard had met Sept. 9 in the newspaper's counting room to form a new association. A separate article said the association would function "not as a military body but as a club," although apparently some prospective members did have military experience. The article concluded, "It is designed to perpetuate this club so long as any two members shall exist; to draw together this band of men, among whom has existed for years naught but the most friendly and almost fraternal affection."[133] Who should be one of the two secretaries for the club? Mark H. Kellogg.

SANDY BARNARD

The newspaper's next reference to Kellogg in September 1865 is notable, for it clearly indicates he had changed his employment from the newspaper to the grocery business:

"HEADQUARTERS — Kellogg & Co. (Mark H. Kellogg & Patsey Daley) have purchased the Flour and Feed store and business of J.B. Williams on Third Street and will hereafter keep a larger and better stock of articles in that line than ever was kept in La Crosse and serve things out to their numerous customers right lively and at living rates. Everybody in town knows the parties, and knows they will not be undersold. They will have fresh butter, game, vegetables, etc., besides flour and feed, and will spare no pains or attention to win the leading patronage of the city. We wish them all the luck in the world."[134]

On Sept. 18, 1865, the *Daily Democrat* began carrying a 2 inch by 1 column ad for the new firm. The company, located on Third Street next to the prominent Harrington House, promised to deliver goods to any part of the city.[135] With Kellogg's departure from his newspaper, Pomeroy promoted John Symes to serve as "general superintendent" of the printing company authorized to act for him in his absence.[136]

Besides his other community duties, Kellogg remained an active Mason. In December, his name was included among a listing of officers selected for Smith's Chapter 13 on Nov. 13. Installation was set for Dec. 27.[137] But even as that event approached, the first in a series of tragedies struck Kellogg's life. He had prospered, personally and professionally in his community. Now misfortune would seemingly interfere with every enterprise he tried. The event would mark the first step on a long road that would take him to the Little Big Horn more than 10 years later.

On Dec. 28, the city was struck by a series of three fires that caused an estimated loss of $56,000, only $25,000 of which was covered by insurance.[138] The second fire was catastrophic for Kellogg & Co. "During the same evening, flames were discovered issuing from a building owned by Mrs. Gregory, on Fourth street, between Main and State streets, occupied by Mark H. Kellogg & Co., as a grocery and feed store, and so rapidly the fire extended its ravages, that in less than two hours every building on that side of the street...was nothing but a pile of ruins."

Noting many people lost everything in their homes or businesses to the flames, the *Daily Democrat* reported, "The entire stock of Kellogg & Co. met with a similar fate."[139] Kellogg's losses amounted to $1,500, but only $900 was covered by insurance. Kellogg printed a short notice of thanks that followed the fire story: "We are under obligations to, and wish in this way to thank our numerous friends for their exertions to save our property from the devouring flames last night."

Pomeroy still supported his former employee: "PLUCKY — Kellogg & Co., we understand, will be ready for business again the 2d of January. We are glad to note their pluck and energy, and they wish us to announce to their numerous patrons that they will be ready to serve their wants on and after the time above mentioned. Location will be given in due season. This firm should have patronage. They are such as build up and help sustain a town, and are never found wanting in times of emergencies. — Help them, that you may receive benefits therefrom."[140]

On Dec. 30, the *Democrat* pointed out that the city once had two "good and efficient fire companies," who "vied with each other in efforts to succeed and take the lead in promptness and efficiency. It does not seem to be so now, and it is time some decided action should be taken by the proper authorities."[141] Despite Pomeroy's strong endorsement of Kellogg's grocery enterprise, evidence suggests the business failed to thrive after it reopened. According to the *Democrat* of Jan. 15, 1866, the business may have lacked the resources to sustain itself:

"A NEW DEAL — Mark Kellogg is again in the field with a stock of flour, feed, family supplies and nix nix [sic]. With the new year a leaf is turned over and the credit system is abolished. He is a good fellow and all that, but 'business is business,' and it takes money to buy peaches. Hereafter, 'down with the piece,' will be requested in all cases. His friends and customers will take due notice and be governed accordingly. This step is necessary in order to sustain and support the concern. — All parties indebted to the late firm of Kellogg & Co., are earnestly requested to walk up to the Captain's office and settle as funds are now much needed and all little donations of that kind will be greatly appreciated. He will be found at his post at Chas. Robinson's building on Main street, one door east of Dunlop's ever ready to supply the wants of all who call."[142]

Charles Robinson was his father-in-law. The change in Kellogg's credit policy suggests his grocery business was failing financially. Significantly, no ads were published for the business in the new year, and no mention of Kellogg or the business appears in the *Democrat* for much of 1866. The La Crosse City Directory for 1866-1867 fails to include Kellogg's business, but does list his residence as the northwest corner of King and 6th streets. His father (and presumably his mother, although women were not listed) was living with him.[143]

SANDY BARNARD

In March, the La Crosse Light Guard members elected permanent officers to serve one-year terms, but Kellogg did not appear on the list. His personal situation demanded his full attention. Despite having played a strong secondary leadership role in his community for many years, in 1866 Kellogg virtually disappeared from community view. Later that year, the name of Kellogg's wife Martha appeared in the paper as one of a number of women offering their names in a testimonial for the Champion Wash Machine. "It does not rub, or beat the clothes, but cleanses them by forcing them through boiling suds so rapidly as to expose every part of the fabric to currents of hot water, and doing an ordinary washing in from one to two hours," or so the published claim stated.[144]

SANDY BARNARD

Chapter 4
Baseball Comes to La Crosse

The next year, 1867, would prove to be one of the most eventful of Kellogg's life. Yet amid great personal tragedy and changing circumstances, Kellogg would write some of his most humorous pieces. Also, despite being 34 years old, he would immerse himself in athletic adventures by his involvement with a baseball team in La Crosse.

Baseball may have been more than a simple pastime for Kellogg that year, as his personal life experienced a series of reverses, beginning with the death of his father Simeon in January. The Kellogg family likely was never rich, as La Crosse property records indicate Simeon frequently mortgaged his hotel and other property. Ill health forced him to sell the Kellogg House in the spring of 1863. His obituary appeared Saturday, Jan. 12, 1867, in the *La Crosse Democrat*, an unusual event in itself as the newspapers of that era published few obituaries. Simeon died at 3 a.m. that day and a funeral service was conducted at 2 p.m. the next day in the First Universalist Church. The account stated, "Mr. Kellogg has long been failing." It added he "was one of the honored pioneers of La Crosse.... Hand in hand with others he labored to build up the city — and has lived to see much of his hoping more than realized."[145] A separate story called for all master Masons to attend a special service at noon Sunday for Simeon. Mark himself was a master Mason and had been entered into the apprentice degree Aug. 19, 1864, in Frontier Lodge No. 45.[146] He was raised to a master Mason Dec. 2, 1864.

The Masons also figure in a strange incident involving Kellogg early in 1867, but only sketchy information about it is available. On Jan. 14, Kellogg filed charges through the lodge against a fellow Mason, whose name was not cited. However, the man was found guilty and suspended by the lodge. No other details could be learned.[147]

With his father's illness, Mark apparently became the family's anchor. Fifteen months before, Simeon's illness might have compelled Mark's entry into the feed and grain business, as he sought a more permanent means of providing for his family. He needed a job that offered more financial reward than his position as locals editor and cashier for Pomeroy. He may have been assisted in the enterprise by his wife's brother, John W. Robinson, whose own newspaper ads referred to him as one of the town's leading grocers. But after Kellogg's business failed to recover from the disastrous fire, in early 1867, he turned to a steady position in the city clerk's office to support his family.

He also remained active with the local fire department, as newspaper accounts make clear. On Sunday, morning Feb. 3, another fire engulfed the building next to Pomeroy's newspaper plant. Pomeroy was absent on a tour of the South, but either assistant editor Charles Lobdell or city editor James H. Lambert wrote, "For weary hours the battle raged — the destroying demon licking up buildings and inflammable material with an insatiate and unappeasable greed, blackening the walls...heating almost to burning point the outside of the building stocked with the treasures and souvenirs, the costly printing material and machinery of the proprietor and editor of the *La Crosse Democrat*...."[148]

Kellogg apparently directed the fire department's efforts to save Pomeroy's building, according to the newspaper: "Mark H. Kellogg, formerly cashier of the establishment and Brick's right hand man in the early and less prosperous days of the *Democrat*, was early on hand, and rendered efficient and valuable services." The story's author continued: "We should like to see a good fire department in this city with Mark installed as chief engineer. No better selection could be made. Brave, daring, and possessed of a rare executive talent in times of peril and excitement, he would make an admirable chief."

Nothing came of that proposal, but the paper's newsmen continued to back Kellogg in other ways throughout the year. In late February, the *Democrat's* Lambert left La Crosse for several weeks to join Pomeroy on his tour. Likely, with both men away, Kellogg resumed working at least part-time for the newspaper.[149] A few days later, the newspaper again called for Kellogg's appointment as head of the fire department, praising him as "a man of judgment, pluck, and bravery."[150] With Pomeroy and Lambert away, the column likely was written by Lobdell.

In late March, the city prepared for local elections to be held April 2. At a Democratic convention March 29, among the party's nominees was Kellogg for city clerk. Running at the top of the ticket for mayor was John M. Levy, who many years earlier had sold the Western Enterprise Hotel to Kellogg's father. The campaign was brief but pointed. The *La Crosse Republican* backed Kellogg's opponent, Howard Cramer, and predicted he would win "by a large majority." It added: "He has the confidence of men of all parties, which Mr. Kellogg, his opponent, has not. If Mr. Kellogg is elected he will give the public printing, which he has control of, to the *Democrat*, which does not reflect the views of the Democracy of La Crosse. If Mr. Cramer is elected, his printing will be done at the *REPUBLICAN* office."[151]

The *Democrat* responded with a strong front page endorsement of Kellogg:

"Probably, judging from present indications, the greatest fight tomorrow will be on City Clerk. The Democratic candidate is MARK H. KELLOGG, who is well-known to our citizens, being, although a young man, one of our old residents, and identified with its history for more than half a score of years. MARK is capable, straight-forward, industrious, one of the workingmen of our city, full of energy, pluck and vim — and we appeal with confidence, not alone to merchants, business men, and other interests, but to the laboring poor men of La Crosse, one of whom Mark is. The office will be a good thing for Mark, and Mark a good man for the office. Give him a lift with your ballots tomorrow."[152]

On its page 4, the newspaper printed a separate review of each Democratic candidate, including Kellogg, who was "well-known to all our citizens, as an industrious, intelligent and thoroughly competent young man. He has served the city in times past as a volunteer fireman, in which position he proved himself brave and reliable. He has recently been connected with the clerk's office, and he is thoroughly familiar with the business of the same. He has never asked for office at the hands of any party in the city before, and his election at this time would give universal satisfaction."[153]

Despite the political rhetoric of both statements, the front page endorsement may be more interesting for its description of Kellogg as one of the "laboring, poor men of La Crosse." Equally interesting is the suggestion the office would be good for Kellogg, who perhaps needed a steady job. On the other hand, his ties to Pomeroy likely were a detriment, as the *Republican's* editorial suggested.

On election day, Cramer triumphed over Kellogg, winning by 58 votes in the day's closest race. Kellogg was one of only two Democrats to lose a key city office, suggesting the *Republican's* interpretation about the competition between the newspapers was correct. In noting Cramer's victory, the *Republican* claimed he won "because he is much the better man for the place. This was also a contest between the daily newspapers, in which the *REPUBLICAN* came out ahead."[154] The *Democrat* offered no interpretation on Kellogg's loss, preferring, instead, to focus on the Democrats' victories in other races.

Having lost the clerk's race, Kellogg was now without a job. He suffered a more tragic loss when on Saturday, May 18, 1867, his wife Martha died, "after a long and painful illness," according to obituary notices in both the *Republican* and the *Democrat*.[155] She was only 28 years old. The funeral was held at 2 p.m. Sunday at her father's house, the corner of 5th and Main streets. That fact suggests the Kelloggs may have been living with her parents at the time.

The *Republican* also published a touching tribute to Martha Kellogg on page 1: "The intelligence of the death of Mrs. Mark H. Kellogg...will be received with sadness in this entire community. Mrs. Kellogg was universally esteemed as a lady of rare excellence. The sympathies of numberless friends will be sincerely expressed toward the bereaved families in this severe dispensation of an All-Wise Providence. A kind mother, an affectionate daughter, a devoted wife, and an exemplary and useful woman has departed to another and a better world. May God, in His infinite mercy, vouchsafe all needful good to the young children who have been deprived of a faithful mother's care; and may this community be long shielded from a similar calamity."[156]

Mark Kellogg, now 34, had always been close to his family. But following the deaths of his wife and father, he never again would be as close to his family. By mid-1867, many of his siblings had already moved from La Crosse with their own families, and his mother Lorenda soon followed. After living 16 years in La Crosse, Kellogg himself spent only the remaining spring and summer months in the city, occupying his time writing for the *Democrat* and playing baseball.

Writer Bill O'Neal has noted, "The American love affair with athletics began in the mid-19th Century." No place were these early games more popular than on the emerging frontier. O'Neal said, "Indeed, no section of America responded more readily to aggressiveness, competition, team cooperation, and physical stamina and skill than the West, for these were the very qualities essential for frontier conquest." [157]

Prior to the Civil War, Alexander Cartwright's game of "rounders," or baseball, captivated Easterners, and their love of the game swept westward with the California gold seekers. But the war itself provided a major spurt in baseball's growth in popularity. "The War between the States caused a phenomenal growth in baseball, as soldiers from North and South learned the game on countless campgrounds between battles and drill sessions. After the war, returning veterans took the new game to every corner of the land," [158] O'Neal stated.

Rules of the game in this period differed significantly from today's; the ball itself was soft, not hard. Baseball quickly gained popularity in Wisconsin and Minnesota. It was played in La Crosse as early as 1853, and another game was reportedly played "on the Square" in 1860. [159] After the Civil War, interest and participation in baseball exploded in the town and Kellogg played a role in this emergence. According to the *History of La Crosse, Wisconsin*, "Organized baseball played by teams, or nines, seems to have begun in 1867 when the Gateway City Club had grounds on Seventh near Badger Street. That year it played a game with another team, the Intrepids; the score was 77 to 38 in favor of the Intrepids. These teams played against teams from Sparta, Onalaska and North La Crosse; in a tournament at Madison, the Capitol Junior team gave the Intrepids a drubbing to the tune of 17 to 62." [160]

Today's sports fans expect indepth coverage by the print and broadcast media. Such interest developed early, as events in 1867 La Crosse indicate. Besides Kellogg, several editors and writers for the town's newspapers helped organize and played for its first two baseball teams. Perhaps most involved was Pomeroy's city editor Lambert. Pomeroy himself was a non-player but he encouraged his staffers to participate. Halfway through the baseball "season" he promoted Lambert, who captained the Intrepids, to associate editor.

In mid-April 1867, with spring at hand and municipal elections past, Lambert took note of the community's reawakening with an item in his "Urban and Rural" column: "BASE BALL — Several of our young men were engaged on the public square yesterday and today, playing the favorite game of base ball. We understand there are several good players in the city, and wonder why it is that a Base Ball Club has never been formed here." [161]

A response was not long in coming. On Tuesday, April 16, Lambert wrote, "The pleasant invigorating weather of the past week has at last induced the young men of this city to organize for outdoor sports. Last evening a number of the most active boys met and organized a base ball club." Indicating a second meeting was scheduled for Thursday evening, the city editor listed the names of the fledgling organization's officers, including its vice president — J.H. Lambert. By Thursday's paper, Lambert was challenging other teams to play his own. Dubbed the "Intrepid," the team played its "initiatory game" at 6 o'clock that evening. He concluded: "We hope to see the 'Intrepid' in trim to give or accept a challenge from any club in the state by July first."[162]

In his May 4 column, Lambert reported the Intrepid club had been meeting regularly. The previous evening the first nine had been chosen and playing time decided, apparently by vote. He noted, "J.H. Lambert was chosen captain," and added, "Did not modesty forbid we should be pleased to remark that it is a first class nine, and will hold its ground against anything that will be brought against it." Among the names of the "2d nine" he listed was rightfielder John Symes, the superintendent of Pomeroy's *Democrat*.[163]

A week later (May 11) Lambert noted that a meeting would be held May 13 to organize a second team. On May 14, he mentioned that club had been organized, its temporary officers elected, and a second meeting scheduled for that evening. On Wednesday, May 15, he wrote that the new team would be called the Gateway City Club. Among its directors were M.H. Kellogg and Charles Lobdell, Pomeroy's assistant editor. Lambert concluded his column entry with a prediction: "As soon as the clubs are a little practiced there will undoubtedly be some match games and rare sport, not only among the clubs here but with others outside." References to the teams' practices appeared regularly in Lambert's columns, but the Gateway team suspended its session for Saturday, May 18: "Gateway City Club — In consequence of the decease of the wife of one of the members of this Club (Mr. M.H. Kellogg), the meeting for practice appointed for this evening will not take place, but is adjourned to Monday at 6 p.m."[164]

Not only did Kellogg play on the Gateway Club against Lambert but he wrote about his experiences in one of a dozen columns of humor he wrote that year for the *Democrat* under the *nom de plume* of Jentleman Jerks. On Tuesday, June 4, Lambert published an item that not only ties Kellogg to the Gateway baseball team but also helps confirm his identity

44   SANDY BARNARD

as the writer of the Jentleman Jerks columns. Kellogg was listed as the shortstop on the Gateway team's first nine, a position the Jerks writer stated in his baseball column that he played. Another La Crosse newspaperman, Leonard Lottridge of the *Republican*, was listed as the Gateway's starting pitcher and was elected captain of its first nine.[165]

The next day, June 5, Lambert's column announced that a match game between the Intrepids and Gateway City was scheduled for 4 p.m. Saturday, June 15, on the grounds of the Gateway Club in the city's First Ward. How important was baseball to the community's young men? According to the *Democrat*, "There is probably no sport in which young men and youths can engage that is less likely than base ball playing to lead to bad habits and evil associations. A mean or unprincipled man or boy is usually a lazy one, and such have no business in base ball clubs." Fines could be levied against a member using profane or obscene language.[166]

The big match game was held late Saturday afternoon before several hundred spectators. On Monday, June 17, the *Democrat* not only reported the Intrepids' victory by a 77 to 38 score but included a lengthy inning by inning summary and a box score.[167] Kellogg began the game playing shortstop for the Gateway Club. It appears he had at least three hits in seven at bats (Lambert's account for the eighth inning left unclear how the individual Gateway players did during their at bats that inning). The box score credited Kellogg with four of the team's outs, but he also scored three runs. He batted in at least two runs, although that also is unclear from the game summary. In the field he made at least one error, when he threw wild to first base in the fifth inning. By the seventh inning he had moved to the catcher's position. For his efforts, Lambert, who was the Intrepids' pitcher, caused four of his team's outs but scored seven runs. As the article appears in his column, Lambert likely wrote it.

For Kellogg the game marked both his formal baseball debut and his farewell. On game day (June 15), in a Jentleman Jerks column, entitled, "Jerks as a Base Ballist," he wrote humorously of his early efforts on the field, first as an outfielder, then as shortstop, and finally, as catcher, where he noted, "We did better here. Catching everything — but the ball. Caught the devil from the captain, and all sorts of mean and low remarks from the outsiders."[168] He continued: "Spectators should never be permitted on a base ball field. They must always get up more base bawl [sic] than the players. Which ain't right."

When his on-field efforts proved less than successful, Jerks decided to try umpiring. "This disgusted most every one, including us. All sorts of good things were said about us, such as: 'Partial cuss,' 'don't know nothin' about the rules,' 'Darned old fool,' and such like compliments, pleasant to sensitive people." That led Jerks to conclude that his opening remark — that baseball was good for health and amusement — did not apply to the players themselves: "The amusement part of the game is all with the spectators. We don't know where the health is, unless it is in a black eye, broken finger, sprained ankles, and stiff joints generally. We have resigned, and retire in as good order as possible. Not anymore baseball for Jentleman Jerks."

Apparently, his teammates thought as little of their own playing abilities. Within days, on June 21, the *Democrat* reported the Gateway team had disbanded. However, the account embarrassed Lambert, who was not its writer, by labeling him "the best practical ball player in the city."[169] The next day Lambert responded: "Personal explanation. — Our native modesty, assiduously cultivated and encouraged from childhood, compels us to make a personal explanation, made necessary by the appearance of the item in these columns yesterday relative to the victory of the 'Intrepids' over the 'Gateway City' baseball club, and the disbanding of the latter. The item was not written by the local editor, nor was it intended for the local columns, but by an error of the foreman found its way there."[170] The *Democrat's* foreman was none other than John Symes, also his teammate.

Almost immediately the Gateway team was replaced by a new one, the Creightons, which included several Gateway players, including assistant editor Lobdell as its vice president. It's doubtful Kellogg joined the new team, as his name never appeared in connection with it. Throughout June and July, the *Democrat* continued its extensive coverage of baseball and the two local teams, and occasionally speculated about the outcome of a game between the two. In early July, Lambert noted, "Baseball fever seems to rage quite extensively and alarmingly, but Connecticut seems to be far more severely afflicted than our Western country."[171]

On July 9, Pomeroy reorganized his newspaper's management by promoting Lobdell to co-editor and Lambert to assistant editor. John Symes, previously superintendent, replaced Lambert as local news editor. While Kellogg went unmentioned, he likely was working in some capacity and doing some writing for the paper. Several more Jerks columns were published during the summer, the last on Sept. 26, 1867.

SANDY BARNARD

As noted earlier, that Kellogg later wrote the "Frontier" columns published in the *St. Paul (Minn.) Pioneer* in the early 1870s is easy to establish. After Kellogg's death, the *Pioneer* stated: "Mr. Mark H. Kellogg, reported among the killed of General Custer's command, was a former correspondent of this paper, writing over the *nom de plume* of 'Frontier'."[172] For his "Jerks" writings no similar references tie him to these columns. Instead, his authorship can be pinpointed by eliminating each of the principal staffers of the *Democrat*: Pomeroy himself, co-editor Lobdell, assistant editor Lambert, and John Symes, the ex-superintendent who replaced Lambert as city editor. The most critical factor concerns publication dates of the Jerks material. The first column appeared Feb. 7, 1867, and the last Sept. 26 that year, just before Kellogg moved from La Crosse to Council Bluffs, Iowa. From all indications he never again lived permanently in La Crosse. After his departure, the Jentleman Jerks *nom de plume* also never appeared again in the paper.

The columns' subject matter also offers strong evidence of Kellogg's authorship. He is the only staffer who not only played baseball but also ran for office that spring. Also in his columns, the writer twice focuses on the weather, a favorite subject in Kellogg's later Frontier columns. Too, it's known Kellogg served as assistant local editor at various times for the *Democrat*, probably including while Lambert was away that spring with Pomeroy. One column deals with the trials of editing the locals page, a task that Kellogg frequently handled on his newspapers.

Finally, Kellogg is often portrayed as a man of wit and good fun, which tags him as someone capable of writing humorously. In his later writings he particularly liked to spoof people, and in the Jerks column "Sketches of the South," he takes off on Pomeroy himself. The latter spent from late January to early April traveling through the Reconstruction South, returning just in time for the April election. Jerks kids Pomeroy for his numerous long, rambling letters sent back for publication. While Pomeroy could be bitter or humorous in his writing, it's unlikely he would spoof his own political letters. Also, he was neither a "baseballist" nor an April office seeker.

Lobdell, the assistant editor whom Pomeroy raised to co-editor, played baseball but unlike Kellogg did not seek local office. Also, as editor during Pomeroy's absence he would not have addressed local issues through the spoofs. Finally, unlike Kellogg, he does not appear to have been a man of great humor. Another staffer,[173] John Symes, who in the 1870s became owner-editor of the *La Crosse Democrat*, also can be eliminated as a possibility. In early 1867, he merely ran the printing back shop. Also, when the first columns appeared in February, he was traveling with Pomeroy.

The strongest candidate would be Lambert, who joined the paper in early January 1867. At that time, Pomeroy described him in glowing terms: "Mr. Lambert is a graceful and accomplished writer of ability — a fine businessman, a scholar, a gentleman and a young Democrat in whom we are well pleased, as the public will be." Such a man would seem well-suited to write the satire apparent in the Jerks' columns, no matter the subject — railroad travel, the weather, local politics or baseball. From a content standpoint, a fair case could be made for him as Jerks. However, he did not seek office in the April election as Jerks did. Also, in the baseball column Jerks referred to himself as the shortstop, a position Kellogg played, and to the team captain. Lambert, who pitched, was himself captain of the Intrepids. He would have been unlikely to refer to himself in the third person. Also, as noted earlier, Lambert was embarrassed when he was labeled the best ball player in town. Perhaps most important, Lambert continued with the *La Crosse Democrat* for at least a couple of years, until he may have gone to New York City with Pomeroy at the end of the decade, when the latter started a paper there. The Jerks columns and references ceased after September 1867, about the same time Kellogg departed for Council Bluffs.

Chapter 5
The Council Bluffs Experience

During the war years Kellogg had established a close relationship with the *Democrat* and Pomeroy, and in the post-war years the men retained some ties, even though Kellogg did not figure prominently among Pomeroy's editors. In early 1867, he likely was a part-time local editor. On his numerous trips that year, Pomeroy often had his employees accompany him. In January, Symes traveled with him. On other occasions Lobdell and Lambert joined their boss on his journeys. In September, when Pomeroy spoke in Council Bluffs, Iowa, and other places to assess the chances for the Democrats in the 1868 election, who accompanied him? It was Mark Kellogg, whose lengthy letter from Council Bluffs, full of praise for Pomeroy, was published Oct. 7, 1867.[174]

In that letter (written Oct. 1), Kellogg said he was returning to La Crosse but his stay in his home town was brief. Within weeks he returned to Council Bluffs, sent there by Pomeroy to work for him and the Democrats. Only his young daughters, Cora and Mattie Grace, tied him to La Crosse, but even those bonds did not keep him in the Wisconsin city. When he moved to Council Bluffs that fall, Kellogg left the girls in the care of his in-laws, Mr. and Mrs. Charles Robinson. Except for a brief period in 1870, Kellogg spent the remaining nine years of his life wandering and writing about the frontier.

Kellogg's string of bad luck with jobs continued in Council Bluffs. His Iowa stop proved the most controversial experience of his life as well as his most unrewarding and bitter, as his farewell comments in the *Council Bluffs Democrat* made clear in August 1868. It also destroyed whatever closeness had existed between Kellogg and Pomeroy. With the La Crosse publisher as principal financial backer for the *Council Bluffs Democrat*, Kellogg spent the next seven months getting the new *Democrat* ready but its first issue wasn't published until May 3, 1868.[175] This new paper provided another vehicle for Pomeroy to advance his venomous political views.[176] In August 1868, after just three months, Kellogg was forced to yield his editorial position and whatever financial interest he might have had in the paper. The *Democrat* limped along under the editorship of one of his partners until late fall, when Pomeroy finally pulled the financial plug.

In a bitter parting column on Aug. 20, Kellogg wrote, "For seven months previous to the establishment of the *Democrat*, we labored here with pen and by word of mouth."[177] His remarks in this column indicate how terrible an ordeal his Iowa experience must have been. He began by saying he had "no regrets in the movement," an ambiguous reference either to the newspaper or perhaps to its rabid political views. His distress immediately becomes evident: "We have labored strenuously for the interest and advancement of this city, and have *starved nearly to death* while so doing...and as yet we have to witness a cent remuneration, or an exhibition of appreciation in any shape whatever." The italics are Kellogg's.

His final three paragraphs are less bitter: "To the few who have shown us kindness, we wish to return thanks in all truthfulness, and with the full warmth of a grateful heart.

"In withdrawing from the DEMOCRAT, we do not wish it understood that our identity as a citizen of Council Bluffs is lost, for we propose remaining in this, our adopted home, for many years, if our life is spared.

"We have struggled hard, and bestowed much labor for the interest of the city, and we retire from the DEMOCRAT for reasons that are not necessary to make public at present, but without a pang of regret or misgiving, and we bid adieu to the readers of the paper in all kindness."[178]

What brought about such a personal and professional disaster isn't clear. Professor Leonard F. Kellogg blamed Pomeroy for persuading Mark Kellogg to pull up stakes from his long-time home town on the Mississippi River to gamble on success in the Missouri River town of Council Bluffs.[179] The new newspaper would further Pomeroy's agenda, but beyond that the La Crosse editor had little concern for his friend.

In his article, "Colonel Custer's Copperhead," historian Lewis O. Saum essentially agrees that the primary culprit was Pomeroy, but he theorizes Kellogg himself may not have been an innocent bystander. Saum says, "[Kellogg] was very much a part of the untidiness."[180] Saum quotes an August 1875 column that Kellogg penned under his Frontier *nom de plume* for the *St. Paul Daily Pioneer-Press* to suggest that the reporter was ca

SANDY BARNARD

pable of writing the angry "red hot" copy evident for the few months he spent with the *Council Bluffs Democrat*. In 1875, Kellogg, writing about Indian depredations near Bismarck, criticized the Republican administration's Indian Peace Policy: "Bah! I say, turn the dogs of war loose, and drive them off the face of the earth, if they do not behave themselves." Saum concludes: "The auras of 'K.K.K.'s Council Bluffs of 1868 and 'Frontier's' Bismarck of 1875 bear a great deal of resemblance."[181]

In tone they may, but Kellogg's remarks of 1875 were in a different, less political context. In the 1870s, Kellogg was much the frontiersman both in his journalism and in his community involvement, first in Brainerd, Minn., and later in Bismarck. At times he wrote admiringly of Indian life and lamented over what he saw as their predestined fate. As a white man in the latter half of the 19th century, he supported corralling the Indians to ease white civilization's advancement. Pomeroy and Kellogg's key partner in Council Bluffs, Alf. S. Kierolf, may have shared a deep devotion to the Copperhead political philosophy, but Kellogg's beliefs did not run as deeply. Financially and intellectually, he seems no more than a secondary partner in the Copperhead enterprise the *Council Bluffs Democrat* represented. Also, while Kellogg's name appeared on the masthead as assistant editor for about three months, a substantial portion of the time he spent traveling and may have been ill while out of town.

Besides Kierolf and Kellogg, the other key figure in the Council Bluffs fiasco was Benjamin F. Montgomery, a La Crosse lawyer. He also made his way to Council Bluffs sometime in late 1867 or 1868 and initially had a business role in the firm styled as "Alf. S. Kierolf & Co."[182] Kierolf, a journalistic and political hack, had bounced about from state to state. Having achieved a degree of notoriety for his perverse political views while editor of the *Sentinel on the Border*, published at Louisville, Ky., he served as editor of the Council Bluffs paper. After Pomeroy's arrival in La Crosse, mentions of Kierolf had appeared periodically in the paper, but the extent of their political and social relationship is difficult to determine. The *Omaha Herald* praised Kierolf for having "a fine reputation as a writer and a journalist," adding that he had "the character and manners of a gentleman."[183] As Saum documents in his article, Kierolf was anything but gentlemanly in his writing and political attacks. The *Herald* also noted Kellogg's presence as locals editor: "We have enough acquaintance with his ability and experience to know that he will readily reach the higher standards of localizing."

The Council Bluffs paper's motto, positioned beneath its nameplate on p. 1, gave clear indication of its politics: "The World Is Governed Too Much." The newspaper's masthead is the only one with copies available today that displays Kellogg's name. References to Kellogg and examples of his writing also can be found, especially in the locals columns. He spins anecdotes, drops names, boosts advertisers and the town, and offers opinions, political views and homespun wisdom. Here are some examples from the May 16, 1868, issue:[184]

- "The ladies in the 'Bee Hive' are as busy as you please. Mrs. Whitaker and Walcott, who have charge of the ladies department, are giving entire satisfaction, and we commend them cheerfully."

- "Professor Mueller, the well-known photographer and dealer in pianos, of this city is the largest advertiser in the New Northwest.... This means 'push,' and such men not only make money, as they should, but are the very life of every town."

- "We took a run through Mr. Mueller's gallery yesterday and were much pleased with the display of plain and colored photographs we found there. The oil paintings are excellently executed and very natural.... Those desiring 'shadows' [photographs] should give Mr. Mueller a call by all means."

- "TOO LATE, CAP. — At our hotel[185] we have several waiter girls who attend to 'biz.' Lucky among them is a damsel of several summers and many moons, who has a peculiar vernacular and a singular expression of delicacy, and we were struck yesterday with a case in point. While we were partaking of our noon meal, a gentleman took a seat near us and called for a dish which, it seems, was out. The handsome maiden promptly replied to his request by stating, 'You're too late, Cap., that's played!' Plain and conclusive, we thought."

- "A DECIDEDLY SCRUBBY PETTY-GROWTH — We have had returned to us from Glenwood, in this state, a package of DEMOCRATS, with this superscription on the wrapper, which is made in the most ignorant and unintelligible scrawl:

SANDY BARNARD

Councel (sic) Bluffs Democratt (sic)
Refusee (sic)
Postage du (sic)
Two nice a man to take
Such a filthy sheet

C W Pettegrew

"We do not remember now to whom these papers were sent, but the name was probably given us by some good friend, who evidently misapprehended the party to have been a gentleman, even though a Republican. If the papers were sent to this noble Petty Growth at Glenwood, he is certainly modest in claiming for himself that he is 'Two nice a man to take such a filthy sheet.' Go and wipe your nose, Pet, wash your dirty face, and carry out your 'har!'"

The newspaper's May 26 edition carried a series of comments from other newspapers about the *Democrat's* birth. The *Plaquemine (La.) South* noted that Kierolf had associated himself with Kellogg and Montgomery, "two able and true champions of the good cause of constitutional liberty," while the *Chatfield (Minn.) Democrat* referred to Kellogg as "our young friend and former fellow citizen (in La Crosse)." The editor added, "He is a spicy and lively writer and will make his 'mark' as a localist."[186] Later, the *Bowling Green (Ind.) Aurora Borealis* referred to Kellogg as Kierolf's "able, accomplished and experienced partner."

Kellogg continued to write his column through early June. On June 3, he praised Council Bluffs as "all right and always will be. Even her enemies concede that she will be a good town one of these days. We never had a doubt of that, and we expect to live to see here the most important city in the New Northwest."

In another brief, he suggested, "This city needs a first class hotel as bad anything we know of…. The city has felt this want for some time and it is hoped that an effort will be speedily made for the erection of such a house as will be a convenience to the traveling public and a credit to us as a city."[187] Several times he indicated his dissatisfaction with the Pacific House where he was living.

More important, his role with the newspaper changed after June 9, the last day his name is listed as assistant editor. He was replaced by lawyer Montgomery. Why the change was made is unknown. Likely he continued working for the paper through the date of his final column, Aug. 20. However, little that appears in the paper between June 9 and Aug. 20

seems to match his earlier writings in La Crosse and Council Bluffs, or those later in the *St. Paul Pioneer* and *Bismarck Tribune*. In the locals column of July 25 appears the following: "PERSONAL — M.H. Kellogg, after an absence of several weeks in Chicago on business connected with this office, and visiting among his numerous friends in Wisconsin, returned home last evening. During his absence his health has been quite poor, but he is now feeling much better."[188] Nothing suggests exactly how long he was away or what his health problem was.

The next reference to Kellogg is his valedictory address of Aug. 20. Kierolf wrote, just above Kellogg's remarks, that the breakup of the trio of partners stemmed from "causes...beyond my control, and are needless here to mention. Suffice it to say, they are my Appomattox!"[189] His comments are far less bitter, and he expresses confidence that Montgomery will sustain the newspaper's "character, as an enterprising and wide-awake journal."

Despite his own statement, Kierolf apparently remained involved at least as an employee for several weeks. Sometime in late September he regained control of the paper, which published for at least another month. According to a history of the city's early journalism, "The last issue of the memorable paper was on Oct. 31 when it was published under the title of RED HOT, which contained some very bitter and denunciatory articles. On Dec. 12 the press and materials were sold to M.M. Pomeroy under a chattel mortgage."[190]

Montgomery stayed on and practiced law there for many years. Kierolf's later years are well documented by Saum, who places him working for newspapers in such scattered locales as Bellefonte, Pa., Lexington, Mo., and Carrollton, Mo. Political soul mates Kierolf and Pomeroy turned on each other in 1869. As Saum recounts the situation, in 1869 Kierolf had written an expose of Pomeroy's shady dealings and views, or so a prepublication announcement for "Brick Pomeroy Unmasked" indicated. The book apparently never was published, but somehow, Pomeroy obtained at least excerpts, which he printed in his New York newspaper, *Pomeroy's Democrat*. His old *La Crosse Democrat* published portions also.[191]

According to "Brick Pomeroy Unmasked," Pomeroy furnished Kierolf with $5,500 to start the *Council Bluffs Democrat*. Supposedly Montgomery, described in the article as "well known and respected in this city," removed from the copy hook "several articles, written by Kierolf, denounc

SANDY BARNARD

ing Pomeroy in the vilest of terms." When Montgomery challenged him, Kierolf said the newspaper "must take that course to get up a large circulation."

"'But it is not true,' says Montgomery. 'Damn the truth of the matter,' says Kierolf. 'We must look out for No. one'."

The article relates that while Montgomery was away, Kierolf changed the *Democrat* to "the resurrected and loathsome *Sentinel-on-the-Border*," Kierolf's former paper. That was "the last blow needed to kill" the *Democrat*, which survived just a few more weeks. Later, Pomeroy refused to hire Kierolf for a job on his New York newspaper. That supposedly prompted Kierolf to undertake the effort to discredit Pomeroy.

At this point in the article, Pomeroy turned on Kellogg, whom he said Kierolf relied on "for the greater portion of the *truth* of his work." He sarcastically wrote, "This fellow Kellogg is pretty well known to this community, and we don't propose to take measure of his character here. If any one at a distance wishes to know of him, we refer them to the 'Wide-awake' order of this city, of which he was once the chief actor, and no man can boast of burning more oil than he." Was Pomeroy referring to the fire that destroyed Kellogg's business, perhaps suggesting Kellogg torched the place himself?

His next comment seems to support such an interpretation. "We also refer them to Patsey Daley, who was once his business partner, a better boy than whom don't live. Also we refer them to Jesse B. Williams, ex-alderman of this city, and if from the above named persons they are not satisfied in regard to Mr. Kierolf's authority [Kellogg], then we refer them to any of our other citizens. Mr. Kierolf made a decided mistake when he took Kellogg for authority, and if nothing else, this fact alone would cause the people of this vicinity to scout the work as false and silly."

At this time, the La Crosse paper was owned and edited by John Symes, who had worked for Pomeroy as general superintendent and as an editor earlier. Symes said in a companion brief that he himself cared nothing about the matter between Kierolf and Pomeroy, "but we have to acknowledge that knowing all the facts as we do, our indignation is somewhat aroused by such Judaism."[192] His statement adds nothing to understanding Kellogg's role.

Never again did the paths of Kellogg and Kierolf cross. Ironically, Kierolf died just a few months before Kellogg was killed at Little Big Horn. On Feb. 25, 1876, in Carrollton, Mo., an editor of another Missouri newspaper, I.N. Hawkins, confronted Kierolf. After Hawkins failed to heed a warning not to come closer, Kierolf shot him five times. Hawkins, who apparently was drunk, died the next day; Kierolf posted bail, but soon died of a heart attack at age 40.[193]

Despite Pomeroy's discrediting of Kellogg, he wasn't unwilling in July 1876 to claim the reporter as his own Little Big Horn campaign correspondent. As for Kellogg, after the Council Bluffs' episode of 1868, he virtually disappeared from late 1868 through 1869. As noted earlier, Kellogg lived at the Pacific House during the period. The next Bushnell city directory, issued as of May 15, 1869, did not list him. However, a separate directory for 1869-1870, issued by J.M. Wolfe, listed him still at the Pacific House.[194] That may mean Kellogg stayed in Council Bluffs well into 1869. How he supported himself is undetermined.

Chapter 6
Wandering on the Frontier

The City Directory for La Crosse for 1868-1869 does not list Mark Kellogg, indicating he had not returned to the town at the time the book was compiled. By 1870, Kellogg had emerged again from the mists. As Saum noted, the 1870 census lists him living in La Crosse with his daughters, Cora and Mattie Grace, in the house of his in-laws, the Charles Robinsons.[195] According to the La Crosse City Directory for 1870-1871, Robinson ran a boarding house at 98 Main St. The 1870 census gave Kellogg's occupation as a printer. Just as interesting are the occupations of three other men living in the household who were unrelated to either the Kelloggs or the Robinsons. Three are telegraphers, including Frank Burton, who was on duty six years later when news of Kellogg's death at the Little Big Horn came down the telegraph line from Bismarck. While the 1870-1871 City Directory reported Kellogg as one of the boarders at the Robinsons', it gave his occupation as telegraph operator.[196]

How long Kellogg stayed at home in La Crosse with his children and in-laws can't be ascertained. Other writers theorized that Kellogg spent much of the period between mid-1870 to mid-1873 working for the Northern Pacific Railroad. Close review of pertinent historical records and period newspapers seems to bear that out. In fact, Kellogg's own writings placed his arrival at Aitkin, Minn., in the winter of 1869-1870. In a Frontier column, he wrote from Aitkin in January 1876, "The weather up to date has been very similar to the winter of 1869-70, in this part of God's acre. I remember it distinctly, it having been my first winter spent so far north in Minnesota."[197] That would suggest he went home in the spring to La Crosse for a longer visit, when the separate recorders for the census and the city directory reported him living with the Robinsons. But Kellogg was more than just a railroad worker or telegrapher during the three-year period. His story is closely entwined with the railroad's.

A railroad across the northern tier of states had long been desired by many Americans. On April 2, 1864, President Abraham Lincoln signed the railroad's charter, giving formal authorization for a line to be constructed from Lake Superior in eastern Minnesota to Puget Sound in Washington, but railroad historian Charles Wood said "The steps necessary for building such a road had their beginnings more than three quarters of a century before."[198] Exploration of this wild northern country went on throughout the period, predating the Lewis and Clark Expedition of 1804-1806 by 17 years. In the 1850s, several possible routes were surveyed, including one across the Northern Plains led by Isaac I. Stevens, governor of Washington Territory who would be killed in action as a Union Army brigadier general in 1862 at Chantilly, Va. Despite his favorable report on the feasibility of such a route, national politics doomed any chance for the first road to follow his proposal. The first transcontinental railroad followed a central path across the country, and the gold spike ceremony at Promontory, Utah, on May 10, 1869, marked the completion of the Union Pacific Railroad, amid great national celebration. In the meantime, Josiah Perham, an eastern promoter of railroads, pushed for a northern railroad and by 1864, his efforts were rewarded by Lincoln's signature. But Perham lacked the financing to fulfill his dream and died in 1868 with not a rail laid. A group of eastern financiers headed by J. Gregory Smith as president lobbied Congress for several years before receiving permission to issue $100 million in construction bonds. Jay Cooke and Company, which had extraordinary success selling government bonds during the Civil War, became marketer for the bonds. Wood said, "Jay Cooke, in addition, to his background in banking and his valuable contacts in high office, also had a flair for promotion on a grand scale. Enthusiastic and optimistic by nature, his one failing was that he made no provision for the inevitable downturns of business."[199]

Cooke's financial scheme eventually installed his company as the railroad's controlling manager and positioned it to earn huge profits. The railroad was granted generous land rights within the existing states and the territories it would cross. By the summer of 1870, Cooke's company was selling bonds, raising about $30 million by late 1871. Groundbreaking ceremonies for the Northern Pacific took place at Thomsons Junction, just west of Duluth, Minn., on Feb. 15, 1870, and actual construction began that July. At the junction the NPRR met another Cooke enterprise, the Lake Superior and Mississippi Railroad, that ran from St. Paul to Duluth, a boom town thanks to the railroad.

SANDY BARNARD

"For a thousand miles west of Duluth, there was no town or village worthy of the name on or near the railroad," Wood's railroad history notes, adding, "With the largest communities 2,000 miles from St. Paul at the western end of the railroad, it was largely up to the Northern Pacific to create its own markets."[200]

Initially, construction moved quickly. By the winter of 1870, the railroad's headquarters town of Brainerd in central Minnesota was effectively connected to Duluth. By late 1871, the line had been extended west from Brainerd to the Red River towns of Moorhead, Minn., and Fargo, Dakota Territory. Traffic moved along the route, and survey teams were in the field in the territories of North Dakota and Montana and along the great rivers of the Northwest, the Snake and the Columbia. Construction slowed in 1872 and financial disaster followed in 1873.

Throughout these years, Kellogg was active in the arena dominated by the NPRR. In October, 1871, the *La Crosse Republican and Leader* reported, "Mark H. Kellogg is in the city and will remain here a few days. Mark is telegraphing for the Northern Pacific Railway, and is enthusiastic over the resources and prospects for the new northwest."[201] Apart from his own writing, that was the first direct tie of Kellogg to the railroad, but other signs point to an even earlier relationship. On Aug. 16, 1871, the newspaper published a letter, written July 10 from Duluth, whose author noted, "Some weeks have elapsed since we penned an article for your journal."[202] The account, full of details about the railroad, was signed with Kellogg's familiar "Frontier." His letter suggested he was living at the Clark House. With the streak of boosterism frequently seen in his writings, he commented favorably about Duluth's prospects: "This is the dawn, out the darkness which has hung like a pall over the future; and *now* its citizens are loud in the expressions of satisfaction, and still louder in their protestations of the bright future of their new place of adoption. May be — may be not — time will show."

After mentioning J. Gregory Smith and other railroad officers had recently visited Duluth, he predicted, "Full work will commence on this great thoroughfare on the [July] 15th. Track laying will be renewed on that date; and be pushed forward at the rate of from two to four miles per day until the line reaches Red River, which it will do in early October. The grading west of the Mississippi River is nearly completed to Red River; and the road, when completed, will be as good a one as can be found in the west."

Continuing his boosterism, Kellogg predicted, "Everything now looks cheering and prosperous; and ere another year has rolled around your correspondent expects to address your readers of the *Leader* from Montana, which is destined to be the wealthiest State in the Union."

Sometime that fall, Kellogg met John P. Dunn, a druggist who remained his friend for the next several years, both in Brainerd and Bismarck.[203] Dunn arrived in Brainerd that fall, setting up its first drug store[204] but remained less than a year. By June or July 1872, he had relocated his business to Edwinton, D.T., a village later renamed Bismarck.[205] Again, his drug store was a first — the first west of the Red River. They renewed their friendship after Kellogg moved to Bismarck in May 1873.

A second, even more chatty, letter from Kellogg was published Nov. 25, 1871, by the La Crosse newspaper, six days after it was written. Kellogg opened with an apology: "Since my return to the NPRR my time has been so fully occupied that I have neglected you somewhat. However, I will endeavor to redeem myself as best I can, for that neglect, by giving you what 'spice' I have gathered in the meantime."[206]

He updated readers on construction of the line toward its Minnesota terminus: "Work on the NORTHERN PACIFIC R.R. has progressed nicely, and the 'End of the Track' was, last night, within 15 miles of its Minnesota, Western terminus, viz: Moorhead, more familiarly known as the 'Red River Crossing.' From one and a half miles to two and a half miles of track per day have been laid during the fall. A heavy fall of snow accompanied by a strong gale of wind commenced on Friday night. The snow continued to fall until Saturday night. Of course all work was stopped during the storm, but will be again vigorously pushed on tomorrow; and every available means used to carry the track through to Moorhead before the end of this month. The snow that has fallen is more of an advantage than otherwise, as it will keep out the frost."

In this column he made his first mention of former Confederate Maj. Gen. Thomas L. Rosser, a close friend of George Custer's while both men were cadets at West Point a decade earlier. The two tangled with each other several times during the Civil War. Now Rosser was working as the NPRR's division engineer.

Kellogg next reported at length about the new railroad headquarters town of Brainerd itself. While impressed with the town and its growth, he regretted, "I cannot speak as well for the morals of the place. It certainly has a large element of a rough character within its limits. There are no

SANDY BARNARD

Sabbaths; there is no cessation of dissipation and rioting. While nothing of a serious character has yet occurred here, still there exists an element ready at any moment to do an evil deed. This element is kept under in every mind through a dread of the strong arm of the law, which steps in whenever the demonstrations indicate trouble of a serious nature."

In his conclusion, he described in near poetic language life in the new northwest: "As we write the snow is falling slowly and lazily. No wind is stirring here. We rarely feel the winds here in the forest, but every evidence of winter is at hand. This fact, not the inclemency of the weather, is decreasing the labor of improvement or the march of civilization. With steady blows, the hardy pioneers are turning forests into cities, and populating vast prairies with a strong, hardy race, who are ready to battle with life for a livelihood, or against a foe, traitor or invader. This is what this great International Railway is doing for a hitherto almost unknown region."

In the wilderness of central Minnesota, the NPRR selected a village at Brainerd to serve as its headquarters. Some 115 miles from Duluth, it was situated at a place dubbed The Crossing, after construction engineers found it a desirable place to bridge the Mississippi River. Brainerd's founding date is uncertain, but is believed to have been in the summer of 1870. In any case, in March 1871, the first construction train rolled into the "City of Pines" followed a month later by the first passenger train. For a time, Brainerd's prospects looked golden as the NPRR constructed large facilities for trains and maintenance in the area. In September a townsite plat was filed for recording with the Crow Wing County Register of Deeds and the place officially became known as Brainerd. Its name derives from the family of the wife of NPRR President Smith.

In ending his Nov. 25, 1871, column, Kellogg promised to write again about the towns along the line, but no such column was found. Once again he slipped away from view for about six months until the first of his Frontier columns appeared from Brainerd July 12, 1872, in the *St. Paul Daily Pioneer*. He remained proud of the town's development: "Brainerd is beyond a doubt the champion town on the line of the NPRR. It possesses the largest hotels, the most beautiful church building, the finest stores, more saloons and fastest horses, more great hearted men, handsomer women, and the best schools and brightest scholars of any other point on the road."[207]

In much of the rest of the column, he offered an extended report of a fishing outing that he clearly enjoyed. In his next *Pioneer* column, July

27, 1872, he played police reporter by detailing the aftermath of the murder of a young woman by two Indians, who later were lynched by a mob in Brainerd. A young woman, Helen McArthur of Crow Wing, a town south of Brainerd, disappeared in May. The Indians were seized after authorities learned they had raped and murdered the woman. After the Indians' trial was delayed, angry citizens acted. Kellogg wrote that "a small number of citizens," with the help of Sheriff Jack Gurrell, demanded one of the accused, To-Be-Sko-Gesheick-Wabe, confess.[208]

"He declared himself innocent, was very reticent and stubborn. Then the committee applied a little hemp to the neck of the Indian, hauling him up for a short time, then letting him down again. A few doses of this sort brought the fellow to a CONFESSION," Kellogg reported. The Indian's confession outraged townspeople.

"About half past 9 o'clock 300 citizens or more, followed the lead of men not citizens of Brainerd, to the building where the Indians were confined. Arriving there, the crowd soon burst open the door, surrounded the sheriff, who could not resist, and forcibly carried the two Indians out into the street, and thence to a saloon called 'The Last Turn,' which is situated on the corner of two business streets. Before this building stands a large Norway pine tree with branches extending towards the building. Ropes were in readiness, and immediate preparations were made for stringing up the Indians." The other Indian, Gee-Gee-Once, stolidly but persistently declared his innocence until the end.

To-Be-Sko-Gesheick-Wabe also declared himself innocent but promised to show where the girl's head was buried. "A slight impatience became visible in the surging crowd; and again cries of 'hang him!' 'String him up!' &c, were repeatedly given, and 'hang him up' it was. With a heavy, rapid pull, he was carried clear to the limb from which he hung." The Indian struggled so fiercely that he burst the fastenings on his feet and arms, and clutching to the rope over his head, he held on the limb of the tree and attempted to haul himself up.

"At this juncture some bystander fired a ball from a revolver into his neck. Instantly, crack, crack went the shots from several revolvers held in the hands of those on the ground, most of which shots took effect in the Indian's body. Of course, his hold loosened, the rope having been slacked, he fell to a level with his brother and they were left dangling there until morning."

SANDY BARNARD

The coroner's inquest the next day elicited little information. Did Kellogg know who committed the act? Undoubtedly, but he wasn't about to reveal any identities. "Not a known Brainerd citizen had a hand in the matter. Your correspondent has a large acquaintance here and on the line of the Northern Pacific, and I state positively the hanging was done by others than citizens of this town, or employees of the Northern Pacific Railroad Company. The general expression of citizens, however, endorsed the act."

Some people expressed their fear to Kellogg that Indians might seek revenge for the hangings, but he had no concerns. "No fears need be entertained for the safety of Brainerd. We do not dread or fear the Indians, in the least," he said, an ironic statement considering his own end in 1876.

His Aug. 1 column in the *Pioneer* also suggests he may have spent some time along the line of the Union Pacific Railroad in the middle of the country. If so, it probably came during the 18-month gap between 1868-1870 when his whereabouts appears less clear. Brainerd's own reputation as a railroad town is "anything but good," he wrote but it's "a paradise compared with [Julesburg], Cheyenne and other towns that sprung up on the line of the Union Pacific Railroad during its building."[209]

According to the column, Kellogg may have viewed himself more as a journalist than a mere occasional letter writer: "A serious accident, which was telegraphed you, occurred near the round house and machine shops of the NPRR yesterday afternoon." Unfortunately, he offered his readers no more information about the incident.

In closing his Aug. 1 column, written only two days before, he sought to reassure his readers about the dangers of life in a "frontier country:" "The chain of incidents, tragedy and death that have occurred at this point during a week just passed has created some gloom and solemness of thought; but such incidents, and similar affairs, are the history of all the frontiers, and this feeling soon passes away. Like a tornado have these things rushed by, and we now expect months of tranquillity and peace. The element of peaceable, law abiding citizens is now largely predominant here.... Lawlessness is at an end; the terror is past, and we predict that no more horrors will be heard from in Brainerd, unless occasioned by an outside or foreign element."

Kellogg's boosterism tendency surfaced again the next day: "I did not expect to intrude upon the columns of the *PIONEER* so soon again, but the outrageously false statements of a [St. Paul]*Press* reporter relative to Brainerd published in the *Press* on the 27th inst., makes a contradiction imperatively necessary in order to do away with false impressions which will naturally arise from a perusal of that highly drawn, imaginative tissue of falseness."[210] Kellogg refuted the reporter's charges about Brainerd's gambling den, saloons and houses of prostitution. He pointed out that Brainerd's at least were run with open doors while in St. Paul such places are covered "with a cloak that hides their misdeeds from the eyes of the passer-by."

The unnamed reporter was severely criticized by the obviously outraged correspondent from Brainerd: "It is of no use to particularize farther, but I will simply say that the youthful reporter of the *Press*, while striving to cover himself all over with glory, has brought *anethemas* upon his head, and a newspaper published in St. Paul called the *Press*, will soon realize the fact. His statements in regard to Brainerd, in the main, from first to last are grossly false, as the *PIONEER* reporter will endorse, or any other gentleman who investigates the matter."

Kellogg next favorably compared his current town to other railroad towns he had known, specifically citing LaSalle, Ill., of 1851-1853, Cairo, Ill., Council Bluffs and Omaha, and many others he did not name. His outrage subsiding, he ended his letter with some recommendations for his readers: "Believe no sensational reports from this section. Take no stock in canardish statements. There has been no prospect of a riot in or a raid upon Brainerd at any time during her brief existence, and today she is as safe from such things as St. Paul."

Kellogg hadn't worked regularly on a newspaper staff since Council Bluffs four years earlier. That soon changed. The *Brainerd Tribune* on Aug. 31 reported a new newspaper would soon begin publication. "It is to be a Greeley paper from now till the November election, after that an agricultural journal.... a Greeley paper in Brainerd would, no doubt, be a financial success."[211] The first tie of the Greeley newspaper to Kellogg appeared in the Hopkins history of the Kellogg family: "He was a telegraph operator and correspondent for several Eastern papers, and was connected with several papers in Western states, among them being the *La Crosse Democrat*, *Greeley Wave* and *Bismarck Tribune*."[212]

Originally, the *Brainerd Tribune*, Republican in its politics, was owned and edited by M.C. Russell, but by 1876 a local political figure and businessman named W.W. Hartley bought him out. Until August 1872, Hartley had been a strong regular Republican, but that year he opted to turn to ward the party's liberal wing. A group of national Republican Party reformers set out to defeat President Ulysses S. Grant for reelection in 1872 by organizing the Liberal Republican Party. It called for civil service reform, an end to corruption in government and the withdrawal of troops from the South. The Democratic Party joined with Liberal Republicans in supporting Horace Greeley, founder of the *New York Tribune*, for the presidency. An editor for more than 30 years, Greeley was a great molder of public opinion in the period just before and during the Civil War. For this purpose, he never hesitated to use his newspaper, which he had started as a Whig daily in 1841. Previously, Greeley had advocated a high protective tariff, the organization of labor, temperance, a homestead law, and women's rights, and opposed monopoly, land grants to railroads and slavery. His editorials were widely quoted. He was one of the first members of the new Republican Party, although he denounced President Lincoln's border-state policy and embarrassed the administration by his anti-war sentiments. Following the Civil War he favored African-American suffrage and amnesty for all Southerners; he defied public opinion by signing the bail bond to release former Confederate President Jefferson Davis from prison. Greeley was known for his inconsistencies, and this was no more evident than in his quest for the presidency in 1872. In this campaign he ran against the Republican candidate despite the fact he was one of the founders of the Republican Party. In early November 1872, Greeley was badly defeated by incumbent Grant. On Nov. 29, just a few weeks after his defeat, he died in New York City.

When news about Kellogg's death reached Brainerd in early July 1876, Hartley, who had been auditor for Crow Wing County in 1872, wrote about Kellogg: "For a time he was employed by the Northern Pacific as train dispatcher and [telegraph] operator, and was afterwards associate editor with ourself of the *Daily Greeley Wave*, a presidential campaign paper, published at this place in 1872."[213] Hartley, the crucial figure in the operation, wrote many years later in an historical recollection for *the Brainerd Daily* Dispatch: "I published a daily paper, called the *Greeley Wave*, nominally and earnestly supporting the presidential ticket indicated by its name, but primarily in the interest of our local ticket."[214]

Kellogg had been a Lincoln Republican in 1860 and a Copperhead Democrat by the end of the Civil War. In 1872, he changed his political stripes once again — to an amalgamation of various personal political philosophies under the banner of Liberal Republican. In a column written

Aug. 21, 1872, Kellogg took note of the *Greeley Wave's* debut, but he didn't mention his own role: "The *Daily Wave* is the name of a daily and weekly newspaper which appeared this morning, edited and published by Messrs. Hartley & Steele. It is a supporter of Greeley and Brown, and will do great service during the coming campaign."[215] This Aug. 21 column was his last for several months. In the meantime, two activities dominated his time. First, he worked as the *Wave's* assistant editor, and he sought election again, this time having been nominated for the state legislature by the Liberal Republicans.

Despite their political differences, Hartley, Russell and Kellogg must have remained friends. Russell, in typical good-natured frontier editor fashion, welcomed his new journalistic and political competition:

THE "GREELEY WAVE."

The above is the title of a little daily paper which made its appearance on Thursday morning last [Aug. 22, 1872] in this place, published and edited by W.W. Hartley and J.W. Steele. It is a professed 'campaigner,' run in the interest of and with the hope to make a few votes up this way for the motley ticket headed by the Horrors of Baltimore. In this object they have a decidedly small share of our sympathy — otherwise they have our good wishes."[216]

Another article in the same paper revealed Kellogg as a fiery speaker on the political stump. Under the title, "A Greeley Fizzle," the newspaper reported two men, M.F. Keating and M.H. Kellogg, had spoken at a Greeley for president rally. Kellogg, the newspaper said, "just about tore off his shirt to start with, and harangued the boys vociferously, which amused the boys, and they all cheered for Grant."[217]

Other newspapers marked the new publication's debut. The *St. Paul Pioneer* called it "a sprightly little daily."[218] The *Duluth Tribune* borrowed the *Pioneer's* language in welcoming the Wave: "The *Daily Greeley Wave* is the name of a sprightly little daily paper, about half the size of the *Tribune*, which has just made its appearance at Brainerd."[219] Whether its use of Tribune was referring to itself or to the *Brainerd Tribune* is unclear, but it pointed out the new daily was "the only straight-out Greeley paper on the line of the Northern Pacific." Its editor also wrote, "Although its publication is doubtless intended as an experiment during the campaign...the publishers say that if they meet with sufficient encouragement, they will make the publication of their little paper a permanent thing."

From the editor's quips and snipings that appeared over the next few weeks in the *Brainerd Tribune*, it's clear the two papers fussed at each other over politics, if not personalities. No copies of the *Wave* are known to exist to provide its side or to determine exactly when Kellogg joined its staff. On Aug. 31, Russell said he didn't like "wrangling either in a newspaper or out of it, and abhor personalities, especially in print. Besides, you see, there are two of them and only one of us."[220] He evidently was referring to Hartley and Steele, suggesting Kellogg wasn't on the paper's staff initially. Later that fall Russell stated several times his friend/competitor Hartley was ill. Perhaps Kellogg took over as associate editor at that point.

A *St. Paul Pioneer* brief of Sept. 12 makes clear Kellogg was on board by at least Sept. 8: "The *Brainerd Greeley Wave* of the 8th is received, bearing the name of M.H. Kellogg as one of its editors. Mr. Kellogg is a newspaper man of large experience, a ready and forcible writer, energetic in all that he undertakes, enthusiastic in his support of Greeley and Brown and the principles which they represent. His connection with the *Wave* means business, and will result in good to the cause of reform, the prosperity of the paper and the business interests of the young, wide-awake city of Brainerd."[221]

The *Wave* was usually referred to as a campaign sheet. A September item in the *Duluth Tribune* indicates it may have been no more than that. The Duluth paper quoted unknown sources in Brainerd as calling the *Wave* "a poor little seven by nine diaper."[222]

Kellogg's connection with the Liberal Republican campaign sheet soon overlapped with his own candidacy for state representative from the state's 30th District, made up of Crow Wing (including Brainerd), Sherburne, Benton, Morrison and Mills Lac counties. On Oct. 5, the *Tribune* reported Kellogg's nomination at the District Convention held Oct. 2 at Sauk Rapids:

"THE OPPOSITION CANDIDATE

"At the District Convention of the Liberals, held at Sauk Rapids, on Wednesday last, for this District, that numerous (?) [*Tribune's* question mark] body elected Mr. M.H. Kellogg, of Brainerd, as their legislative standard-bearer, in opposition to T.F. Knappen, Esq., of this place, Republican candidate for the same position. Well, this is as it should be; an easy victory is always preferable to a hard and expensive one, and now a Republican sweep in our local politics is a foregone conclusion. Come, Kellogg, mount the old potato-barrel again, on Front Street, and let us know what you know about not knowing how you're going to get the Legislature this fall — we'd like to know, you know."[223]

The Oct. 6 *St. Paul Pioneer* noted the nominations of the two men but made no further comment. On Sept. 27, 1872, the *Pioneer* carried a three-paragraph item from "Carlos" in Brainerd. It began, "In the absence of 'Frontier,' your regular correspondent, allow us to trouble you with a short communication."[224] Carlos is not identified and the name did not appear again. But obviously "Frontier" was off doing other things — running a newspaper and preparing to be nominated for state representative.

The election campaign and the newspapers' competition were spirited but apparently friendly. It seems the two newspapers were published out of the *Tribune's* office, or so H.L. Bridgeman, a visitor to Brainerd, reported sometime that fall of 1872.

"The leading journal of the town is the *Brainerd Tribune*, weekly, with 750 circulation and an enterprising manager who came up here from Nashville, Tenn. A campaign sheet called the *Greeley Wave* is also issued from the same office by an individual who makes his appearance in his own columns as publisher and proprietor, editor, county auditor, judge of probate, deputy clerk, real estate and insurance agent, liberal candidate for judge of probate and 'will also solemnize marriages.' The whole force of printers in town consists of two men and a boy, and they work on in contentment, ignorant of the typographical union.[225]

The man from Nashville certainly was *Tribune* editor Russell, and the man with all the jobs fits Hartley. Whether one of the printers was Kellogg is unknown, because the date Bridgeman visited Brainerd, which he described as a "roaring camp of vice," is also unclear. His references to a militia company and a fire department, both of which were being organized in October 1872, suggest the letter was written that month, when Kellogg was on the paper's staff. Recall, also, the 1870 census for La Crosse, Wis., listed Kellogg's occupation as printer.

The *Tribune's* columns give good evidence of a spirited campaign and suggest the *Wave* was not a reluctant participant in the electioneering. A critical letter the *Tribune* published from local businessman John A. McLean Oct. 26, 1872, makes this evident. According to the letter, which referred to Kellogg as editor, a *Wave* article had criticized McLean for paying Knappen, a lawyer. McLean claimed he merely acted as an agent for a business that owed Knappen for legal work and that the bill had been paid in June, long before the campaign, not in September as Kellogg apparently wrote.

"We are sorry that the editor of that paper, who is a candidate for the legislature, is so hard up for political matter with which to beat Mr. Knappen, candidate for the same position, as to resort to utter and contemptible falsehoods.... Also, non-resident Kellogg! We are sorry for you that you can't have an opportunity to gobble onto somebody's money for electioneering purpose. As for Knappen if he has not money enough to defray his expense of the campaign, we know that his friends will furnish it for him, and that you will probably find out next November. Don't misconstrue testimony of witnesses into falsehood for your own political aggrandizement."[226]

McLean's reference to "non-resident Kellogg" is puzzling. Undoubtedly, Kellogg had lived in Brainerd for many months. For example, Russell, in noting Kellogg's nomination, referred to him as "of Brainerd."[227] Precisely when Kellogg came to Brainerd remains unclear, but a Frontier column comparing the winter weather of 1872-1873 with earlier years supports the belief he had been in the area for years: "Having had an actual experience in, and knowledge of Minnesota since 1850, and this being my third winter in this vicinity, and having had peculiar advantages for gaining information regarding the country, its climate, its resources, disadvantages, etc. I am prepared to give truths and facts, against fiction and untruths, and I wish it understood that I can sustain with undeniable proof any and all statements I may make in this connection."[228]

In the end, it was McLean who appeared mysterious, not Kellogg, who was certainly no Johnny-come-lately to the relatively new pioneer town. If Kellogg himself no longer appears mysterious, the election results of his bid for the Minnesota Legislature certainly do. The election was held Nov. 5 and four days later, the weekly *Tribune's* editor, Russell, was beside himself as he conceded the state representative's race to Liberal Republican Kellogg and scolded his own Republican Party:

"We have waited until the last moment possible, in hopes to get the full results of the election on representative in this District and are even at a late hour compelled to go to press without the definite result. Enough returns [are] given below, however, to indicate the election of Kellogg, by a slight majority, which, to say the least of it, is an inglorious defeat for the Republican candidate, Mr. T.F. Knappen, when considering the sweeping victory for the Republican Party on their National, Congressional and county tickets. The lesson may be a wholesome one to the Republican Party in the future, however, which is the only consolation we are enabled to dig out of this little side-show transaction, which was let go by default in its early stages, so far as the better and more intelligent portion of the party was concerned, for which said 'better portion' of the party owe themselves, individual and collectively, a good, square cowhiding all around."[229]

According to Russell's preliminary results, Kellogg won by 108 votes. In its Nov. 14 edition, the *St. Paul Pioneer* noted Russell's remarks and his scolding of his party: "The *Brainerd Tribune* (Rep.) concedes the election of MARK A. (sic) KELLOGG (Dem.) to the House over Mr. KNAPPEN, the Republican candidate, and then proceeds to read its party friends a lecture for placing KNAPPEN on the track."[230]

But two days later, Nov. 16, Russell reversed his previous report and hinted Kellogg might have been robbed of election. "The question as to whether Knappen (Rep.) or Kellogg (Dem.) is the elected from this District seems even yet to be somewhat veiled in mystery, although the St. Paul papers, in their legislative slates, seem to concede the election of Mr. Knappen — and they ought to know. We had come to the conclusion that we were mistaken in our estimate on the election given last week, and this week be able to positively announce the election of Mr. Knappen; and from the first lights before us we feel sure that his election must be certain — for he ran like a Trojan even in some of the Democratic strongholds south of here, coming in away ahead of his ticket in several instances. But, presto! In comes Mr. Kellogg with the following statement which is said to be a correct compilation of the official vote of the District, compiled by friends of Mr. Kellogg."[231]

Kellogg's statement showed him with a 98-vote majority. However, Russell added in a shirt-tail paragraph that official results gave Knappen a 22-vote majority, but he made no further comment that day. Finally, on Dec. 7, he noted that the votes had been officially canvassed at Sauk Rapids (Nov. 30) and Knappen "was duly awarded the certificate of election, which finally answers the oft asked question of, 'who's elected?'."[232]

Did Kellogg lose because of vote fraud? The *Tribune* and the *Pioneer* considered the election matter closed and made no further mention. However, R.C. Mitchell, editor of the *Duluth Tribune*, raised the possibility of fraud on Nov. 14: "FEELS SAUCY — Our Democratic friend, Kellogg, the editor of the *Brainerd Wave*, feels pretty saucy about carrying his own country, even if he *was* defeated for the Legislature, as will be seen by the following paragraph, which we clip from the last number of that paper:

SANDY BARNARD

"'BRO. MITCHELL — Ye editor of the Duluth TRIBUNE — 'Old High-cock-a-lo-run.' tenders his compliments with 187 majority from Crow Wing County.'

"Well, Mark, all that we have to say is that you did well, and that the above shows what a splendid run you would have made, had you not been on the *wrong ticket*."

After reporting the *Tribune's* story on the possibility that Knappen had lost to Kellogg, Mitchell concluded, "Now, as the understanding down here, and at St. Paul also, has been that Mr. Kellogg was defeated, we would like to know how this thing really is."[233]

Two days later, Mitchell responded again to Russell's suggestion that Republicans needed a good cowhiding: "Pshaw! Russell, what is the use of beating round the bush. Why don't you say right out and done with it that Knappen is one of the most infamous political scalawags and corrupt scoundrels in this section of the country — and that was the reason he was defeated at the polls. Our only surprise is that his opponent's majority was not thrice as large. We do not know Mr. Kellogg, but if he can't discount Knappen, in point of honor, and then beat him out of sight, he is a poor stick, indeed."[234]

The Frontier columns resumed two months later but never mentioned his unsuccessful campaign. This was in keeping with the private Mark Kellogg, who seldom revealed himself in his columns. With the election behind him, Kellogg busied himself with other community activities for several months. Back in August, local Masons formed a lodge. The new Aurora Lodge was perfected Oct. 14. Masonic records indicate Kellogg was one of the original petitioners for the lodge, and he was listed as a charter member Jan. 15, 1873.[235]

In mid-October, his name also appeared in stories about a Minnesota State Guard military company that had been formed in the town. He was appointed to the committee on constitution and bylaws.[236] Russell was on the committee on name and uniforms. In December, Kellogg, bearing a corporal's rank in the company, sat on a court-martial for two men, but no charges were mentioned. Kellogg also helped organize the fire department, not surprising given his La Crosse experience. In late November, he served as secretary for its organizing committee. After permanent officers were selected, he was appointed to a three-man committee that wrote the department's constitution and bylaws.[237]

With the new year of 1873, Kellogg resumed writing as Frontier, and again showed himself a stout defender of Brainerd's reputation. Yet early 1873 would not be good for him. In February, the *Tribune* listed him among several men dropped from Headquarters Company E, Third Regiment, Minnesota State National Guard, for "continued absence from drill and non-payment of dues."[238]

Worse, according to Masonic records, on May 1, 1873, he was expelled from the Masons. Information is sketchy, but Kellogg may have committed some serious offense. Masonic historian Carl Zapffe wrote that Kellogg was subject to a hearing that required invoking the penalty of expulsion: "The proceedings of the Grand Lodge published in 1874 state that at the annual communication in 1874 a committee had reviewed [Kellogg's hearing] and reported in these words: '...the testimony shows such an entire disregard on the part of the accused, of his Masonic obligations in regard to the funds of the Lodge, that no doubt can be entertained of the entire propriety of the disciplinary action...and they therefore recommend...be affirmed'."[239]

Zapffe concluded: "His case is designated A.L. 5873, which means that expulsion is recorded as a fact for 1873. It has been impossible to find out just what Kellogg did with Lodge funds. He was not an officer of the lodge, which deepens the mystery."

Grand Lodge records for Minnesota were lost or destroyed by fire in the late 1800s, so, more recently, Harvey Hansen, grand secretary of the Grand Lodge, could add little to Zapffe's interpretation written in 1948. However, Hansen suggested that if Kellogg's offense was as simple as failure to pay his dues, he would have been dropped from the rolls and no Masonic trial would have been ensued. "Therefore, the matter would have been much more serious than that, to have had the matter brought to trial."[240]

Kellogg's first column of 1873, published Jan. 29, covered familiar subjects — weather cold but pleasant, city affairs in good shape, railroad doings. In closing, Kellogg suggested he lacked news of "sensations" and could not provide "any food for gossip" for the *Pioneer's* readers. However, one comment suggested the town was feeling the constraints of the economic downturn that later in the year worsened into the Panic of 1873: "Business is still light and the money stringency still continues."[241] The shortage of money had slowed construction on the railroad in 1872 and forced the resignation of President Smith in August 1872.[242] Jay Cooke sought desperately to shore up his banking house's crumbling walls, but on

SANDY BARNARD

Sept. 18, 1873, his doors closed in the financial panic of 1873, the country's worst financial disaster since 1837. The banking system was paralyzed and thousands left unemployed. Construction along the railroad was halted on the east bank of the Missouri River, 300 miles west of Brainerd at Bismarck. The railroad was thrown into receivership and, by 1875, faced reorganization.

Masonic historian Zapffe said Brainerd was hit hard economically. "By this calamity the new city was given a set-back and became denied the benefits of a boom which accrues to new cities. Brainerd saw the railroad headquarters moved to St. Paul, in 1873, and many families left the city."[243]

It's unclear what Kellogg did during this time. He had been dropped from the state guard unit, but in mid-February when it was called to Oak Lake to arrest an Indian suspected of murder, he tagged along. "I will keep you posted, if necessary, by courier," he told the *Pioneer* Feb. 11.[244] The next day he reported the militia's return to Brainerd. On Feb. 13, he wrote an even longer account about that episode and a second about a shooting that resulted in a man's death. Kellogg lamented the bad effects of such incidents on the town's reputation: "Citizens feel that these doings, these terrible affrays, have a tendency to injure the place, and strong efforts will be made to do away with the evils that cause such disastrous endings, and give Brainerd so hard a name abroad."[245]

On Feb. 20, Kellogg described a long trip he took on a Northern Pacific train dispatched to clear the tracks of snow, what he called "a fight of man against nature." Whether he was working for the railroad is unclear. He suggested NPRR Supt. C.F. Hobart invited him. After a pleasant evening on the road, he enthusiastically related his ride in the cab of the snow plow "whose heart...was penetrating and scattering [snow] to the four winds of heaven, its particles enveloping us to the exclusion of any sight whatever of surrounding objects."[246] The trip didn't end until they reached Fargo. "I returned to Brainerd more than pleased with my trip, my experiences, the courtesies extended to me by all, and found my adopted home quiet, orderly and behaving herself as becomes a metropolis."

On Feb. 28, he debunked recent stories reporting the railroad planned to move its general offices from Brainerd to St. Paul. "Your reporter must have got 'mixed' some way or another. I was informed by the officers of the road now here that there is no foundation for the assertion. They were surprised to see the publication of such a statement, and knew nothing of the matter until read in the columns of the *PIONEER*."[247] Despite his optimism, his sources eventually proved inaccurate. In the wake of the country's worsening economic situation that year, the offices were moved to St. Paul.

In February, Kellogg was at his most active as a string correspondent for the *Pioneer*, but in early March, poor weather on the railroad led him to apologize to the newspaper's editors for delaying "my usual weekly contribution to the *Pioneer*." He added that the weather was improving and he expected no more delays for the NPRR that season.[248] At one point in this column, he chastised another reporter, H.V. Redfield of the *Cincinnati Commercial*, for his support of the Southern Pacific Railroad Co. and his willingness "to be a crushing foe to the interests" of the NPRR.

At this point of mid-March, Kellogg expected to remain in Brainerd. Some people are leaving the town, he said, "but a majority of the freeholders and business men of this place have an abiding faith in the future of their young city and will cling to her destinies for awhile longer." Despite his prediction, Kellogg did not linger much longer in Brainerd. In just a few weeks, he joined the exodus by following his friend, druggist John P. Dunn, from the river crossing over the Mississippi at Brainerd to the projected Missouri Crossing at the new frontier town of Bismarck. In all likelihood, he went there because of the possibility of a railroad job. In this column, he highly praised Custer's friend, Thomas Rosser: "Gen. T.L. Rosser, assistant chief engineer of the Northern Pacific Railroad, left Brainerd Thursday morning, for the Missouri river. He will be absent some time, and will complete his arrangements so far as possible at once, for the summer's campaign. The General is in excellent health and spirits, and will push all work in the department vigorously. The NPRR Co. were wise in their choice, and fortunate in the acceptance of General Rosser for the position he now holds."

Did Kellogg work for the railroad, if not Rosser? His next comment suggests that possibility: "Having known him intimately and well since the commencement of the work of building this road, I can safely say that he has made no enemies, and all who have known him on the line rejoice at his appointment and return." A friend like Rosser could assure him of continued employment in the increasingly hard times, but even so, with the focus of construction in eastern Dakota, a move would be in order.

Two days later, he outlined the latter's construction plans: "ACTUAL WORK will soon commence on the NPRR. General Rosser has already gone West. Forces are being organized for the opening of the Dakota Division, which will be opened about the 1st of May. A steamboat line has

SANDY BARNARD

organized from Ft. McKeen, on the crossing of the Missouri River, which will be in readiness to co-operate with the railway as soon as the road reaches the Missouri River, which will be, at the farthest, during the first week of May."[249]

Three more columns were published in April 1873, mostly dealing with two of his favorite subjects — the weather and the railroad's people and construction. A letter published April 3 predicted track laying would begin across Dakota Territory to the Missouri River in a few days. "Trains will be run to the crossing of that river by the middle of May. Then business will 'boom' at that point."[250]

About a week later, he reported Rosser and a large force left Fargo April 8 to clear the track to the end of the line, which rested 38 miles east of the Missouri River. He expected completion of the line by May 15. "PUSH is the word this spring; and the management of the Northern Pacific Company will drive things with a vigor and speed that will be surprising."[251] His role for the railroad at this time is unclear, but his column suggested he was involved with it. He revealed he had traveled the line between Duluth and Fargo during the past week and found the track in excellent condition. Unless he worked in some capacity for the railroad, why would he have made such a trip or been so observant?

This column additionally revealed how extensive his ties to the NPRR were and supports the possibility he accompanied Rosser's surveying parties across Dakota Territory a year or two earlier. After discussing the quality of the country between Fargo and the Missouri, he added, "West of the Missouri I will speak at length of the soil, the climate, the advantages, etc., of Northern Dakota in the future. Having traveled across it by wagons I have had an opportunity to gather much satisfactory information regarding those matters." Unless he traveled with Rosser, he would have had no reason to travel by wagon in the dangerous wilderness that lay west of the river.[252]

On April 23, he returned to Brainerd from Fargo, having stayed in the Headquarters Hotel there. Both Fargo and Moorhead presented a "lively appearance" to him, but he did not expect the Minnesota town on the east to progress as much as its western neighbor in Dakota. Snow had slowed Rosser's construction crew.

Late in April, Kellogg offered another clue about the date of his arrival in Minnesota. Writing April 27 from Aitkin, 28 miles east of Brainerd, he said, "Nearly three years ago your correspondent arrived, ahead of the track, at a point on the line of the NPRR called Mud River [Aitkin vicinity] after the name of a stream topographically so called."[253] Inasmuch as the railroad construction began in mid-summer 1870, this letter seems a solid indication he went to work at that time, probably as a telegrapher. In this column, Kellogg pointed out where he lived that summer: "At that time there were two log houses 'mudded up' built here, one by N. Tibbetts called the 'O'Jibway House,' O'Jibway being the pronunciation by the aborigines of Chippewa; and the other erected by the Engineer Department, the latter being my headquarters for some months."

From his further comments, Kellogg obviously liked the community and was inspired to make another prediction: "The future of Aitkin is very promising, and those of us who live five years will see here a busy, bustling, live town. It is inevitable." Kellogg would not live to see that come true.

The next month, May, he wrote his last column from Brainerd. He failed to mention he had been expelled from the Masonic Lodge three days before. Instead, his focus is on the "Front" — the railroad pushing west toward the Missouri Crossing: "WORK AT THE FRONT is going ahead rapidly. A large force of men and trains will shove the track to Bismarck, on the Missouri Crossing, early in June. Every possible means will be taken to complete the track to the river, and prepare it for the heavy traffic which must pass over it this season.

"The rush to the Missouri River is very large. Two coach loads daily from this point hardly accommodate the demand. People are flocking thitherward from all sections of the country. Bismarck promises to be a 'red-hot town' during this summer and it will have varied experiences and some tragedies, before it settles itself down to a staid, quiet city like Brainerd."[254]

Sometime in early May, Kellogg, too, rode the train from Brainerd to the end of the line and continued overland to Bismarck. Across the Missouri River was the new Fort Abraham Lincoln, home to the 7th U.S. Cavalry commanded by Lt. Col. George Armstrong Custer. It was just three years before his death.

SANDY BARNARD

Chapter 7
At the Front

A buoyant and enthusiastic Kellogg, writing as Frontier, documented his departure from Brainerd and arrival in the central Dakota village of Bismarck in a column dated May 10 and published May 16, 1873: "On the morning of Tuesday last [Tuesday May 6], I left Brainerd, the future capital of Minnesota, for the future capital of Dakota, viz. Edwinton, alias Bismarck." If he left Brainerd under the cloud of his expulsion from the Masons, here he appears optimistic that his fortunes would change in his new home.

"At the Front — To an old pioneer, the 'Front' is a word talismanic. To the uninitiated, or, perhaps, the inexperienced, the phrase is, to a certain degree, meaningless. Let the case be as it may, your correspondent is at the present extreme front of the Northern Pacific Railway; and from this point he proposes to give to the readers of the *PIONEER* his experiences and observations as he journeyed hitherward, and to have his say as to matters hereaway — adding nothing, nothing extenuating; but writing as he *sees* and *knows*."[255]

He went on: "The trip out was one of but little incident. The ride to Fargo was 'on time,' and en route I observed that the rays of a spring sun was (sic) rapidly developing vegetation. A new life has taken hold of the people along the route; the result of which will be an improvement, and an increase of population hardly comprehended."

For himself, perhaps new life would take hold in Bismarck and his fortunes would improve. But Kellogg did not dwell on his personal circumstances for his readers. Instead, he had railroad news to report. While the rails had not yet reached the town itself, he praised the site selected for the crossing as "one of the most beautiful, being a table land very level in its formation, extending from the river bottoms east as far as one wishes to travel — on foot." With some 700 people already living there, "all in business, no idlers or blood suckers hanging around," Kellogg predicted that by the next year, 3,000 would call Bismarck home. Eventually, he predicted, the town would become the "largest and most important interior city on the line of the Northern Pacific."

Dakota Territory was organized in 1861, although settlement was opposed by Indian tribes living in the region. Steamboat traffic had sailed the Missouri River for about 40 years.[256] Bismarck, as true of most towns along the line, owed its establishment to the NPRR. In May 1872, the first settlers, representing railroad interests, established a townsite named Edwinton, after Edwin Johnson, the NPRR's chief engineer at the time.[257] In the spring of 1872, the Army established Camp Hancock on the site of what became Bismarck on the Missouri's east bank and across the river set up Fort McKeen as an infantry post. During that year, other settlers, intending to set down roots and including Kellogg's druggist friend, John P. Dunn, began arriving.[258] The stage was set for the town to prosper as the railroad moved closer. According to the *History of the City of Bismarck*, "Early in 1873, the barriers at Fourteenth Siding, 50 miles east of Bismarck, where grading had been halted by an early snowstorm the previous October, were removed and work resumed."[259] The first train rolled into town June 5, 1873, thereby changing the lives of many individuals up and down the NPRR. According to early histories, the "towns of Brainerd, Moorhead and Glyndon, Minnesota, nearly emptied at this time."[260]

For Kellogg, the most important arrival in the spring of 1873 was Col. Clement A. Lounsberry, who came to the village of 150 cottonwood shacks and tents May 11. A 30-year-old Civil War hero and previously a journalist in Minnesota, he gave up secure newspaper ties to seek success in the rough and rowdy village that was Bismarck that summer. He decided to launch his *Bismarck Tribune*, but before he could begin his career at the Missouri Crossing, he had to await the rail line's completion. His Washington hand press, fonts and other supplies arrived June 5 on the first train into town. The first *Tribune* rolled off his press July 6, 1873.[261]

Lounsberry also filed a soldiers' homestead claim nearby. North Dakota historian Frank E. Vyzralek wrote: "Lounsberry saw Bismarck as the future commercial, industrial and political center of the region and bent the full efforts of himself and his newspaper toward achieving that end. Active in political and civic affairs, he lost no opportunity to 'boom' Bismarck and aid in its growth. Often these activities brought little or no personal profit."[262]

SANDY BARNARD

How well Kellogg and Lounsberry knew each other before their arrivals in Bismarck is unknown, but their paths crossed early that summer. In the meantime, Kellogg continued writing his upbeat letters for the *Pioneer*. On May 31, he humorously offered his first impressions of his new home: "It is now three weeks since I arrived at this goal of the Northern Pacific Railroad, since which time I have cruised in all directions excepting west; and as my acquaintance with the Sioux who occupy the country in that direction is so limited, my modesty forbids an intrusion on my part into their peaceful habitations — besides I have lost no Indians and have no particular wish to seek game in their happy hunting grounds — and by the way, hair dealers have appeared in this region, which has a tendency to 'rise hair'."[263]

The town had been quiet, he said, despite the presence of a variety of people from "nearly every nationality and every known social element of the country." But he sensed that in such an environment it was only a matter of time before "tragedy will be a startling fact." He criticized as untrue Eastern reports that claimed the Sioux had attacked the town and Fort Abraham Lincoln across the river. "I will keep the *PIONEER* posted on matters occurring hereaway, and the reading public can rely upon facts."

He reported the Yellowstone Expedition under General David Stanley and Custer would depart June 15 and promised to give details shortly. He also informed his readers that track construction was within 12 miles of Bismarck on Friday May 30 and was expected to reach the town by the next Thursday, June 5. However, this column was not published before he sent a special message on June 2 to the newspaper announcing the track's completion to Bismarck: "Considerable excitement and much rejoicing of the citizens is occasioned by the arrival of the track of the Northern Pacific. The Mississippi and Missouri, the two great navigable streams of the continent, are again linked and joined by hands of men, through the energy of the Northern Pacific Railroad Company."[264]

In his letter of June 16, full of details about the Yellowstone Expedition that would protect the NPRR's surveying crews across the countryside of Dakota and Montana territories, Kellogg mentioned George Custer for the first time (although he spelled the name Custar). Simply, Custer would "assist" Stanley. Kellogg clearly had access to the military commanders as well as Rosser. He even recalled the place in Montana where Rosser's men were driven back the previous year. With some 2,000 soldiers and civilians making up this expedition, Kellogg thought the Indians would be "but little annoyance.... The escort is too large and too well armed for the Indians to make an open attack upon, yet it is a possibility that they may do so, for they have a strong repugnance against surveying parties whom they look upon as the first trespassers upon a section of country they wish to keep intact, and for their own use.[265]

To his mind, Bismarck continued to "thrive famously." He provided a lengthy report of his "stroll" about the town, including an inside look at Ed Morton's huge open-doored gambling house, where he enjoyed a hot sherry cobbler. "All is peaceful, quiet and orderly."

About a week later, June 24, Kellogg criticized the government's Indian policy after a reported attack on trappers near Fort Benton, far up the Missouri River in Montana Territory. Basing his report on the stories of two men who had come down river by steamer, he expressed the anti-Indian sentiments of Western frontiersmen, harshly labeling the Indians as "the little creatures who govern government affairs" to the west. An incensed Kellogg seemingly called out for their extermination: "If 'Uncle Sam' will give your correspondent a hundred dollars for each Indian scalp taken, he will undertake to rid American soil of its native inhabitants in two years — and he will employ western men only. No more Quakers in his [sic]. This scheme would save largely, and future ages would loudly eulogize an economy of the great statesmen of this age."[266]

After once again detailing Bismarck's continuing development, Kellogg mentioned Lounsberry's presence for the first time. "Colonel Lounsberry, lately of *Minneapolis Tribune*, has his office nicely under way and will make an issue very soon. He has a pleasant office and favorably located and will run a newspaper on frontier principles." By this time Lounsberry had probably hired Kellogg to help put out the new paper. The first edition was published July 6, 1873, amid signs that Lounsberry's enterprise would prove as chancy as the town's own existence. In his July 11 edition, Lounsberry called for all the town's businesses to support him in producing a strong local paper. "A town is always judged by its local paper. If it is lively and bristles with advertising and business notices, a stranger at once concludes the town is a live one." Lack of support would suggest the town is "dead," he added. "Will not the Bismarck people contribute largely toward making the *Tribune* a paper that will do credit to the place, and its publication a business that will give a fair return for the time and money expended?"[267] Even so, his lack of supplies forced him to leave out about two and a half columns of advertising that day.

Kellogg reportedly received the newspaper's second copy, the first going to foreman Charles Lombard. As Lounsberry offhandedly labelled him, Kellogg was an "attaché of the Tribune in its early days."[268] However, it appears Kellogg was more than a mere attaché that summer. He likely filled in as editor of the *Tribune's* third and fourth issues — July 23 and July 30, 1873 — during the first of Lounsberry's several absences that year. Even in the July 11 issue some columns seem to reflect his voice. For example, "Libels on Bismarck" begins, "A number of editorial scribblers have selected Bismarck and some of its people for target practice and the result is some of the most outlandish lies." After several paragraphs of defending the town, the writer concluded in language strongly reminiscent of Kellogg's, "Such stories are uncalled for, wholly untrue and injurious to the town."[269] Another column, headed, "Railway Business," included considerable detail about the NPRR and its personalities, far more than Lounsberry himself probably possessed at the time, especially compared to Kellogg.

The paper's lead editorial of July 23, 1873, also sounds much like Kellogg, the boomer: "We look forward to a day not very far distant, on which it will be announced to its sister states, and the world, that Bismarck has become the capital of the State of Dakota."[270] It's unlikely Lounsberry wrote the piece because the writer mentions having seen such large cities as St. Joseph, Kansas City and Omaha grow. He added, "We are experiencing the same features that we have witnessed in the growth of the west during the last 20 years or more." Unlike Kellogg, who had spent many years along the Mississippi or west of it, Lounsberry was born in Indiana in 1843 and reared in Michigan. He did not travel to Minnesota and the west until after the Civil War.

Most important, the briefs column reported, "Our Chief — The Colonel, departed from the sanctum on the morning of the 18th inst., with his figure head turned toward the east. He will 'slosh' around among his many friends in Minneapolis, and thereaway for a few days, and return to Bismarck on Tuesday next."[271] Again, the language and phrasing strongly suggest Kellogg as the writer. "We know the Colonel needed rest and relief, and that he will have an enjoyable time, yet we wish he were here. It isn't fun much either to 'run' a newspaper; one is so prone to say something that somebody won't like, then 'ye' quill driver is liable to get his head 'mashed,' or his 'globes smoked,' or a Mansard roof raised on his cranium."

While working for Lounsberry, Kellogg continued to submit articles to the *Pioneer*, defending Bismarck against attacks from outsiders and booming its prospects as a quiet, orderly town. "Come what may, thus far Bismarck, in a moral point of view, is the moral town of the Northern Pacific, even if it is situated on the Missouri River."[272]

Another *Pioneer* letter writer, using the pen name Omega, thanked Kellogg for his assistance during a recent visit: "Those who contemplate visiting Bismarck and wish to see all there is to be seen, and to have the same exhibited in a proper and agreeable light, should call on Mr. M.H. Kellogg, an occasional correspondent of the *Pioneer*, and at present temporarily connected with the *Bismarck Tribune*. The writer is indebted to him, and J.A. Stoyell, Esq., for this courtesy."[273]

The colonel, who returned to Bismarck Aug. 5, praised Kellogg for his able assistance during the editor's absence and confirmed Kellogg's role as editor of the July 23 and 30 issues: "The editor who returned yesterday is under obligation to Mark H. Kellogg for whatever of excellence has appeared in the columns of the *Tribune* during his recent absence and is so well pleased that he will not hesitate to again leave the paper in Kellogg's hands on a like occasion."[274]

Despite that impressive start in the colonel's service, Kellogg never was more than a part-time employee for Lounsberry, who frequently boasted in the paper's early years about how he willingly tackled numerous obstacles to assure publication. Such battles did not make him a rich man. So he had no room on his full-time staff for Kellogg. Instead, Lounsberry's money problems forced him to take on a financial partner, Amos C. Jordan.[275] Kellogg, a poor man, ended what likely was his only full-time employment with the *Tribune*, but continued assisting the paper. When Lounsberry, much the absentee owner, headed east later that month, Jordan took over, noting, "We feel very much as did the boy who rode the elephant; the [editor's] seat looked much more comfortable when someone else was sitting in it."[276]

Fortunately Kellogg was nearby: "Our old friend Mark Kellogg has kindly come to the rescue, however, and promises to extend his aid in the emergency, from which we draw much consolation and our readers much benefit." That appeared in the Aug. 27 issue, and the locals column reflects Kellogg's writing style.

Jordan's warm feelings soon iced up. In the Sept. 24 *Tribune*, a reprint from the *Duluth Tribune* noted, "Mark Kellogg, who has been run

SANDY BARNARD

ning the *Bismarck Tribune* during the absence of Colonel Lounsberry, came down last evening and left for St. Paul this morning." Beneath that brief, Jordan wrote, "The editor of the *Tribune* MOST EMPHATICALLY objects. For such favors as I have been placed under by Mr. Kellogg, he has my hearty thanks until better paid; but I wish most decidedly to put a veto to the impression which seems to have been circulated that he has been 'running the *Tribune* during the absence of Colonel Lounsberry.' I am alone responsible for the utterances." In closing, Jordan claimed he alone was due the "benefit of the reward."

Jordan may have been the editor, but Kellogg's writing style is apparent in the *Tribune* during this month. That fall, according to the *Brainerd Tribune* of Oct. 4, Kellogg passed through Brainerd en route to St. Paul to represent the Northern Pacific Railroad at the state fair: "Mark H. Kellogg, an old-time Brainerdite, spent a day in this city this week on his way from St. Paul to Bismarck, which latter place is his home now. Mark was down to our State Fair, in charge of a lot of N.P. products, including a large 'bullberry' tree loaded with fruit."[277]

The *Bismarck Tribune* of Oct. 15 reported, "Mark Kellogg has returned from a three weeks' trip east." That same day the *St. Paul Pioneer* reported Frontier's account of an upper Mississippi River trip with editor M.C. Russell of the *Brainerd Tribune*, apparently taken Saturday Oct. 4.

The court calendar published Oct. 15 in the *Bismarck Tribune* included an intriguing reference: "Samuel Betting vs. Harry Bose; a case transferred to Justice Kellogg; Justice absent, no appearance." Kellogg had been absent. Also, noteworthy — the plaintiff's attorney was Kellogg's lawyer friend J.A. Stoyell.

His early months in Bismarck seem to refute the notion Kellogg was some mystery man. In just a few months in the town, he had edited the *Bismarck Tribune* newspaper, represented the railroad at the state fair in St. Paul and may have held court as a justice of the peace.

By late October, whatever business arrangement existed between Lounsberry and Jordan had ended. The latter eventually worked for newspapers in Minneapolis, St. Paul and Iowa. In December, Lounsberry traveled east once again to spend the winter covering the legislature for the *Minneapolis Tribune*. He left his own *Tribune* in the hands of Nathan H. Knappen. According to Vaughn, "Knappen soon incurred the wrath of the rowdy element of the community by his realistic descriptions of their activities in the columns of the paper."[278]

Kellogg too would become caught up in the turmoil that surrounded one of the first murders in the community. Sometime prior to Nov. 11, a soldier named Frank King was killed by a gambler named Spotty Whalen in a quarrel over a woman named Maud Seymour. Seeking revenge, a group of soldiers came to the gambling hall of Dave Mullen, well known in towns along the NPRR line, and demanded admittance. Instead, a gunshot from the house killed another soldier. His comrades fired into the building, hitting Mullen in the brain and killing him. A second man was wounded.

Kellogg wrote extensively about the incident in the *Pioneer* but seemed to side with the dead man. As Kellogg related the tale, Mullen agreed to open the doors of his establishment to the enraged soldiers, who thereupon shot him down with a volley. After the shootings the soldiers scattered, their identities unknown to local authorities. Kellogg feared the situation was ripe for a "riot." About 70 armed soldiers were supposedly heading to town, while the townspeople prepared for a renewed attack by the soldiers, ostensibly their protectors.[279]

In covering the shooting, Kellogg not only wore his usual hat of a reporter, but also a special hat as foreman of the coroner's jury investigating the crime. He provided his readers an insider's look at the murder scene: "The scene within the house where THE MURDER was committed beggars description; but as I saw it I will try to open the picture to your readers: As I entered the door of the saloon I saw on my right, near the counter, where Mullen fell after being shot, a pool of blood covering three feet square, of the floor, with considerable brains mingled in. The counter was spotted with blood. From the front door, clear the whole length of the main room, through the hall, out to the back door of the house, was one steady stain of human gore, which had followed from the wounds of 'Denny' Minnehan [the second man], who went in search of water after being shot. On the platform at the rear of the main or dancing hall lay the remains of Dave Mullen. Upon examining the corpse I found a ball had entered the forehead above the left eye, and passed through the head and out at the back crushing and carrying away the skull and portions of the brain. In the walls of the building, through doors and windows were the marks of the many bullets which had been fired by the soldiers."

Kellogg's sense of righteous indignation rose: "THIS TRAGEDY is wholly the fault of men wearing the garb of U.S. soldiers. If they had been kept in their quarters, where they belonged, this bloody and murderous

SANDY BARNARD

scene would not have been enacted. There have been telegrams sent eastward which are untrue; and, having heard the testimony in the coroner's inquest held on both the deceased, I do not hesitate to pronounce this act of the soldiery one that was decidedly a premeditated and cold-blooded murder, and such is the general verdict of the citizens. The hope is that this will be the end of this cruel kind of work: but blood has been spilled, the bad passions of bold, bad men are aroused, and it is difficult to predict the end."

Dr. B.F. Slaughter convened a coroner's jury that included Kellogg as foreman. The original brief report of the jury, signed by its members, including Kellogg, mirrors the reporter's conclusion in the *Pioneer*: "We the jury in the above entitled cause after due deliberation do hereby give the following verdict, to wit: That David Mullen did on the morning of Nov. 11th, 1873, come to his death from a gun shot wound fired by a person dressed in the garb of a soldier. Said gun shot ball entering his forehead and passed directly through his brain."[280] It's possible Kellogg wrote the document.

Lounsberry claimed the feud that culminated in the death of Mullen may have directly resulted from articles published by his newspaper.[281] After a series of shootings at the gambling den run by Mullen and his partner Jack O'Neil, the *Tribune* editorially urged the formation of a vigilance committee to handle the lawless characters in the absence of any civil organization competent to deal with them. Soon after the *Tribune* containing this article appeared both Mullen and O'Neil, heavily armed, approached the *Tribune* office. "Colonel Lounsberry met them and said he had heard that they threatened to do some shooting on account of the *Tribune's* position; that if there was any shooting to be done the quicker it commenced the better it would please him; that he had seen bullets fly before."

Lounsberry's stance apparently cooled the men. They blamed any previous violence at their saloon on their need to protect themselves. They also promised to avoid "any unnecessary trouble" and asked the editor to "refrain from inciting attacks upon them."[282]

In his next column, written three days later, Kellogg reported Bismarck had survived its "Reign of Terror" without further loss of life. He reminded readers of his prediction a few months earlier that "the slumbering volcano was liable to break out at any time."[283] While community leaders apparently were stirred by the murder to force "the warring ele ments" to leave town, Kellogg complained the military still allowed armed soldiers to roam Bismarck's streets at will at night. However, he remained optimistic about the future: "Like all frontier towns on the line, we have had our 'dance of death,' and do not expect any more such horrors." His only lament concerned the expected seasonal closing of the railroad, which would make mail scarce.

Kellogg likely spent the winter at Bismarck, inasmuch as he gave no indication he was leaving. However, a "Frontier" column, written at Pembina in the far northeastern corner of Dakota Territory on Dec. 27, 1873, and published by the *St. Paul Pioneer* on Jan. 4, 1874, at first seemed to suggest he might not have stayed. The column used several phrases common to other of Kellogg's writings, but Professor Leonard F. Kellogg believed this particular one was written by someone else. His theory is undoubtedly correct inasmuch as another Bismarck-based column, written Jan. 1, 1874, was published Jan. 28 by the newspaper. With the railroad closed for the winter, it would have been impossible for Kellogg to return to Bismarck from Pembina in just four days in late December.

Kellogg criticized the Northwestern Telegraph Co. for its slowness in repairing its broken line, which had been out for a month. That fact, along with the lack of trains and mail, made people feel isolated. Also, the soldiers had been no more problem, because of Custer's presence. "Gen. Custar's [sic] arrival was opportune, and by his presence and action has kept in check the bad passions of the men in his command. It is well."[284] He indicated the community's optimism remained high, despite the poor prospects of any further construction of the NPRR west of Bismarck. "This is a hopeful people, possessed of the nerve, pluck and energy such as builds countries and towns and cities. They are a people inured to hardships and exposure, and laugh at the idle stories told in Eastern papers about the *sufferings* of the Dakotians." He signed himself off as "Isolatedly yours, Frontier."

His next letter wasn't published until Feb. 4 and included a lengthy account of the shooting death of a soldier at Whiskey Point, a collection of saloons and dance houses on the east bank of the Missouri opposite Fort Lincoln. He wrote the column Jan. 19 but held it to include the results of a trial that resulted in William Riley being convicted of manslaughter in the soldier's death.

The harsh Dakota winter isolated the community after its rail and river connections to the outside world were lost. Mail service relied on

SANDY BARNARD

military couriers traveling overland, which meant that often Kellogg's columns were not published for two weeks or more after they were written. For example, his Jan. 18 column wasn't published until Feb. 6. But these circumstances didn't mean residents had to forfeit all forms of merriment until spring, as Kellogg reported in that January column:

"Members of the 7th Cavalry, stationed at Fort A. Lincoln, have been treating this people to MINSTREL ENTERTAINMENTS during the past week. They draw large houses, and their performances compare favorably with the most (sic) of minstrel troupes traveling through the Eastern states. Their programme is long, versatile and amusing. It is really a wonder to see an exhibit of so much talent. Think of it. Away out here on the frontier in a supposed barren wilderness, the very end of civilization, the good citizens, isolated as they are, are nevertheless allowed to be entertained in a cosmopolitan manner. Negro minstrelsy; good ballad and comic singing; necromancy, horizontal bar 'iron jawed' exhibits, ground and lofty tumbling, and all excellently executed, go to make up a pleasant evening's entertainment."[285] Custer himself was known to have participated in such shows, although Kellogg makes no mention of him on this occasion.

Kellogg described at length a rainbow-like phenomenon he observed Jan. 14. In a revealing comment, he added, "In the Rocky Mountain regions I have seen the rainbow by moonlight, and many other strange, bewildering phenomena." When did he visit the Rocky Mountains? Inasmuch as his writings seem to pinpoint his whereabouts for much of the 1870s, his visit must have taken place during that undocumented post-Council Bluffs period when he seemed to disappear. He probably visited family members in the Denver area.

In late February, Kellogg reported Custer's command in the spring would be ordered into the Black Hills, a sacred area for the Sioux and one promised to them by the Treaty of 1868. But Kellogg didn't hesitate to reveal the expedition's anticipated true purpose: "From the relations of old and experienced miners there is every evidence to believe there are immense gold deposits in these yet undeveloped and unprospected sections of country. If this proves to be a fact, then we may look forward to another '49' and 'Pike's Peak' rush during the coming two years."[286]

Kellogg again debunked tales in Eastern newspapers about Indian slaughters in the Bismarck vicinity. "Your correspondent has given to the *PIONEER* credible and reliable information on all matters of interest from hereaway, and unless you receive information from me relative to such matters, you can rely that there are no truths in the [Indian] reports."

Boomer that he was, Kellogg showed his indignant side again in a letter published March 28 refuting comments critical of Dakota Territory by Gen. William B. Hazen, who was stationed at Fort Buford in northwestern Dakota.[287] He called the general's comments "ludicrous." He suggested his "connections," otherwise unspecified, made it his duty to respond. Citing long-time settler Louis Agard as his source of information about Dakota Territory, he defended the area's climate, soil and rainfall. Kellogg even predicted Custer's soon-to-be published field notes of the 1873 Yellowstone expedition would refute Hazen's criticisms of the territory's prospects. "I am willing to stake my reputation on their production. [Custer] will treat upon the soil, climate, water, agricultural advantages of that belt of country over which he traveled, as well as to the immense mineral resources of the large amount of territory over which he traveled, and I am firm in the belief that his statements will bear me out in every particular."

Kellogg concluded: "To sum up the whole thing in a nut shell, I aver that all of the correspondence which has heretofore been published relative to that portion of Dakota over which the Northern Pacific Railroad is now constructed, and that portion of Dakota west of the Missouri river to the Yellowstone Valley or Powder River, which is selected by said company as their future route, that is derogatory or against said section of country is a living lie, which is easily controverted by actual facts and figures, lying Bohemians to the contrary notwithstanding."

How Kellogg supported himself that winter is unclear. Lounsberry was back in Minneapolis all winter, but Kellogg seems to have had little involvement with the *Tribune* during the winter. By mid-April 1874, Lounsberry, referred to as the paper's "summer editor," returned.[288] A Minneapolis man, George W. Plumley, who had bought an interest in the paper, ran its mechanical department. The paper remained independent politically, "preferring however, Republican candidates where all things are equal, but it will not hold itself bound by party nominations when better men are running in opposition."[289]

Minutes of Burleigh County Commission meetings for this period suggest Kellogg had a county job, likely as a jailer. At least a number of orders listing Kellogg as payee were presented over a couple of years, some going unpaid for lack of funds. Records, while incomplete, cover much of 1874 and 1875. They give no indication Kellogg ever received his money, which ranged in amounts of $10 to $30. If the county didn't pay its debt to him, Kellogg apparently gained a small measure of revenge. In 1874, his personal property was valued at $200 for which he owed $4.50 in taxes. A year later, the amount rose to $5.50 after a $1 penalty for non-payment was added. Burleigh County records give no indication he ever paid his delinquent tax bill.

Kellogg has been criticized for his reports during the 1876 military campaign that tended toward hero worship of Custer. But in April 1874, Kellogg was anything but a hero worshiper. A local man, C.H. McCarthy, was seized cutting timber on government land and Custer had him jailed at Fort Lincoln. That outraged local citizens, who, banding under the Pioneer Association, passed a resolution condemning Custer for his "unwarranted exercise of military authority."[290]

The resolution called for its publication in the *Bismarck Tribune* and *St. Paul Pioneer*. Kellogg immediately made the resolution the focus of his letter written April 16 and published April 23. Adding his own opinion, he said, "The action of the Pioneer Association is a just rebuke to overwhelming authority, and it is but fair that Mr. McCarthy should have all the rights extended to all American citizens, viz: The right of trial in civil courts, if he be guilty of what is charged namely, cutting timber on a government reservation. There is no military law that allows a citizen to be incarcerated in a military prison for such, or any other amenable act, where the civil and U.S. Courts are in existence and full sway."

However, Lounsberry, a Custer apologist, delayed publishing the resolution until May 6. Even then, he criticized the Pioneer Association for its censure of Custer. "While it might have been proper enough for Mr. McCarthy's friends and neighbors to have adopted resolutions condemning the arrest and imprisonment in the guard house of a citizen, earnestly protesting, the *Tribune* does not believe it was good policy for the Pioneer Association to make Mr. McCarthy's grievance theirs. The protest would have been more forcible too, had it been couched in language less severe. It is saying a great deal to charge General Custer with wantonly disregarding the dearest rights of an American citizen. The *Tribune* doubts if censure so severe as this was intended, and if intended we fail to see that any good can be accomplished by it and believe the only effect would be to grieve those who admire the General for his distinguished services and esteem him for his personal worth."[291]

About the same time, Lounsberry was giving away with subscriptions a 19 x 25-inch picture of Custer that he called "a faithful portrait of this brilliant and popular Cavalry Commander, which alone is worth the price of subscription." The former Union Army colonel was certainly enamored of Custer.

Kellogg himself may have been critical of Custer in April, but in late May he expressed confidence in the cavalry officer's ability to handle whatever Indian problems might arise. Indians from reservations south of Bismarck reportedly had been leaving to spend the summer roaming in the western country set aside for them by the Treaty of 1868. Now Custer would scout this area. Kellogg asserted Bismarck and other points east of the Missouri were "as safe from Indians as St. Paul."[292]

But to the west was a different story. "There is no doubt that a large portion of the country west of the Missouri, running across Dakota and in eastern Montana, are largely infected with hostile bands of Indians, but General Custar will keep them at bay, and moving until they tire and sicken on making raids on the whites."

After many months of writing regularly from Brainerd and Bismarck, Frontier was about to take a break. Kellogg combined two short pieces into one column in early July. His key news brief, datelined July 3, noted the departure of the Black Hills Expedition, led by Custer, that morning. The expedition actually had departed the previous morning of July 2. Whether the error was Kellogg's or occurred in transmission or publication is unknown. He said reports indicated 6,000 to 8,000 hostile Indians were believed to be congregating on the route. Well armed, they would give Custer "a warm reception." Kellogg did not travel with the expedition, as Nathan H. Knappan represented Lounsberry's newspaper. Kellogg, instead, became "Hay Baler."

Vaughn wrote at length about this episode in Kellogg's life.[293] Because so little rain fell that summer, hay contractors supplying Fort Lincoln were in trouble. Lawyer John Stoyell, a friend of Kellogg's, organized a hay camp north of Bismarck on the bottoms south of Painted Woods Lake. Kellogg was his foreman. Living in the vicinity was Joseph H. Taylor, a Yankton editor who had met Kellogg in 1868. Vaughn said Taylor was working as a county justice, but in his own memoirs Taylor said he was also a game provider for the Stoyell hay crew.[294] One morning at daybreak, while trailing a wounded doe through the dark forest, Taylor came across "the fleshless skeleton of a large man." He recognized the

SANDY BARNARD

remains as those of a harmless, deranged man known as French Joe. He returned to the camp to report his finding and to summon an informal jury to investigate. At the camp he met the new foreman, "M.M. [sic] Kellogg — Editor Kellogg," who had just come up from Bismarck.

"When Mr. Kellogg was informed of the finding of the corpse, he kindly agreed to accompany us, and assist at the inquest and burial. After the identification of the remains had been settled upon as those of the unfortunate Frenchman, the Editor proceeded to deliver a temperance talk that under the circumstances, the time and place, made an enduring imprint upon the minds and hearts of his few but attentive listeners."

After a lengthy discussion of the dead man's unfortunate life, Kellogg concluded, "This is a hard end." He looked down for a moment on the skeleton and then on the gloomy woodlands around the group. "I hope and pray that my end — and our ends may be different, that we can hope for a good Christian burial."

Taylor wrote about Kellogg's remarks: "Poor Kellogg! The book of fate well hid from him the leaf that bore in character his pre-destined end. How little he knew — how little we all know what the future has in store for us."

Kellogg provided more insight into the episode and pinpointed when it occurred in his "Hay Baler" column written July 15 but not published in the *Bismarck Tribune* until Aug. 19. On the morning of July 15, Taylor and County Commissioner W.H. Mercer asked for Kellogg's assistance in the post-mortem examination of French Joe's body. The men recognized the man by his clothing. Kellogg noted: "The remains would have proven nothing, as the turkey buzzards had stripped all the flesh from the bones, as clean as if done with a knife."[295]

In Joe's pants were $3 and nearby was another 60 cents. Kellogg concluded, "This man must have suffered a terribly agonizing death; there were three places near each other that showed terrible and shocking evidence of his death...It was a sad sad sight; three miles from an isolated homestead, a mile from any water, with no companions, this robust man was suddenly cut down, and died, friendless, and alone, with no eye, save that of his maker upon him."

Kellogg theorized that Joe, a known alcoholic, had been drinking hard, wandered into the forest, became lost and eventually died of thirst and starvation. "It was a short volume, but one full of the most touching and heart-rending temperance teachings, it has ever been our lot to learn. It was a horrible death, and teaches a fearful lesson."

That fall, Kellogg was once again involved in politics, supporting the congressional candidacy of M.K. Armstrong, who was running against J.P. Kidder. The *Bismarck Tribune* in October listed Kellogg among the Bismarck men who did "some tall work...at the polls" for Armstrong.[296] Kidder, the Republican, won, but other supporters of Armstrong included John P. Dunn.

Kellogg resurfaced as Frontier in December, an indication he remained in Bismarck for a second winter. In his Dec. 14 letter, he focused on the "Carnival of Death" — a series of nine accidental deaths and murders — that had struck the community recently. Foremost was the shooting of Jack O'Neil, the former partner of Dave Mullen whose death at the hands of some 7th Cavalrymen Kellogg had investigated the year before. Two other men were killed near the Standing Rock Agency of the Sioux. In the absence of "reliable information," Kellogg wasn't ready to blame the Indians for the deaths. He also reported the drownings in the Missouri River of Sheriff C.H. McCarthy and Deputy U.S. Marshal C.J. Miller, who had fallen through the ice: "Words are inadequate to pen picture the deep regret of our citizens at the loss, and untimely end of these two prominent and useful men."[297]

This letter is also important for another reason — Kellogg's savage criticism of Orville Grant, younger brother of President Grant. It provides a clear indication Kellogg was involved in investigating scandals involving Indian trading licenses and military post tradership appointments. By 1876, Custer's involvement in trying to air the facts behind the scandals would almost cost him his command of the 7th Cavalry during the Little Big Horn campaign. As historian Robert Utley put it, the younger Grant "carried influence peddling to new levels of brazenness."[298] In 1874, Secretary of the Interior Columbus Delano revoked all Indian trading licenses on the upper Missouri. To obtain renewals, traders had to deal with Grant. "Those who failed to meet his terms saw their licenses awarded to others," Utley said. The interior secretary controlled the monopoly in traderships at the Indian agencies, while the secretary of war handled military post appointments.

By the fall of 1875, this and other scandals forced the ouster of Delano, but similar practices existed in the appointment of the military post traders, something the experienced Custer would certainly have known. In the summer of 1875, the *New York Herald*, whose editor, James Gordon Bennett Jr., was among the strongest critics of the Grant administration, began investigating corruption at the forts and trading posts of the upper Missouri. Reporter Ralph Meeker, using the alias J.D. Thompson, made inquiries along the river towns and posts. Supposedly, only Custer — who numbered Bennett among his friends — Lounsberry, and Bismarck Postmistress Linda Slaughter knew the real purpose of Meeker/Thompson and supported his efforts. Meeker's investigative reporting led to a series of stories in the *Herald* during July-October 1875 that brought down Delano and would have repercussions into the next year. As Utley observed, "Custer's complicity with Meeker and the *Herald* would form one of the strands in the rope that almost strangled him."[299]

In the aftermath of Kellogg's death in 1876, the *Herald* acknowledged a role for him in Meeker's investigation: "Last year when the *HERALD* was investigating the Indian frauds in that region Mr. Kellogg furnished facts which had come under his personal observation."[300] In his article on Kellogg, Hixon played down that statement, suggesting Kellogg played at best a minor role assisting Meeker.[301] Kellogg's precise role remains unknown, but his own writings indicate he possessed substantial knowledge of agency and trading post frauds. Writing Dec. 14, he referred to previously published charges against Orville Grant, noting, "All that was said, and more too is true as holy writ."[302] More important, he added, "...we endorse those charges from a certain knowledge of the facts."

In March 1875, he referred briefly to "ye noble frauds" and promised to write a more lengthy report when space permitted. "I can say however, though, the common practice exhibited by those connected with the Indian Bureau during the past 14 years loses none of its spice or villainy in this section."[303] That summer, Kellogg returned to the subject after criticisms of Indian management policies were published by Yale Professor O.C. Marsh: "As you well know, I have had many opportunities of seeing and learning of the management of the Indian ring, for many years, and I endorse generally all that Professor Marsh has stated, and can produce at any time affidavits of men whose integrity stands unimpeachable and beyond reproach, showing the gigantic thefts which Indian agents and contractors have committed on the Indians and the government and the people."[304]

Kellogg continued that two summers earlier he reported for the *Pioneer* an interview he had with tribal leaders of the Mandans, Gros Ventres and Arikaras at Fort Lincoln. "Before these representatives of three tribes left here, I had an interview with three or four of the head chiefs, through an interpreter, and learned many things of which I was ignorant at the time relative to the treatment of themselves by various Indian agents, at different posts in their section of the country, which I have since traced to the end and found to be true."

Next, he related two lengthy examples of common fraudulent practices in the past. In one instance, a steamer laden with goods for the Indians landed at Fort Berthold, but only a third of its cargo for the tribes was unloaded. The other two-thirds went up river to Fort Peck, a place he labeled "that robbers roost for Indian agents along the Missouri River for many years past," or to Fort Benton. He blamed the deceit on "these dishonest agents and their scheming confederates." In the second instance, he accused two Indian agents named Irish and Balcombe of accumulating fortunes even though their salaries were only $1,500 a year.

He stated: "I cite these two cases only as a parallel for others of later date occurring within my knowledge, which I will soon unearth and bring to light. There will be grave doubts in the minds of the general eastern reader as to the truthfulness of developments which will henceforth be made through the columns of leading journals of the land — but those statements will emanate from such sources, and be backed up by such evidence eventually as to not only entitle them to belief; but call down on the heads of these cormorants of the government, heads of departments and all concerned, such a whirlpool of indignation as will cause the perpetrators to hide their very heads in shame, and seek in foreign climes an unknowness that will sink them, in utter oblivion." His strong condemnation of the agents' fraudulent actions against the Indians came in the middle of Meeker's investigation, underscoring the probability that Kellogg assisted the *Herald* reporter.

The fiery, indignant Kellogg next re-emerged: "This particular portion of God's acre, along the Missouri river, which comes under the supervision of the Indian ring, is now under the control of Orville S. Grant & Co. Orville is the well-known brother of Ulysses the Great, and of course is considered immaculately honorable — but then he aint, (sic) you know. Well, this ring governs, aye, governs, all Indian agencies along the Missouri River. They have, through the decrees of the powers that be, extended lines of reservations, so as to drive out and away other traders, outside of the government agents, post traders, and such, who were too honest to lower themselves to the common level of thieves, and become the lowest kind of thief, namely: a pilferer from Indians; and they do so manage, and by their cunning, dirty work so endeavor to manipulate — and then cover up their ugly work — that no one but the select few shall be any the wiser of their doings; but thank God, they cannot close the eyes of men, shut up their ears, or paralyze their arm, or will to do right, and little by little these wrongs come to light, and ere long the aggregate developments will startle the country.

"The subject is so prolific I can hardly express myself in a single letter, and will defer further comment for the future on this single line of fraud which is constantly being committed on the nation's wards."

Lest his readers misunderstand his motivations in exposing the agency frauds, Kellogg earlier let it be known that he was no romantic Easterner in his approach to the Indian: "I have no romance in my nature as regards Indians. I look upon them as a whole, as a lying, thievish set; dirty, lazy and degraded; among the lowest of God's creatures, from whose treachery and evil work I have suffered, and with all my heart wish they could be safely 'corralled,' or colonized that they might never more be brought into contact or communion with the white races. Longfellow's 'Hiawatha' is a beautifully written masterpiece, full of that sort of romance and ideality that leads the eastern novel reading mind astray; but the hardy pioneer of the uncivilized west, let his mind be ever so cultured and his theoretical sympathies be thoroughly aroused by the beautiful word painting of that poem, yet the reality, as known by his own experience is so widely at variance with the ideal therein depicted that the poem falls upon, his mind, in common fact, 'flat, stale, and unpalatable'."

Left unclear is how Kellogg may have suffered from Indian "treachery and evil work" earlier in his life. Even La Crosse of the 1850s, wilderness that it was, was not in danger of Indian attacks. While he considered it inappropriate to steal goods or mistreat the Indians who had subjected themselves to reservation life, he would not hesitate to use force against "the red devils" who continued to wage war against whites. In August 1875, a series of raids against whites brought this saber-rattling response from Frontier: "And thus they go, making raids here and there, killing inoffensive white citizens, raiding off stock, and doing pretty much as they please, with the utmost impunity — and yet the present Indian policy cries out for 'Peace! peace! — christianize the poor unfortunates, treat them with kindness,' and all that sort of bosh. Bah! I say, turn the dogs of war loose, and drive them from off the face of the earth, if they do not behave themselves. Border citizens will brook this lukewarmness on the part of the Indian Department but little longer, but will arise in their might, and make 'good' Indians of every mother's son of them, viz., send them to the 'happy hunting grounds'."[305] Historian Lewis Saum cited that passage as an example of Kellogg's Copperhead political views. Instead of politics, it more accurately reflects his anti-Indian frontier views about the Indian role in the Western society of the future: Subjugate the Indian and compel him to live in peace in a white-dominated society.

Early in 1875, Bismarck became an incorporated city, a decision criticized by Kellogg. Sarcastically labeling the city government structure an "elephant," he wrote in the *Pioneer*, "We needed to be metamorphosed into a city as much as a hack needs five wheels, and besides it will be such fun to pay $10,000 to $12,000 additional tax each year to keep up our lick."[306] What he worked at, besides some county-related job, that winter is unknown but evidence in the *Bismarck Tribune* suggests he may have filled in at the paper. After another winter in Minnesota, Lounsberry returned by mid-March. The March 17 paper reported he was off to Yankton and on April 7 it said he was expected back the next week. Interestingly, an April 7 editorial, offering much the same view Kellogg expressed earlier in the *Pioneer*, criticized the creation of a city government that might become "an expensive elephant." The editorialist added: "The writer saw no occasion for a city organization, and still believes the people would have been better off and better satisfied without it, but since the legislature — it cannot be said in its wisdom, for it possessed but little of that — gave it, we are glad to second the fact that the people are true to themselves."[307]

On April 15, Kellogg sought to dampen expectations about the Black Hills, suggesting no one in Bismarck was making a dash yet for the Hills. Pointing out Custer's "rigid" instructions from Washington to prevent whites from entering the Indians' sanctuary, he added, "I expect large numbers of people will rush in, despite the orders of the war department."[308]

On April 21, Kellogg's name appeared in a lengthy list of Bismarck residents subject to jury duty. The same issue of the paper noted Charles Lombard had returned on the steamer <u>Josephine</u>. Terming him "the architect of the first few issues" of the paper, it said he would go on to Montana as the paper's special correspondent and business agent.[309] In June, Kellogg, ever the boomer, offered *Pioneer* readers a long comparison of the advantages of the Great Northern Route from Chicago to Helena, Mont., over the central Union Pacific route. He had no doubt about his view, believing that once the "moving bands of Indians...are corralled" the New Northwest would develop quickly. "It is as inevitable as fate.... Mark the prediction."[310]

Hixon found it puzzling that Linda Slaughter, the wife of Dr. B.F. Slaughter and one of the first women to settle in Bismarck, never mentioned Kellogg in her extensive writing about the early community. By the summer 1875, she had served nearly two years as postmistress, when abruptly she was replaced. Many years later, she wrote in Lounsberry's *Fargo Record* magazine that she was ousted because of her connection to Ralph Meeker, the *New York Herald* investigator. Meeker supposedly asked for her help in investigating abuses at Fort Berthold Indian Agency up the Missouri River from Bismarck.

"This I accomplished through the help of a commandant of one of the upriver posts, and Meeker went to work as a common laborer on the agency farm.... His letters were dated Bismarck and mailed at this office, having been sent under cover to me for that purpose," Slaughter said.[311]

Orville Grant learned of her involvement in the investigation and "hastened to Washington and secured my summary removal." That upset the community and about 200 people signed a petition to have her reinstated. Among the signers were John P. Dunn and Mark Kellogg. Friends in the U.S. Senate also intervened with Postmaster General Marshall Jewell, and she was reinstated Aug. 15, 1875, for several months. She resigned in March 1876 to serve as the local school superintendent and was replaced by Clement A. Lounsberry.

Why did Lounsberry want such a job? It paid $750 a year, and achieving financial success as a frontier editor was difficult. On Sept. 6, 1875, Lounsberry outlined the *Tribune's* business history. In 1874, he had reorganized the operation as the *Bismarck Tribune* Co., issuing 120 shares of stock. He owned 79, or about two-thirds of the shares, while the others were held by three men with Minnesota newspaper and business interests.[312] A little earlier, Lounsberry said that the departure of George W. Plumley, the head of the mechanical department, from the paper was motivated in part by tight economic times, "rendering it almost impossible for the *Tribune's* earnings to support two families."[313]

The slowdown in business may explain why the county had not paid Kellogg's bills as county jailer. In October and December, the *Tribune* carried references to the County Board of Commissioners' approving pay ments of $60 and $74 to him for services as jailer.[314]

His lack of opportunity with the *Tribune* may explain Kellogg's decision that fall to go east for the winter. The *Tribune* reported on Nov. 3, "Mark Kellogg goes to Aitkin [Minn.] to spend the winter having been engaged by a lumber firm there in a clerical capacity. May success attend him."[315] Before he left he dabbled once more in politics for his lawyer friend John A. Stoyell, who was running for county attorney. The *Tribune* noted that at a political meeting Stoyell spoke about "the great uprising, followed by another from Mark Kellogg in a similar strain...."[316] For once Kellogg backed a winner, as Stoyell defeated two other candidates.

Little is known about what he did that winter in Aitkin, east of Brainerd. He wrote three columns for the *Pioneer* from Aitkin, mostly covering such familiar topics as the weather, the countryside and lumber industry. However, in mid-January, he showed himself cognizant of the political situation that would cost him his life six months later. He stated Custer had been ordered not to interfere with parties going to the Black Hills. He felt compelled to issue a prediction about the Indians' likely response to a government order to return to the reservations:

"Thus the animus of the government is ascertained. The only Indians who have shown an inclination to raid on white parties in that region are Sitting Bull's band of mountain Unkapapas, numbering about 1,500 warriors, well armed, who are a mischievous, devilish set; but they have been officially notified of late that they must stop their raiding, and retire to their own grounds, or war will be made upon them. The red devils will hunt their holes. Thus it will be seen all impediments are virtually set aside regarding the opening of the Black Hills. As soon as these matters become familiarly known, look out for a great rush. Men never have and never can be kept away from the fascinations of glittering gold, and the Black Hills will be no exception to the rule."[317]

In early February, he penned an upbeat letter about all the good that would flow from the expected opening of the Black Hills and its gold fields. His last sentence indicated he would remain in Aitkin about 10 more days before returning to Bismarck. He gave no indication of what prompted his return and made no mention of the Army's possible clash with the Sioux and Cheyenne in the Hills and elsewhere in the West.[318]

SANDY BARNARD

Chapter 8
Claim for Glory

Of Custer's 1876 campaign against the Sioux and Cheyenne, Clement Lounsberry writing in the third person would later state: "Colonel Lounsberry, who represented the *New York Herald* and the Associated Press through its St. Paul office, was the only correspondent who had secured authority to accompany the expedition, but sickness in his family at the last moment prevented his going and he chose Mark H. Kellogg to represent him on the expedition."[319]

Earlier, in 1896, Lounsberry wrote similarly in his *Fargo Record* magazine, "The editor of the *Record* was to go with Custer. Every arrangement was complete but sickness came to his family and Mark Kellogg took his place as a representative of the *New York Herald* and other eastern newspapers, and was the only correspondent with Custer."[320]

Finally, in the *Record* several months later, Lounsberry again wrote, "I was to have gone with Custer myself, but sudden illness in my family prevented me. I would have been with Custer as Kellogg was but for that."[321]

How true were his statements? They certainly influenced history. In fact, Lounsberry's presumed status as the intended correspondent who would travel with Custer for the *Bismarck Tribune* and *New York Herald* now ranks as one of the few undisputed statements associated with the overall story of the Battle of Little Big Horn. Authors writing about Custer's last battle routinely rephrase the boiler-plate language that relegates Kellogg to his traditional role as merely a last-minute substitute for his editor. However, close reading of the historical record and review of the two men's interests and frontier experience lead to an unmistakable conclusion that Lounsberry, prior to the campaign, never intended to travel with Custer. Instead, his oft-repeated claim that he was the campaign's intended correspondent simply reflects his attempt in his later years to tap the reflected glory of the Little Big Horn. With Kellogg himself dead, who would dispute the former Union Army colonel, civic leader, politician and frontier editor? His polished story took root as historical fact. Unfortunately, for Kellogg, Lounsberry's grab for glory reduced him to a footnote in the battle literature — the "accidental" dead reporter of Custer's Last Stand, the mystery man of frontier journalism.

Two aspects of Lounsberry's account are likely true: Custer may have asked him, probably while the two were snowbound in March 1876 on a NPRR train, to accompany the expedition. Lounsberry's wife, who had given birth to the last of their five children several months earlier, might have fallen "ill." But was her illness the primary reason the colonel stayed home? Not likely. Lounsberry had too many business and personal interests that spring of 1876 to think about trekking west with the 7th Cavalry. Even as he struggled to keep his Bismarck newspaper afloat,[322] he was preparing to launch a new paper in the Black Hills.[323] Neither journalistic enterprise could withstand his absence for many months. During the *Tribune's* first three years, the colonel had often strayed from his editorial department, sometimes for several months. But these absences came during winter, when harsh weather locked up the town and froze out the Northern Pacific and Missouri River traffic. Little money could be made in the marooned pioneer settlement. Living more comfortably back in Minneapolis, he had an important job with the *Minneapolis Tribune*. With spring's arrival, the railroad reopened its line. As reliably as the bees and the flowers, the colonel returned, as Bismarck's prospects came alive again. Spring and summer, those were the seasons for Lounsberry to make whatever money he could eke out there.

During this period, especially that winter and spring of 1875-1876, Lounsberry's political pursuits also kept him busy. Two issues dominated political efforts in Dakota Territory: Open the Black Hills and divide the territory into formal north and south units. To Lounsberry and other public-spirited citizens of Bismarck, dispatching the army to tame the Indians was nothing more than a necessary step to enable white settlement of the Black Hills and elsewhere in Indian country. Thus, January and February of 1876 found Lounsberry focused on both issues. If the territory were divided with Bismarck as the northern capital, his town could prosper. That meant more advertising for his struggling newspaper — and perhaps a prime political appointment for himself.

In February 1876, Lounsberry, Mayor John A. McLean and businessman J.W. Watson took samples of Black Hills gold east to Minneapolis-

SANDY BARNARD

St. Paul and Washington, D.C., to plead the area's case before state and national officials. They were preceded by a letter from the Bismarck's businessmen, asking St. Paul's Chamber of Commerce to urge the NPRR to open its rail line early, as "the interests of the citizens of Bismarck and St. Paul in this matter are identical, both to secure immigration and to furnish supplies (to the miners)."[324]

On Feb. 7, 1876, Lounsberry addressed the St. Paul Chamber about "this Black Hills excitement" and provided an upbeat history of the discovery of gold and what it meant for his town and, by extension, St. Paul. In reporting his speech, the *St. Paul Pioneer* included his responses to questions from chamber members.[325] The story's last paragraph summarized the group's purpose:

"To another gentleman, Mr. Lounsberry said what Bismarck asked on behalf of the chamber of commerce was action by the chamber as a body and by members as individuals looking to the immediate opening of the (rail) road and the opening of the Hills to settlement."[326]

A sidebar reported the chamber adopted two motions supporting Lounsberry's request. Apparently buoyed by their favorable St. Paul reception, the Bismarck delegation headed for Washington, D.C., "where they were on the floor of the House of Representatives and exhibited specimens of gold from the Black Hills." Years later Lounsberry recounted in his *History* that the men "were granted an audience by President Grant and Secretary of War Belknap, General Grant remarking, 'That settles the question as to whether there is gold in the Black Hills'."[327]

Another comment by Lounsberry in his St. Paul speech is important: "Mr. McLean and myself will go to the Hills immediately on our return to Bismarck. Mr. McLean to establish trade and to gain information from personal observation."[328] That speech never explained why he was going, but Lounsberry revealed that reason in late March in his *Tribune*:

"A portion of the material for the *Black Hills Tribune* arrived on Monday and it will go forward at an early day. Present arrangements will place the paper in charge of X.S. Burke, late of the *Perham [Minn.] News*, with the Bismarck Tribune Company owning an interest in the concern. Colonel Lounsberry will probably go to the Hills to aid in the establishment of the paper, returning at once to take charge of the *Bismarck Tribune* which he has no thought of abandoning."[329]

The busy Lounsberry had one more non-campaign business interest that spring. On March 15, 1876, his newspaper reported, "Mrs. L.W.

Slaughter having resigned, Col. Lounsberry, editor of the *Bismarck Tribune*, has been appointed postmaster at Bismarck in her stead."[330] Thus, two points become obvious:

 • Lounsberry's focus was on opening the Black Hills and his own business activities, not the Custer expedition.

 • Having two newspapers, which he had "no thought of abandoning," and a post office to run, plus his other political interests, Lounsberry wasn't inclined to spend the summer with Custer rounding up Indians.

It's important to view the Custer campaign from the perspective of Bismarck in the spring of 1876, not from modern hindsight about what happened on the Little Big Horn in June. Lounsberry, Kellogg, and other non-Indians fully expected the 7th Cavalry to handle what they considered the routine task of corralling the "wild savages" who stood in the way of white progress on the Northern Plains.

Lounsberry's personal situation also was a consideration. In 1876, Lounsberry was still a young man, having just turned 33 that March. His wife Lucretia and he had five young children to raise. As recently as Nov. 15, 1875, his wife had given birth to their fifth child, William. Their oldest child, Hattie, was only age 9.[331] No young father with such responsibilities could afford to spend three to five months on a military campaign during the year's biggest money-making season.

Lounsberry's health also precluded his joining the expedition. War-related disabilities plagued him for the rest of his life. Because he limped and carried a cane, he lacked the physical ability to accompany a fast-moving cavalry force against a cunning, elusive foe. Lounsberry's granddaughter, Helen A. Hennessy, related how in 1886 her grandfather's leg, bothered by an old war wound, had to be rebroken and reset.[332] Military planners in 1876 feared the Indians would escape from the soldiers and a summer-long campaign would ensue.[333] Lounsberry, despite his relative youth and veteran's status, was unlikely to be up to the rigors of a hard cavalry campaign.

Perhaps in mid-March, Lounsberry — flush with the joy of being asked by his friend Custer to travel with him — briefly dreamed about going. If he entertained such thoughts of adventure, his failure to identify himself as the intended war correspondent during the weeks before the troops departed is puzzling. Originally, the Custer column was expected to move out in late March or early April. On March 15, 1876, the *Tribune* reported Custer had returned to Bismarck to lead the expedition that would move on Sitting Bull and his warriors "about the 5th of April." It added, "We shall give further details at an early date, with correspondence from the expedition regularly."[334]

Passengers aboard a Northern Pacific train, long delayed by snow, that arrived on Monday March 13 included Lounsberry. The *Tribune's* March 15 issue noted Lounsberry's return from the east after an absence of six weeks "on business connected with the Black Hills business."[335] The next week's issue of March 22 introduced the following notice that was republished several times before Custer's departure in May:

"The *Bismarck Tribune* will send a special correspondent with General Custer's Big Horn expedition of 1876 as it did with the Black Hills expedition of 1874 and those seeking information in relation to the gold fields will find more reliable information in it concerning them than can be found in any other paper, or gleaned from any other source."[336]

Not once was Lounsberry's name suggested as the correspondent. That paragraph emphasizes gold, not Indians. If Lounsberry intended to go as the *Tribune's* campaign correspondent, why did he never state that fact?[337] By comparison, Kellogg's own personal flexibility must be emphasized. Kellogg lacked the permanent roots of job and family in Bismarck. He had displayed his prowess on the frontier. This would become evident anew during the Little Big Horn campaign when he went hunting three times with scout Charley Reynolds, a legendary wilderness figure. Reynolds would not have left the main force with a novice. An outdoors man with no physical disability, Kellogg could handle a weapon and would not be a liability to the soldiers.[338] Kellogg clearly was a more logical choice for campaign correspondent than Lounsberry.

After spending the winter in Aitkin, Minn., Kellogg returned to Bismarck with Custer, his wife Elizabeth (Libbie) and Lounsberry on the same train that became trapped by snow. In her book, *Boots and Saddles*, Mrs. Custer said the general and she were obliged to leave New York City in February because they had run out of money saved for their leave.[339] But in St. Paul, they found the NPRR closed to Bismarck and not expected to reopen before April. The NPRR, "mindful of what the general had done for them," proposed to force open the route, despite the winter weather. From her rather self-centered description of the equipment used and the number of employees enlisted in the effort, it would have been an expensive undertaking by the railroad for just the Custers. However, also aboard the train were several prominent Bismarck citizens, including the Black Hills gold trio of Lounsberry, McLean and Watson, as well as miners. The freight cars also contained goods for local merchants.

The whole enterprise soon bogged down in ice-encrusted snow drifts west of Fargo, and it appeared all would have to wait out the spring thaw. One day a small battery and pocket relay were found in the Custers' car. According to Mrs. Custer's account, a telegrapher was found, the line was cut and connected to the portable instrument, and soon the passengers had contact with Fargo and Fort Abraham Lincoln. As historian Oliver Knight documented in a 1960 article, Kellogg likely was the telegrapher who tapped out messages from the marooned train.[340] Soon after the message was sent, Capt. Thomas Custer arrived by sleigh to retrieve his brother and Mrs. Custer and take them on to Bismarck. All the other passengers, including Lounsberry and Kellogg, had to await the clearing of the tracks or make other arrangements to come across country.

Was Kellogg the telegrapher? Custer himself confirmed his identity, although he, too, failed to name the telegrapher. On June 17, during his final campaign, Custer wrote Libbie that an outgoing mail bag had been lost for five or 10 minutes in the Yellowstone River. Among the items was an article he had written for *Galaxy* magazine. He told his wife, "The latter [article] was recognized by a young newspaper reporter and telegraph operator who came up on the train with us from St. Paul, and he took special pains in drying it."[341]

Kellogg was the only reporter/telegrapher who was at both places with Custer. Kellogg himself would write about the mail bag incident in his own campaign dispatches in June. Of interest is Custer's use of the adjective "young." At age 43, Kellogg was seven years older than Custer himself. That also may suggest that Kellogg still had a youthful appearance.

Mrs. Custer's memoirs commented on the sleeping arrangements during their stay on the train. Her husband invited several citizens to share their bed in their car, much to her chagrin. "The audible sleeping in our bed, however, through the long nights that followed, convinced me that the general had assigned those places to the oldest, fattest, and ranking civilians."[342] Many years later, Lounsberry owned up to being the loud snorer who shared the covers with the Custers.[343]

Kellogg's return was reported March 22 by the *Tribune*: "Mark Kellogg, the well-known newspaper correspondent, returned to Bismarck

SANDY BARNARD

on Monday en route for the Black Hills. Mark is looking better and feeling better this spring than for years before. He goes to the Hills with Dodge's (mining) party which will leave as soon as the snow disappears."[344] This item suggests that in late March Lounsberry had not yet settled on Kellogg or anyone else as his correspondent for the Custer expedition, which at that time was expected to take the field soon. However, Custer soon was recalled to Washington, D.C., to testify before the House Clymer Committee investigating corruption in the administration's granting of traderships in Indian country. Reporting Custer's Washington trip in the March 22 issue, the *Tribune* said, "The General's absence will not delay the expedition, which, however, will not get away before April 15th."[345]

A week later, in its March 29 issue, stories indicate that sometime during the previous seven days Lounsberry must have persuaded Kellogg to wait for Custer's departure and not go with J.C. Dodge's mining party to the Black Hills. At least Kellogg was not listed among the Dodge party members who left March 28 for the Hills. He remained in town. In late April, the *Tribune* reported he attended the annual lawyers' meeting, probably as the guest of John A. Stoyell. Traditional references suggest Kellogg studied law. If so, it would have been with Stoyell, clearly one of his friends in Bismarck of the 1870s.[346]

Sometime that spring, prior to the departure of the troops, Kellogg wrote a letter to his daughters in La Crosse. After his death, John Symes of the *La Crosse Liberal Democrat* paraphrased its contents in an article published July 16: "Mr. Kellogg wrote to his two little daughters in this city, who are orphaned by his death...that he had made a claim in the Black Hills, but that he had no money to work it; that he also owned a share in a coal mine near Bismarck, and that he expected to be worth enough to educate and take care of his children.

"He also stated that he was going with Custer into the Indian war as correspondent for the *New York Herald* and *Chicago Tribune*, and that he should also sketch and write some for *Harper's Weekly*. He seemed to be unfortunate as far as money matters went, all through life, yet preserved a healthy good nature through all his bad luck, and was just beginning to get a foot hold when stricken down by the red skins."

The article concludes, "Last winter he visited the Black Hills, as correspondent for the papers mentioned above."[347] How much of the article is accurate is hard to gauge. Kellogg is not known to have worked for *Harper's Weekly*, either as a writer or an artist. That he went to the Black

Hills prior to moving to Aitkin doesn't seem likely either. The writer's comments on Kellogg's misfortunes in money matters seem on target. While his relationship with his daughters cannot be assessed, it's easy to conclude he was shaping his situation in a positive way for them, perhaps to give them hope of being reunited as a family once again.

At Fort Lincoln, preparations for the expedition continued that spring. Finally, by May 17, everything was ready, and Kellogg rode with Terry and Custer — nearly seven weeks after Lounsberry likely asked him. And Lounsberry? He stayed busy. In early May, his paper reported the departure on Sunday, April 30, of "the *Black Hills Tribune* outfit," headed by X.S. Burke and a man named Emmeluth, "two of as good men as ever shoved a lead pencil."[348] Perhaps that explains why Lounsberry tapped Kellogg to go with Custer. Lounsberry needed Burke and Emmeluth to set up his new shop. However, he did not travel with them to the Black Hills.

In his May 24 issue, a week after the troops headed west, Lounsberry puffed up his paper's status: "The *Bismarck Tribune* is the only newspaper which sends a special correspondent with General Terry's Big Horn Expedition, therefore those who desire early and reliable information concerning the discoveries and prospects in the Big Horn and Wind River region, as well as reliable information in relation to the Black Hills should subscribe to the *Tribune*."[349]

Again, Lounsberry expected "discoveries" but made no mention of fighting Indians. According to Lounsberry's expectations, this expedition would be as successful as the one in 1874, just in a new locale farther west. The troops would solve the Indian dilemma as a simple secondary exercise to their real purpose — finding new wonders to benefit the town's trade. So confident was Lounsberry that he, despite his wife's reported illness, didn't stay long in Bismarck. Before the end of May, he traveled east, according to the *Brainerd (Minn.) Tribune*, which noted his passage through town.[350] A week later, on the colonel's return trip, the train carrying him to Bismarck wrecked near Brainerd but he "only received a slight scratch on the hand. Lucky boy."[351]

Lucky he was. Much luckier than his reporter Kellogg, destined to die with Custer in about two weeks.

Chapter 9
Covering the Little Big Horn Campaign

On Wednesday May 17, 1876, Clement Lounsberry published the first of Kellogg's four campaign dispatches. It began simply enough: "Your correspondent joined the expedition Sunday [May 14] and went into camp."[352] The Terry-Custer column originally was scheduled to depart at 5 a.m. Monday May 15, but a severe rainstorm Sunday evening forced a delay until Wednesday morning May 17. The Saturday night before he crossed the Missouri River for Fort Abraham Lincoln, Kellogg took his final home-cooked meal in Bismarck at the home of the John P. Dunn family. Mrs. Christina Dunn recalled many years later that she offered him "a beef steak dinner served with mashed potatoes, peas, turnips, and spinach, oxtail soup with crackers, home made apple pie with cheese and topped with home made ice cream."[353] She stated that the dinner, lavish by pioneer standards, was served May 17, but that would have been impossible as the troops and Kellogg departed at 5 a.m. May 17. Perhaps he re-crossed the Missouri River to partake of the meal Tuesday May 16, but more likely they dined together Saturday night May 13. Joining the Dunns and Kellogg were Lounsberry and the Dunns' 2-year-old daughter Fannie.

In the late 1940s, Dr. Fannie Dunn Quain wrote in a letter that Kellogg "had been a personal friend of the family and had dinner with them afternoons when he was off duty," but because of her age in 1876 she had no memory of him.[354] Christina Dunn described Kellogg as "an intimate friend of Mr. Dunn's," who used to "almost live at the (drug) store." Kellogg was "a quiet sort of man [who] said very little about his people. Mr. Dunn knew that he was a widower with two children and this was about all that he knew of his personal life."[355]

Custer himself had just returned from near political exile in Washington, D.C. He had been recalled in March to Washington to testify before the Congressional Committee on Expenditures in the War Department, chaired by Heister Clymer. Earlier, Secretary of War W.W. Belknap had been forced to resign under the threat of impeachment, but the Clymer Committee kept up its investigation. Custer's testimony of March 29 and April 4 about his knowledge of post traderships amounted to little more than hearsay, and he hoped to return to Fort Lincoln to oversee preparations for the march. But the possibility he might be called to testify at Belknap's impeachment forced him to remain in Washington until April 20. No sooner had he departed when a politically motivated summons finally was issued for him to testify at the impeachment hearing. Custer had stirred the wrath of President Grant, whose brother Orville was implicated in the scandals. Grant ordered Custer removed not only from command of the expeditionary force itself but also from his regiment, the ultimate insult for him. Replacing him as the expedition's overall commander was Brig. Gen. Alfred H. Terry, commander officer of the Military Department of Dakota. Even Custer's friends, Generals William T. Sherman and Philip Sheridan could not extricate him from his dilemma. "By publicly attacking the president's official and personal family, Custer had lent himself to partisan Democratic purposes and now everyone fell in line to carry out the president's determination to punish him," Utley wrote.[356]

At the same time, Sherman and Sheridan weren't happy at the prospect of having Maj. Marcus A. Reno lead the 7th, and General Terry himself, while a highly competent Civil War veteran, had never campaigned against Indians. Terry dictated a telegram for the contrite Custer to send through channels appealing for reinstatement. Fortunately for Custer and his superiors, opposition newspapers were pummeling Grant, who politically had little choice by May 8 but to allow Custer at least to lead his regiment on the campaign.

Modern critics of Custer often cite Kellogg's presence with the Dakota Column as a sign of the general's massive ego at work. Sherman had advised Terry, "If you want General Custer along, [the president] withdraws his objections. Advise Custer to be prudent, not to take along any newspaper men, who always make mischief...."[357] However, in July 1876, Lounsberry pointed out that Kellogg traveled as the expedition's only accredited correspondent, "as we are prepared to prove by General Terry himself, of whom the writer obtained for Kellogg permission to go."[358] As the years passed, Lounsberry's recollections on this point changed. For example, in August 1895, he wrote in his *Fargo Record*, "The writer was the only correspondent invited by Custer to accompany the expedition."[359]

SANDY BARNARD

In October 1911, Lounsberry told researcher Walter M. Camp that "Custer had furnished a horse and means of subsistence for Kellogg who went in my place, and he was known as the only correspondent."[360] It's probable that Custer's early offer aboard the snow-bound train was effectively rescinded by his problems with Grant. Fortunately, Lounsberry obtained a later invitation from Terry.

After Kellogg's death, when other newspapers, including the *New York Herald* and the *Chicago Tribune*, also claimed Kellogg as their correspondent, the colonel puffed indignantly that he alone had outfitted the reporter and paid "the entire expense…all arrangements for his work were made by the *Bismarck Tribune*, and to it belongs the credit of sending with Terry the only newspaper correspondent with him."[361]

On the day of his death, Kellogg was riding a mule, and some have wondered whether such an animal carried him all the way from Bismarck. Lounsberry indicated otherwise. In his *Early History of North Dakota*, the colonel also wrote, "Accompanying [Custer] was Mark Kellogg, bearing my commission from the *New York Herald*, who rode the horse that was provided for me — for I had purposed going in his stead — and who wore the belt I had worn in the Civil War, which was stained with my blood."[362] Hixon interviewed one of Lounsberry's children, Mrs. C.E.V. Draper, who did not recall Kellogg. She did remember playing with her father's belt, which was short and better suited for a small man.[363] According to the memoirs of Company M's First Sgt. John Ryan, Kellogg was armed with a Spencer carbine.[364]

Despite the rainy cold weather of May 14, Kellogg's upbeat account of his tour of the 7th's tent city, laid out on the flats two miles south of Fort Lincoln, suggests he was excited by his assignment: "The appearance of the camp is very inspiring." The table of land on which the camp sat was "peculiarly attractive," and "officers and men are in the best of health and spirits, notwithstanding the depressing effects of the weather, and eager to move."[365] He provided a lengthy order of battle for the 7th and all the other units making up the column. As Knight observed, "He was not overly careful in giving figures for the various components; his figures do not add up."[366] Utley says that Terry's command numbered about 1,000 men, and the 7th Cavalry counted 32 officers and 718 enlisted men.[367]

Throughout the campaign, Kellogg had the run of the camp and the trust of the officers, a point supported by Lounsberry: "Being well known to the 7th Cavalry, he became its guest, and was ever with them, in camp and on the tramp."[368] That was evident in his first column, as Kellogg noted, " I have visited every department and every position of the camp and find everywhere perfect preparation, order and system. Everything is moving along like clockwork."

In his 1911 correspondence with Camp, Lounsberry shared a sense of Kellogg's work habits during the campaign: "It was Kellogg's way to make notes from day to day and in the evening or other times of delay write them up for publication, having matter always ready when the opportunity should come to send out his letter."[369]

For his first column, Kellogg gained two interviews with Terry, who obligingly outlined his plans and his route for early in the campaign. The troops would move due west, following the previously surveyed route of the NPRR to the banks of the Yellowstone River. At that point they would link up with Colonel Gibbon's force and set up a supply depot. Kellogg and Terry, a former lawyer, were little worried that the reporter's story would alert Sitting Bull and other Indian leaders to the commander's plans. Kellogg praised Terry for his "well-known executive ability," adding, "His courteous manner and kindly tones win fast the affections of the men in his command. Nothing seems to escape his notice."

The second interview came Monday afternoon May 15. Terry informed him that "There was to be no child's play as regards the Indians. They must be taught that the government was not to be trifled with, and such measures would be taken as would learn the Indians to feel and recognize that there existed in the land an arm and power which they must obey."

In this pre-departure column, Custer himself caught Kellogg's notice: "Gen. Geo. A. Custer, dressed in a dashing suit of buckskin, is prominent everywhere. Here, there, flitting to and fro, in his quick eager way, taking in everything connected with his command, as well as generally, with the keen, incisive manner for which he is so well known. The General is full of perfect readiness for a fray with the hostile red devils, and woe to the body of scalp lifters that comes within reach of himself and brave companions in arms."

Lounsberry tacked an editor's note to the bottom of Kellogg's May 17 column, pointing out the troops departed at 5 a.m. that day. The band played "Garry Owen," which was the regimental march, and "The Girl I Left Behind Me," another popular tune. In the newspaper's next issue, May 24, the editor published his reporter's second column, this time datelined the Heart River, the expedition's first camp site. Kellogg opened

110   SANDY BARNARD

by describing the command's departure the previous Wednesday.[370] As the troops moved out, he was impressed by "a cheering and brilliant sight" that he witnessed from the "highest peaked coteau west of Fort Lincoln" and by the inspiring strains of martial music played by the regiment's band. However, as the two-mile long column of cavalry, infantry, scouts and supply wagons made its way up from the river flats to the top of the bluffs on that foggy damp morning, Kellogg's writing captured less symbolism than Custer's wife Elizabeth perceived. She wrote, "As the sun broke through the mist a mirage appeared, which took up about half the line of cavalry, and thenceforth for a little distance it marched, equally plain to the sight on the earth and in the sky. The future of the heroic band, whose days were even then numbered, seemed to be revealed, and already there seemed a premonition in the supernatural translation as their forms were reflected from the opaque mist of the early dawn."[371]

After pointing out the expedition's excellent campsite along the Heart had been Custer's choice, he noted the paymaster paid the troops, assuring "the 'boys' will have a 'stake' in their pockets for a much longer period than they usually keep one there, and yet they are not happy, but think constantly of the girl left behind or other pleasures." Once again, he complimented Terry, who "is in excellent health and spirits, and hopes the Indians will gain sufficient courage to make a stand at or before we reach the Yellowstone River. His equable temper and genial manner show that the responsibilities resting on him, although weighty, wear him not at all."

Next, he penned a picture of the energetic Custer: "As usual on occasions of this kind, General Custer is full of life and spirit, the same true soldier exhibiting the dashing bravery of a man who knows no fear, true to the life in him. His energy is unbounded. Fatigue leaves no traces on him, and whatever care possesses him is hidden within his inner self. His men respect him and will dare to do brave things under his leadership."

Although far from home, Kellogg termed himself "fully contented" but apologized for not having space to thank by name all the officers for "their uniform kindness." Lounsberry added a lengthy editor's note, but it's unknown whether the information came from Kellogg or another source. It dealt mostly with camp details and weather as well as the sighting of a few "evidently hostile" Indians on bluffs near one of the camps.

During the campaign Kellogg was one of a number of men who kept diaries. His motivation likely stemmed from the journalistic need to record details for use in his dispatches. Thus, much of its content reads in short choppy bursts of words, not in full sentences that form a smooth narrative. Today the fragile Kellogg diary is housed with the State Historical Society of North Dakota in Bismarck. After his death, the diary was returned to Bismarck and given to John Dunn. The rectangular sheets of coarse gray paper of the diary are shaped much like the reporter's common notebook of today. The modern notebook is also rectangular, measuring a handy 4 by 8 inches, with a metal spiral binding that allows pages to be turned upon themselves. A reporter can thrust the pad into a coat or pants pocket. Kellogg's "notebook" lacks the spiral binding, but consists of 37 loose sheets of a paper grade similar to today's newsprint. In long form they measure 3 3/4 x 18 1/4 inches, but folded in half, they form a notebook of 3 3/4 x 9 inches, close to the dimensions of today's journalistic pad. He could easily have carried his notes in a pocket. His handwriting is clear and readable; any problems with legibility stem more from fading caused by the diary's age. The document begins May 17 and ends June 9. In later years, the Dunns claimed the remaining pages had been lost. However, Kellogg habitually began his new day's entries on the same page, immediately below the previous day's. Those of June 9 end in the middle of its final page. The rest of that page is blank. That suggests Kellogg intentionally broke off his notes on that day, perhaps placing his early pages, now no longer needed, in his satchel while he carried a new set covering the last 16 days of his life.

In the Little Big Horn literature it has often been claimed the Kellogg diary was blood-stained. However, tests conducted in December 1995 on two samples of stains from the diary by Chief Forensic Scientist Aaron E. Rash of the North Dakota Health Department's Forensic Science Division effectively ruled out the presence of blood. "While not ruling out the possibility that the tests simply fail to work on possible bloodstains nearly 120 years old, Rash expressed '95 percent' certainty that the stains are not blood," according to an article in *North Dakota History*. Rash theorized the stains on the diary could have been caused by a liquid, including a spilled beverage, such as coffee, wine or whiskey, or even some other source such as muddy water.[372]

For about three weeks the troops followed Terry's original route to reach the Yellowstone River at the mouth of Glendive Creek in eastern Montana, near where Gen. D.S. Stanley had established a supply stockade during the 1873 Yellowstone expedition that protected a railroad survey ing party. No Indians intent on hostile activity were seen. Farther to the west, scouts of Col. John Gibbon had twice spotted big villages, on May 16 in the Tongue River Valley and on May 27 in the Rosebud Valley. Gibbon was unable to mount an offensive on either occasion. He also failed to send messages to Terry and to Crook to alert them. So the three ponderous Army columns moved to and fro in Indian country, ignorant of where both their foe and their own support wandered.

Kellogg's third campaign dispatch, his most lengthy to date, was datelined May 29, "in the field near Rosebud Buttes" and was published June 14.[373] After noting the countryside and the lack of hostiles, he renewed his now obligatory praise of the expedition's two leaders. Terry "keeps a close tongue and his opinions seldom become public property," suggesting that even the reporter was not being provided with much information for publication. Kellogg added, "He keeps his command in hand, however, as if he expected attack, and is ever prepared for it."

With Custer, Kellogg penned his most colorful description of the general on the prowl: "General Terry, through his watchfulness and care of his officers and men, and through his kind words and acts has become endeared to all in the command, and the men will stand by him to a man as they ever have by the more dashing Custer, who as the men say, may be seen hell-whooping over the prairie at almost any time of day. Free from the responsibility of command, all of his energies may be employed in the work assigned him, ever in the saddle, only when eating, sleeping or writing, he is generally on the flank, or far in advance of the column with a few trusty scouts, making observations of the country, on the alert for signs of Indians, with which he is as familiar as a white man can be, and occasionally hunting for pastime."

On the march Custer divided his regiment's 12 companies into two wings, each having two battalions of three companies apiece. The wing commanders were Major Reno and Capt. Frederick W. Benteen. Utley notes that Benteen and Custer at best "treated each other with military formality."[374] Reno and Custer barely knew one another, having never served together at the same post. Still, Custer had a low opinion of Reno, whose cold personality and social awkwardness made him difficult to like or respect. The wing organization freed Custer from the mundane tasks of an active regimental commander. As Kellogg observed, "General Terry always leads the advance of the column; Custer is with him when not on the 'scoot,' as the boys have come to call it."

Kellogg again revealed his 19th century, man of the West, political and social views, pointing out, "The bee, the buffalo and the Indian are ever crowded ahead as civilization advances." With buffalo no longer roaming the area surveyed by the Northern Pacific, he added, "The Indian must soon follow. For whites want the country and the Great Spirit has decreed that the red man must pass on." He talked at length about the long tangled relationships of the Arikaras with the whites and their mutual enemy, the Sioux. "It does the soul of Bloody Knife [an Arikara scout reputed to be Custer's favorite]...good to tell of the bloody battles which have been fought [with the Sioux] on the ground west and south of Berthold." Kellogg believed the scouts greatly respected Custer, the "long haired chief...though he long since abandoned those golden ringlets, and now wears a fighting cut, as all good soldiers should."

Along the way the column passed the grave of a 7th Cavalryman, Sgt. Henry M. Stempker, who died of disease in August 1874 during the Black Hills expedition.[375] Kellogg's words in portraying the sad scene in his report echoed with as much irony as his hay camp temperance speech of two years earlier. "This brave soldier died here surrounded only by his brave comrades, hundreds, perhaps thousands of miles from mother or sister, or the home of his childhood. Life is beset with hidden footfalls.

"When we least expect it death approaches. The sensitive mind always becomes sad when in the presence of death but to meet with the dead on the western plains has a peculiar effect. The churchyard where sleep our friends and relatives may be passed without serious thought. But here death with his grim visage stares at us from unexpected places forcing an entire change in the channel of our thoughts. Shall we leave beneath the sod of the almost limitless prairies the forms of any of those now with us, who are so full of life and hope? We shall see."

Kellogg would have depended on army couriers to carry his dispatches back to Bismarck. Newspapers other than the *Tribune* published his dispatches during the campaign. A story by "Frontier" appeared in the *Chicago Times* of May 25. Stories, either written by Kellogg or rewritten by Lounsberry from Kellogg's original, also were printed May 18, May 24, and July 11 in the *New York Herald*.[376]

Kellogg, apparently, took a two-week break from his regular publishing in the *Bismarck Tribune*. His next Bismarck column, dated June 12 from "Camp of Terry's Expedition, Near Mouth of Powder River," was written over several days, but it wasn't published until June 21. Why he had not sent a dispatch for two weeks goes unexplained. Instead, he opened by promising to update his readers on the command's progress, as it reached the Powder River and met up with Gibbon's troops. As mentioned earlier, his available diary entries end with June 9. However, in his dispatch of June 12, Kellogg relied on "notes from my diary" for June 10, 11 and 12. He outlined the strategy Terry and his commanders had hit upon. If the Indians had moved south away from the Yellowstone and Powder rivers, General Crook's troops, coming up from Wyoming, would presumably intercept them. Gibbon was ordered to go up the Yellowstone to the mouth of the Rosebud to prevent the Indians from crossing to the north. Reno would lead six companies up the Powder, move across country to the Tongue and back to the Yellowstone. Terry, Custer and the rest of the command would leave the Powder and travel up the Yellowstone to the Tongue to await Reno's return.

Utley said, "Custer disliked Terry's plan, as he made clear in dispatches he was sending, for publication without attribution, to the *New York Herald*."[377] Kellogg suggested Custer was in a snit about his superior's plans: "General Custer declined to take command of the scout of which Major Reno is now at the head of, not believing that any Indians would be met with in either direction. His opinion is that they are in bulk in the vicinity of the Rosebud range."

According to his diary entry for June 11 (which he repeated in his column written June 12), Kellogg spent that day off in the badlands on his third side trip hunting with scout Charley Reynolds. His existing diary reveals that the two men twice previously, May 31 and June 5, went off on successful hunts for antelope and Rocky Mountain sheep. On this third occasion he commented that moving in the rugged country of the badlands isn't difficult "if mounted on an active mule." Whether that meant he had lost his horse by this time or was just relying on a more sure-footed animal for his foray into the rugged countryside is unknown.

Some early accounts of the Little Big Horn campaign state Kellogg may have ridden the *Far West* (the expedition's accompanying river steamer) from Bismarck up to the Powder River supply depot, but that wasn't true. That tale may have resulted from Kellogg's own enthusiastic account about his day aboard the steamer June 12 at the invitation of Capt. Grant Marsh. The 86-mile round trip took him to the Glendive Creek base to bring up supplies to the Powder River. The run took just three hours as the boat averaged more than 28 miles an hour. "That's no 'fish story,'

Colonel," Kellogg wrote to his editor, "but a fact, and I think this proves the *Far West* a clipper to 'go along'."

About half way through his June 12 letter, he began fulfilling his promise to fill in the gaps since his May 29 letter. He included a detailed account of his first hunting trip with Reynolds on May 31. He also related with his customary enthusiasm his participation in a scouting party led by Custer June 7. "Your correspondent had the pleasure of accompanying the scouting party, and writes, from personal observation, what he knows to be a fact." After Custer delivered on his promise to reach the Powder River by 3 p.m. that day, Kellogg praised him. "Nothing daunted him, on he goes, never tiring, his boundless energy and will overcoming all seeming obstacles."

Kellogg also praised the men of the 7th Cavalry as "fine appearing, strong, quick, athletic fellows, always cheerfully ready to obey the order of command, whether it is for mount, picket duty, pioneer labor, or police work." He added, "Take them all in all they comprise just such a regiment as one would choose as an escort through the country of a foe, or where it was positive hard fighting would occur." He suggested, too, the men were dedicated to "Leather Breeches," their seemingly affectionate name for Custer. His letter concluded optimistically: "From this point will radiate the cavalry in force, and is the general impression that the hostiles will be found in the course of 10 days."

The campaign was approaching its climax. On June 19, Reno's command reappeared, but he would be roundly criticized for having exceeded his orders. Instead of just scouting the Powder River and Tongue River valleys, Reno continued to the Rosebud, then marched back to the Yellowstone, where he encountered Gibbon's men. Actually, he deserved praise for giving Terry his best information on the Indians' whereabouts. He found recent camp sites that suggested the village, previously spotted by Lt. James Bradley of Gibbon's command, had been moved up the Rosebud sometime earlier. That meant Terry's plan for catching the Indians on the Rosebud would have to be revised. Despite his solid intelligence about the Indians, poor Reno was sharply criticized by all concerned, including Mark Kellogg and George Custer in posthumous letters to the *New York Herald*. In a column published July 11, Kellogg insisted, "For some cause unknown to your correspondent, Major Reno was unfortunate enough not only to exceed but to disobey the orders and instructions of General Terry."[378] If Kellogg ever deserved historian Oliver Knight's trained seal label, it would be for those remarks. They mirrored Custer's own that appeared anonymously in the *Herald* and lambasted Reno. Custer wrote about his subordinate: "Reno, after an absence of 10 days, returned, when it was found to the disgust of every member of the entire expedition, from the commanding general down to the lowest private, that Reno, instead of simply failing to accomplish any good results, had so misconducted his force as to embarrass, if not seriously and permanently mar, all hopes of future success of the expedition. He had not only deliberately and without a shadow of an excuse failed to obey his written orders issued by General Terry's personal directions, but he had acted in positive disobedience to the strict injunctions of the department commander."[379]

Custer further criticized him for turning away from the Indians' trail instead of pursuing them. He suggested, too, "A court martial is strongly hinted at, and if one is not ordered it will not be because it is not richly deserved."

Kellogg's letter, the last published obviously as his, was written June 21 and was datelined "Yellowstone River, mouth Rosebud River." In a private cover note, the reporter apologized to the *Herald's* editor for his previous manuscript that had been soaked for a time in the Yellowstone. "My last was badly demoralized from wetting...and I have feared it would not prove acceptable on that account." Why Kellogg was so concerned about the condition of his manuscript is unknown. Lounsberry always claimed he forwarded Kellogg's work to the *Herald*. This note may indicate Kellogg sent his materials directly and did not always rely on the colonel to mail or telegraph dispatches to New York.

The loss of the dispatch in the river, albeit temporarily with no real harm, seemed to have unsettled the reporter's confidence and he sought to justify his own position with the command. "The officers of the expedition have written generally to their friends to watch for the *Herald*, as they know I am to record their deeds. I will endeavor to give you interesting letters as we go along."

He again noted, "I have the liberty of the entire column, headquarters and all, and will get down to bottom facts in all matters connected with the expedition." He signed the note with his own name, M.H. Kellogg, not his pen name. After detailing the Reno controversy, Kellogg pointed out that the next day, June 22, Custer's regiment would move up the Rosebud in pursuit of the Indian trail discovered by Reno. The rest of Terry's command would march up the Yellowstone to the Big Horn River, Kellogg

This is the most common image of reporter Mark Kellogg. It was originally a carte de visite, c. 1863-1864, taken by La Crosse, Wis., photographer H.C. Heath in the early 1860s while Kellogg was working as a journalist for the La Crosse Democrat.

Courtesy Sandy Barnard

Carte de visite of Hannah Paine Robinson, Mark Kellogg's mother-in-law. According to an inscription on the back of the original image, it was taken Nov. 13, 1863, by photographer H.C. Heath of La Crosse, Wis. Mrs. Robinson was age 58 at the time.
Courtesy Sandy Barnard

Carte de visite of Eliza Jane Robinson, sister-in-law of Mark Kellogg. According to an inscription on the back of the original image, it was taken Feb. 18, 1964, by photographer H.C. Heath of La Crosse, Wis. Eliza was age 18 at the time.
Courtesy Sandy Barnard

The woman is Mattie Grace Kellogg Temple, the younger daughter of reporter Mark Kellogg. She married Dr. Franklin S. Temple in 1892. Their son Frank L. Temple was born in 1893. This photo's location and date are unknown, although it is believed to have been taken between 1902-04.
Courtesy Winifred Temple Stewart

Frank L. Temple, age 43, the grandson of reporter Mark Kellogg, and his daughter, Winifred V. Temple, age 16, the great-granddaughter of Kellogg. The photo was taken in October 1936 in Raymond, N.H.
Courtesy Winifred Temple Stewart

M ark Kellogg's descendants today. Seated (front row) is Winifred V. Temple Stewart, Kellogg's great-granddaughter. Her sons are Richard S. Balch (left) and Ronald L. Balch (right). Ronald's daughters are Stefanie, 13, (left) and Jennifer, 15, (right), who are the reporter's great-great-great-granddaughters.
Chico, Calif., February 1996.
Courtesy Winifred Temple Stewart

Mark Kellogg ate his last home-cooked meal at the home of pharmacist John P. Dunn in Bismarck, North Dakota. Even though Kellogg and Dunn were close friends, Dunn's wife Christina said her husband knew very little about Kellogg's past.
Courtesy State Historical Society of North Dakota

John Piatt Dunn

Clement Lounsberry

In the mid-1890s, long after he had sold his interest in the *Bismarck Tribune*, Lounsberry edited a magazine, the *Fargo Record*, which contained many articles of historical value. This photo appeared in July 1896 in the *Record*, when he would have been 53 years old. However, he appears somewhat younger in this photo.
Courtesy Sandy Barnard

Marcus M. "Brick" Pomeroy

Pomeroy hired Mark Kellogg as an editor, for the La Crosse, Wis., *Democrat*. [c. 1863-1864] and cashier for his newspaper in 1862.
Courtesy Sandy Barnard

L t. Col. George Armstrong Custer apparently arranged for *Bismarck Tribune* coverage of his military expedition in the winter of 1876 while snowbound on a train with *Tribune* Editor Clement Lounsberry. Custer anticipated favorable news coverage of his supposed military triumph, but the biggest scoop of the century turned out to be his demise.
Courtesy The Bismarck Tribune

General Rosser and staff at Brainard · 1871

Thomas L. Rosser (seated, with white hat) was a close friend of George Custer's at West Point. As a Confederate general, he frequently engaged Custer's units during the Civil War. After the war, Rosser was a chief engineer for the Northern Pacific Railroad. When this photo was taken at Brainerd, Minn., in 1871, Mark Kellogg (standing, far left) was working for him, probably as a telegrapher.
Courtesy Burlington Northern Railroad

S . KELLOGG. Proprietor.

M ark Kellogg's father, Simeon, was a prominent hotel keeper in La Crosse, Wis., for many years. Historical accounts say that Mark, as a young man, worked for his father as a clerk in what was known as the "Kellogg House," before he turned to careers in telegraphy and journalism.

Courtesy Area Research Center, University of Wisconsin at La Crosse

M ark Kellogg likely was an early casualty among the men who accompanied Lt. Col. George Custer's battalion. His body was found June 29, 1876, four days after his death, by Col. John Gibbon. Close study of Gibbon's account and the Little Big Horn Battlefield today suggests this site close to the Little Big Horn River may have been the general vicinity where Gibbon discovered the dead newsman.

Courtesy Michael Donahue and the Old Elk Family

124   SANDY BARNARD

Mark Kellogg marker, Little Big Horn Battlefield National Monument

This marker is actually the second to have been erected at the traditional site where Mark Kellogg's body reportedly was found and buried on the battlefield. However, this site bears no resemblance to the area described by Col. John Gibbon, who found Kellogg's body in June 1876. He probably wasn't buried at this place either.
Courtesy Sandy Barnard

Mark Kellogg Memorial Marker, La Crosse, Wis.

In 1867, Kellogg's wife, Martha, died in La Crosse, Wis., and was buried in her family's plot in Oak Grove Cemetery, La Crosse. After Kellogg's death in 1876, a reference to his death in Montana was added to the marker over her grave. In 1976, the La Crosse news media erected this sign that recalled highlights of his career, especially the sacrifice of his life at the Little Big Horn.
Courtesy Sandy Barnard

For the journey westward with Custer's troops, Mark Kellogg packed these items in a black leather satchel: a blue wool shirt, wool socks, cotton underwear, mosquito netting to drape his head and face, reading glasses, pencil, combs, tobacco and flint. Along the way he collected some rocks that appealed to his interest in geography. When Custer split his cavalry from the main command for the ride to the Little Big Horn, Kellogg left his satchel behind on the Far West riverboat. The satchel and its contents were returned to Bismarck, ND, pharmacist John Dunn, who was Kellogg's friend. The Dunn family donated the items to the State Historical Society of North Dakota in 1918.
Courtesy State Historical Society of North Dakota

M ark Kellogg's journal detailed the march to the Little
Big Horn and talked of Custer's confidence. The journal
was given to the Bismarck Tribune by Fannie Dunn Quain;
later, the Tribune donated the journal to the State Historical
Society of North Dakota.
Courtesy State Historical Society of North Dakota

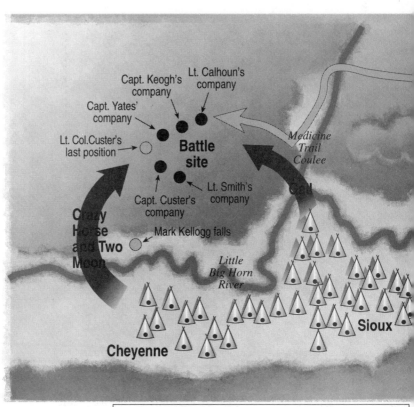

Lt. Calhoun's company

Capt. Keogh's company

Capt. Yates' company

Lt. Col.Custer's last position

Battle site

Medicine Trail Coulee

Gall

Lt. Smith's company

Capt. Custer's company

Crazy Horse and Two Moon

Mark Kellogg falls

Little Big Horn River

Sioux

Cheyenne

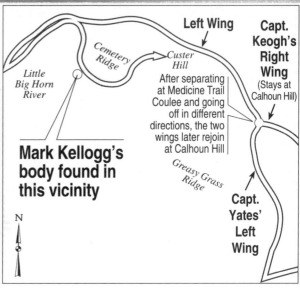

Left Wing

Capt. Keogh's Right Wing
(Stays at Calhoun Hill)

Cemetery Ridge

Custer Hill

Little Big Horn River

After separating at Medicine Trail Coulee and going off in different directions, the two wings later rejoin at Calhoun Hill

Mark Kellogg's body found in this vicinity

Greasy Grass Ridge

Capt. Yates' Left Wing

N

*T*ribune Correspondent Mark Kellogg fell in the vicinity where the left wing of Custer's command met warriors, near the Little Big Horn

SANDY BARNARD

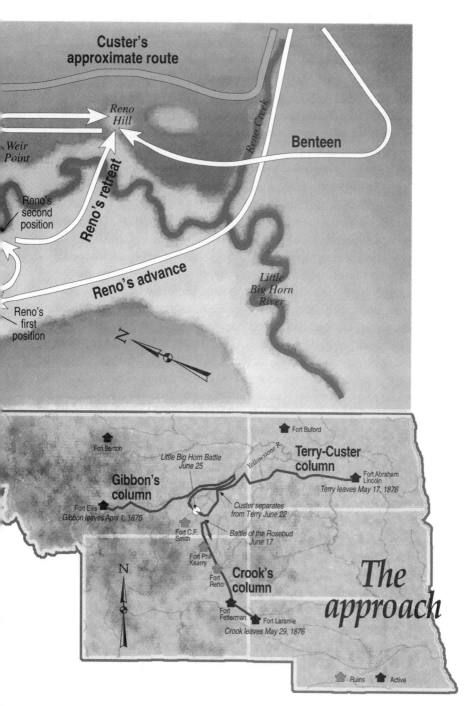

Custer's
approximate route

Reno
Hill

Weir
Point

Benteen

Reno's
second
position

Reno's retreat

Reno's advance

Little
Big Horn
River

N

Reno's
first
position

Fort Buford

Fort Benton

Little Big Horn Battle
June 25

Yellowstone R.

Terry-Custer
column

Gibbon's
column

Fort Ellis
Gibbon leaves April 1, 1876

Custer separates
from Terry June 22

Fort Abraham
Lincoln
Terry leaves May 17, 1876

Fort C.F.
Smith

Battle of the Rosebud
June 17

Fort Phil
Kearny

N

Fort
Reno

Crook's
column

The
approach

Fort
Fetterman

Fort Laramie

Crook leaves May 29, 1876

Ruins

Active

added, "in order to intercept the Indians if they should attempt to escape from General Custer down that avenue. The hope is now strong, and, I believe, well founded, that this band of ugly customers, known as Sitting Bull's band, will be 'gobbled' and dealt with as they deserve."

He offered his readers a lengthy description of the Yellowstone countryside before once more bestowing lavish praise on Terry, who "I find to be my ideal of a commanding general — large brained, sagacious, far reaching cool under all circumstances and with rare executive abilities. He is besides genial, courteous, frank and manly."

And, in this, his last published column, he could not overlook George Custer, whom he described in flowery and overdone language as "the most peculiar genius in the army." More important, this would be one of the last portraits in print of Custer in life, written by someone with little need to gain his favor or risk his ire. Kellogg, while not an objective reporter by modern journalistic standards, saw Custer as "a man of strong impulse, of great hearted friendships and bitter enmities, of quick nervous temperament, undaunted courage, will and determination; a man possessing electric mental capacity and of iron frame and constitution; a brave, faithful, gallant soldier, who has warm friends and bitter enemies; the hardest rider, the greatest pusher, with the most untiring vigilance, overcoming seeming impossibilities and with an ambition to succeed in all things he undertakes; a man to do right, as he construes the right, in every case; one respected and beloved by his followers, who would freely follow him into the 'jaws of hell'."

Kellogg concluded: "Of Lt. Col. G.A. Custer I am now writing. Do not think I am overdrawing the picture. The pen picture is true to the life and is drawn not only from actual observation, but from an experience that cannot mislead me."

During the campaign Kellogg had observed Custer closely on numerous occasions, including when the 7th Cavalry marched from the Tongue River to the junction of the Yellowstone and the Rosebud. The trek was across rough country that Kellogg reported "caused panting breaths and reeking perspiration." Riding at the rear of the column, he observed Custer wore a light-colored buckskin suit.[380]

Did Kellogg send a similar letter to the *Bismarck Tribune*? Surely he must have, as his first loyalty would have been to keep Lounsberry's readers back home informed. Some slight evidence suggests Lounsberry not only received such a letter but failed to publish it before the news of the battle broke late on July 5. In his July 5 newspaper, published just hours before the *Far West* brought the startling news about the disaster on the Little Big Horn, he said, "The letter of our special correspondent with Terry's expedition is laid over until next week for want of room, together with the principal portion of our report of the centennial celebration. All will be published next week together with later and fuller news from the Black Hills."[381] Other news apparently was more important to the colonel than the military expedition in Montana.

As noted earlier, Lounsberry headed his extra of July 6 with Kellogg's prophetic statement: "We leave the Rosebud tomorrow, and by the time this reaches you we will have met and fought the red devils, with what result remains to be seen. I go with Custer and will be at the death." Researchers of the battle have routinely assumed the passage was written aboard the *Far West* on the evening of June 21 as a cover note for Kellogg's last dispatch from the field. However, his intriguing use of the word "Rosebud" suggests this note actually accompanied another "final dispatch," perhaps written as late as June 24, the day before the battle. If Kellogg had written his words on the *Far West*, he would have said, "We leave the Yellowstone tomorrow." At the point where the two water courses meet, the much larger Yellowstone River dwarfs the much smaller Rosebud River.

Also consider Kellogg's phrasing "by the time this reaches you we will have met and fought the red devils." On June 21, prospects for any immediate fighting were uncertain. If written then, that statement should be interpreted more accurately — "Surely in the days and weeks this note will take to reach you, we will have found, we will have met and we will have fought the red devils."

However, by the evening of June 24, the buzz around the 7th's camp was that tomorrow would bring hard fighting. The regiment's Indian scouts were apprehensive about the size of the village the column was trailing. The ever-buoyant, supremely confident Custer might dismiss the scouts' fears of what lay ahead, but among his rank-and-file, concern was growing. Kellogg tapped into this uneasiness with his cautionary phrasing, "with what result remains to be seen." That does not sound like the upbeat "Bring 'em on — we can defeat the world" reporter of the previous weeks on the campaign trail.

On several occasions years later, Lounsberry himself suggested he had received another "final dispatch" from Kellogg. In 1895, he wrote, "Gen. [James S.] Brisbin had forwarded to him [Lounsberry] the manuscript of Mark Kellogg, written up to an hour before the fatal charge, which was found in his haversack, one carried by the writer during the war."[382] In another account five years earlier, Brisbin, a major under Gibbon, recalled that at Kellogg's death site, "His saddle-bags had been cut open and the contents strewn upon the ground. His papers were gathered up, and it was found he had kept an accurate account of the march up to the time when General Custer left the Rosebud to cross over to the Little Big Horn and attack the great Sioux Camp."[383]

The best evidence for whether Kellogg on June 24 had another dispatch ready that went unpublished can be found in Lounsberry's 1911 correspondence with Walter Camp.[384] On Sept. 19, Camp asked Lounsberry a series of questions. On the bottom of that letter, Lounsberry typed a response, probably on Sept. 21, in which he said Dr. Henry Porter, a battle survivor, had given him a "manuscript from Mark Kellogg's haversack." Porter also gave him a pass book with notes written by Brisbin, who asked the editor to forward them to the *New York Herald*, "for the reason that the *Herald* having done him some personal service he had promised that if he ever had an opportunity to give them a scoop he would do so."

Lounsberry added, "There was Mark Kellogg's notes written up to almost the moment of battle (not the ones recovered from his knapsack)." The reference to a knapsack left Camp confused, so on Sept. 27 he asked the former editor for clarification. On Oct. 16, Lounsberry sought to clear up the issue: "This matter (his notes from day to day) was in his haversack and was found scattered about his remains and gathered up by Brisbin and sent me, while the notes proper were left in his knapsack for more elaborate writing, probably, later. The papers found were used as a part of the story telegraphed by me."

What is to be made of this? Kellogg's notes, certainly through June 9, if not later, remained on the *Far West* in the black satchel bag that Lounsberry referred to as the reporter's "knapsack." That bag is among the Kellogg holdings in the State Historical Society of North Dakota. His other notes of the last few days, written up to "almost the moment of battle," were in a different bag that Lounsberry referred to as a haversack. The Indians who killed Kellogg obviously had no use for his written materials so they left them scattered on the ground near the body. They likely confiscated the haversack (although some of Lounsberry's later statements suggested otherwise).

On the afternoon of June 21, Terry and his subordinates, Gibbon, Custer and Brisbin, who commanded a battalion of the 2nd Cavalry from

SANDY BARNARD

Fort Ellis, Montana Territory, gathered in a cabin aboard the *Far West*. The boat was moored to the south bank of the Yellowstone at the mouth of the Rosebud. Terry laid out his plans for tracking the enemy, which Kellogg had reported for the *Herald* and undoubtedly included in a dispatch sent to Lounsberry. No record indicates Kellogg sat in on this strategy session, but his claim to have the "liberty of the entire column" and his precision in reporting Terry's plan strongly suggest he lingered nearby, as his last known works to Lounsberry and to the *Herald* were written aboard the steamer.

For determining Kellogg's movements on June 21, Brisbin, a brevet major general during the Civil War, provided the best information. He usually is credited as the author of a lengthy account written June 28 on the Montana battlefield and sent back to Lounsberry for forwarding to the *Herald*, which published it July 8. It included this oft-quoted statement about Kellogg: "I saw poor Kellogg on the boat the night before the troops marched and he was busy until after 12 o'clock writing up his dispatches and getting his rations ready for the journey. At a little after midnight, June 21, I went out on the deck of the steamer to smoke a cigar and Kellogg came out a few minutes afterward and said he was through with his writing and ready for the forwarding on tomorrow. He talked a long time about the campaign, and was full of hope that they might during the coming march overhaul the Indians and have a good fight."[385] Brisbin's comments seem to indicate Kellogg may have been bunking on the boat.

In 1890, Brisbin again related his story of the Little Big Horn, including some more tantalizing details about Kellogg's last night on the *Far West*. Significantly, he suggested that Kellogg originally intended to travel with the Terry-Gibbon column. "It was late at night when Mark Kellogg [*Herald* publisher James Gordon] Bennett's man made up his mind to go with Custer. He had intended going with us but feared he might miss something if he did not accompany the fiery cavalryman. I went with him to Custer, got him permission to accompany the column, and got him a mount of a pair of saddle-bags [sic] and some provisions from the boat. We fixed poor Mark up for his ride to death."[386]

His account indicates that Kellogg might have recently lost his horse. Brisbin helped him locate a mule for his final ride with Custer.

In any case, by mid-day, June 22, the various elements of Terry's command were ready. Terry believed the hostiles were somewhere up the Rosebud Valley, and had either moved east toward the Black Hills or west toward the Little Big Horn Valley. His strategy, as reported by Kellogg:

Have the 7th Cavalry under Custer head south up the Rosebud, following the Indians' trail spotted by Reno. Gibbon's command, accompanied by Terry himself and the slower-moving infantry, would march west along the Yellowstone to the Big Horn. From there they would follow the Big Horn south to the Little Big Horn River. If Custer found Indians along the Little Big Horn, he would attack and drive them north into Gibbon's blocking force.

Terry's plan offered Custer considerable leeway because no one could be sure of exactly which direction the Indians would take on the upper reaches of the Rosebud. Terry assumed Gibbon's force could reach the Little Big Horn about June 26, but otherwise his orders placed few expectations on Custer. Clearly, Terry's written orders to Custer allowed him to respond to the developing military situation as he saw fit.

Unknown to Terry and Custer, Brig. Gen. George Crook's troops had returned to the campaign trail, only to be attacked by a much stronger Sioux and Cheyenne force than any of them anticipated, far up the Rosebud on June 17. For the second time in the 1876 campaign, Crook retired from the fight and retreated to camp along Goose Creek at present-day Sheridan, Wyo. Waiting for supplies and additional men, he represented no further threat to the Indians. He was unable to inform the other columns the Indians meant to fight the soldiers, regardless of how strong the army might be.

About noon June 22, the 7th Cavalry — 12 companies consisting of 566 enlisted, 31 officers, 24 Indian scouts and about a dozen packers, guides, other civilians and newspaper reporter Mark H. Kellogg — paraded before Terry. Brisbin reported that Custer's men were "all in splendid condition...in the best of spirits and mounted on the finest horses that could be bought in the east."[387] One man was not aboard a horse. "The very last one I saw at the mouth of the Rosebud was Mr. Kellogg, the *Herald* correspondent, who was mounted on a mule and a pair of canvas saddle bags in which were stored paper and pencil, sugar, coffee and bacon sufficient to last 15 days. He sat on the right of General Gibbon, watching the review, and rode away after Custer, General Terry calling him back to say goodby."

As Kellogg urged his mule on to catch up to the departing column, he left behind his columns for couriers to carry back to the newspapers. On board the boat were virtually all of his earthly possessions, contained within a black satchel bag made of oil cloth sewn to a metal frame, with black leather carrying handles. The contents were modest, not surprising for a man of little wealth and simple pleasures. His diary perhaps was most enduring in interest. Some surprising items reflected Kellogg's interest in his environment: Samples of scoria, flint, coal, and petrified wood, all found in western North Dakota. Also, he carried a whetstone with a dished-out top for sharpening his knives. Teeth marks on his small pencil with square lead attest to his apparent habit of chewing on it.[388]

Several personal objects also were found. At age 43, he needed reading glasses. Undoubtedly, he carried several pairs, but the one in his bag had been sold by Marshall Brothers, Minneapolis, Minn. He also carried two combs, one of cow horn, the other of black, hard rubber made by the I.R. Comb Co. Kellogg enjoyed tobacco in two forms, including orally, via plug tobacco. He also smoked Bull Durham tobacco, manufactured by W.T. Blackwell & Co., Durham, N.C. The blue-green piece of paper at the top of the tobacco bag is the remnant of a U.S. revenue stamp, denoting the collection of federal taxes on the product.

Finally, several articles of clothing were contained in his bag and indicate he was a man of small build, probably about 5 foot, 7 inches tall. Blue and white cotton stockings are about size 7 1/2 - 8. Weather on the northern plains in spring and early summer could vary significantly and Kellogg obviously was prepared for the extremes the military column encountered. His heavy cotton undershirt and drawers have glass buttons for closure of the cuffs, collar and fly. The drawers have a cloth tie in back of the waist to tighten them. He also left behind a machine sewn, dark blue wool shirt with mother-of-pearl and glass buttons. Wool shirts were standard apparels on the plains. As wet wool dries, it draws moisture and heat from the body, helping to keep it cool. Warmer weather would bring out the flies, gnats, and mosquitoes on the northern Great Plains, but Kellogg was prepared with a mosquito netting that covered his head, face and neck.

Beginning June 22, for the next three days, Custer pushed his regiment up the Rosebud looking for the Indians. Intelligence provided to the columns suggested the hostiles would number no more than 800 warriors. As true of most of the officers in the field that summer, Custer was more concerned the Indians would scatter if possible, rather than fight the soldiers. He had supreme confidence in himself and his men to handle the Indians, no matter how large their number. According to Utley, "Each man carried a Springfield single-shot carbine and a Colt revolver, with 100 rounds for carbine and 24 for pistol."[389]

On the first day the 12 companies followed the Rosebud for 12 miles. On June 23, they made another 33 and crossed the Indian trail earlier discovered by Reno. On June 24, the 7th covered another 28 miles, passing the site of a Sioux sun dance held earlier in June. Signs at the scene unsettled Custer's Crow and Arikara Indian scouts, amid other indications on the trail that the number of hostile Indians was larger than anticipated. These Indians had traveled up the Rosebud themselves for much of June, all the time keeping a watch on Gibbon's and Crook's forces. By June 16, the village had crossed over the Rosebud to settle on a tributary of the Little Big Horn that whites would come to know as Reno Creek. About that time, scouts from the village realized the danger the advancing column of Crook on the Rosebud represented. On June 17, warriors poured from the village. In a stunning reversal of form, they headed for the Rosebud to attack Crook, forcing him to retreat into Wyoming. The village itself, now full of excited warriors fresh from their victory, moved into the Little Big Horn Valley to await the remaining cast of characters, Indian and white. As Utley said, "Their brethren from the agencies finally began to arrive in significant numbers. On the back trail from the Rosebud down Reno Creek, and down the Little Big Horn itself, the agency Indians converged on their destination. They came in small groups and large, trailing on the ground behind them, in a chaos of size, direction, and age, the marks of their progress."[390]

The village grew ever larger, Utley added, from 400 to 1,000 lodges and from 3,000 to 7,000 people. The warrior total increased, too, from 800 to 2,000, far more than the 600 or so soldiers Custer led searching for them. "In six separate tribal circles they crowded the narrow valley of the Little Big Horn. Oglalas, Miniconjous, Sans Arcs, Blackfeet, Two Kettles, Brules, and a scattering of Yanktonnais and Santees (Sioux, but not Tetons) made up the five Sioux circles, while 120 Cheyenne lodges rounded out the array. Even a handful of Arapahoes cast their lot with their friends."[391]

On June 24, the village arrived at its final camp along the Little Big Horn River, setting the stage for the great battle between the cultures, one seeking to maintain its way of life, the other seeking to change it. Organized by circles, the camp lay about two miles below the mouth of Reno Creek. Some debate exists about the size and extent of the village, which traditionally was thought to have stretched about three miles from the present-day Garryowen Post Office on the south to the vicinity of Medicine Tail Coulee on the north. Cottonwood trees provided shade along the river the Indians called the Greasy Grass, which snaked below 300-foot bluffs on the east. To the west low-slung bench lands provided ample grass for the village's massive pony herd. With so many people and animals in a relatively small arena, the village could not stay together for long. Utley says, "White apologists, seeking to explain the disaster this coalition of tribes wrought, would later endow it with an immensity it never approached. Still, it was big by all standards of the time, and it was more than twice as big as any of the army officers looking for it had anticipated."[392]

The Indians also were prepared to fight, he added. "The coincidence of timing that brought the 7th Cavalry to the vicinity of this village during the few days of its peak strength was only the beginning of a run of ill fortune that ended in the utter collapse of 'Custer's Luck'."[393]

On the night of June 24, the 7th Cavalry bivouacked on the Rosebud. Custer's scouts had ascertained the hostiles must be encamped on the lower Little Big Horn, not its upper reaches. Terry's orders suggested Custer should continue up the Rosebud to the upper Little Big Horn, but that now seemed unnecessary. Meeting with his officers, he told them he wanted the command to cross the Rosebud divide that night, rest the next day while scouts pinpointed the village, and attack at dawn June 26. Gibbon's men should be in position by then. By 2 a.m. June 25, a tortuous six-mile march up Davis Creek mercifully ended, and the soldiers could rest. At daybreak, Custer's scouts reported they could see the village from a small peak known as the Crow's Nest. But when Custer arrived at the summit about 9 a.m., haze blocked any view of the Indian camp just 15 miles to the west. He then received reports that suggested warrior parties in the area might have spotted his troops. His brother, Capt. Thomas W. Custer, told him troopers had exchanged fire with several Sioux when they went back along the trail to retrieve a box of hardtack that had fallen off a mule.

Custer, fearful the village knew of his presence and would flee his approaching regiment, began to make impulsive decisions. An immediate attack in daylight would be launched against a village whose actual location and size would be ascertained on the march. Through all of this, virtually nothing is known about Mark Kellogg's actions except that he took notes for his next dispatch. Soon after the command crossed the divide and reached Reno Creek, Custer made a fateful decision about how to deploy his men that afternoon. Major Reno was assigned command of one battalion of about 140 men, made up of Companies M, A and G. Captain Benteen took a second battalion of three companies, H, D and K, about 125 men. Five more companies of about 210 men would remain under

Custer's own direction, although they would operate in two wings. Companies E and F were under Capt. George Yates and C, I and L under Capt. Myles Keogh. Company B, augmented by men from the other companies and commanded by Capt. Thomas M. McDougall, would guard the slower-moving pack train to the rear.

In November 1868 at the Battle of Washita, Custer successfully stormed the Cheyenne village of Chief Black Kettle after dividing his force into four attack units. However, Custer had been unaware of warriors from other villages along the Washita River who threatened to overturn his victory on that occasion. As he moved down Reno Creek, he evidently recalled the lesson learned at the Washita. He dispatched Benteen's battalion on a scout to the left, or south, toward the upper valley of the Little Big Horn, looking for Indians who might fall on the 7th's vulnerable rear.

Reno's battalion moved along the left bank of Reno Creek toward the Little Big Horn while Custer's group remained on the right bank. Along the route of march, the last known episode of Mark Kellogg's life took place. Brisbin's earlier comments about Kellogg's decision to go with Custer instead of Terry underscore how seriously he viewed his role as the only accredited reporter with the Dakota Column. Comments many years later by white scout Frederic F. Girard further bear this out. "Soon after we had passed the divide, in the morning Mark Kellogg, reporter of the *New York Herald*, came pushing ahead to the scouts," Gerard told researcher Walter M. Camp in 1909. "He was riding a mule that was a little slow, and coming up to me, asked if I would lend him my spurs. As I was not using them, I consented and handed them over to him with the remark that he had better not put them on, as I would advise him to fall back to the command and stay with it. He replied that he was expecting interesting developments and he wished to keep up with the scouts and report everything he could see ahead."[394]

One other episode may have involved Kellogg, although, if true, it probably occurred earlier in the day. David Humphreys Miller, in his 1957 book, *Custer's Fall*, placed Kellogg aboard his mule by Custer's side, as the unit moved forward from the Crow's Nest. Miller, whose research was based on Indian accounts, indicated Indians had dubbed Kellogg as "Man-Who-Makes-the-Paper-Talk." Were those Indians the ones who had conquered Custer and his correspondent? According to Miller's account, which has Arikara scout Jerome Good Elk as its source, Custer's Indian scouts gave Kellogg that name. They were impressed by his scribblings, from which other white men were able to read words. Miller said Kellogg's I-Go-With-Custer note had been translated for the scouts by Gerard. The language shook up the Indian scouts. "The Arikaras felt it was a strange way to talk of an impending victory — even in word pictures. It added to their growing uneasiness about the coming encounter with the Sioux."[395]

If authentic, Miller's tale provides additional support to the theory that Kellogg's statement was written after June 21. Otherwise, why would the words have so worried the scouts if written at the *Far West*? However, if written June 24, the scouts' concerns would be more understandable. Unfortunately, Miller's account is inaccurate on several details about Kellogg, and the book is flawed by its almost fictional style. For example, he has Kellogg riding a mule all the way from Fort Lincoln and carrying his black satchel bag with him during these last few days.

The next reference to Kellogg is Col. John Gibbon's discovery of the reporter's decomposing body on June 29. Only so much is known about Kellogg in the intervening period as is known about the fates of Custer and the other 208 soldiers and civilians who fell with the two men. The historical record states that as the command neared the Little Big Horn River, Custer dispatched Reno's men to attack the southern end of the village, whose people scouts had indicated might be fleeing to the north. Custer issued a vague promise to Reno that "You will be supported by the whole outfit." As Reno launched his attack on the village, which still lay two miles north from the mouth of Reno Creek, the major assumed Custer's men would ride behind him. Instead, Custer, apparently distracted by warriors on the bluffs above the course of the Little Big Horn, turned to the right and headed after those Indians with his five companies. Utley speculates Custer may have hoped to repeat "the old Washita gambit of hitting from more than one direction...to strike panic in the enemy."[396] Still, Custer was acting as a blind man with little sense of the village's size or numbers. Only after he reached a high point on the bluffs, in the vicinity of today's Weir Point, could he see what a challenge lay ahead — a massive village far larger than he could have anticipated. Below him, Reno's men had dismounted to establish a skirmish line against the onrushing warriors flowing from the village toward them.

Custer realized he had to get his men into action as quickly as possible, preferably from the north of the village. He also needed his other two units, Benteen's battalion and McDougall's pack train with its reserve ammunition. Sgt. Daniel Kanipe was ordered to return to the pack train and tell McDougall to hurry forward. As he turned to ride away, he saw the command head down a long narrow coulee, probably today's Cedar Coulee, which runs below Weir Point and the extension of Sharpshooter's Ridge. Shortly, a second messenger, trumpeter Giovanni Martini, was handed a note from Custer's adjutant, Lt. W.W. Cooke, and ordered to find Benteen. The hurriedly scrawled message told Benteen, "Come on. Big Village. Be Quick. Bring Packs. W.W. Cooke. P.[S.] bring pacs [sic]." Martini watched momentarily as Custer's men rode down Medicine Tail Coulee apparently headed for a ford. Then he turned away, one of the last men in Custer's command granted a reprieve from death that day.

Custer probably did not know that Reno's men were soon routed from the village area, and the major led only about two-thirds of his panic-stricken men in a mad dash to cross the Little Big Horn River. Arriving on top of the bluffs, they soon met Benteen coming in response to Custer's final message. Eventually the pack train with the all-important reserve ammunition arrived. The Reno-Benteen contingent made up about 350 men, who soon faced a siege that would last well into June 26. Through-out it all, they had no idea about the fate of Custer, Kellogg and the other 208 men who died with them. On June 27, Terry and Gibbon arrived, long after the Indians had withdrawn from the valley of the Little Big Horn. On June 28, the command buried its dead and continued to care for its wounded.

Since his arrival other duties had preoccupied Gibbon but on June 29, he set forth to visit the Custer battlefield. As Gibbon recalled later: "As we proceeded up the valley, now an open grassy slope, we suddenly came upon a body lying in the grass. It was lying upon its back, and was in an advanced state of decomposition. It was not stripped, but had evidently been scalped and one ear cut off. The clothing was not that of a soldier, and, with the idea of identifying the remains, I caused one of the boots to be cut off and the stockings and drawers examined for a name, but none could be found. On looking at the boot, however, a curious construction was observed. The heel of the boot was reinforced by a piece of leather which in front terminated in two straps, one of which was furnished with a buckle, evidently for the purpose of tightening the instep of the boot. This led to the identification of the remains, for on being carried to camp the boot was recognized as one belonging to Mr. Kellogg, a newspaper correspondent who accompanied General Custer's column."[397]

Gibbon makes no mention of finding Kellogg's notes beside his body, which should have been a tip off to the dead man's identity. That the reporter was still clothed in his civilian dress and had suffered little mutilation by comparison to other soldier and civilian dead seems significant when trying to unravel the puzzling facts about his death and specifically where he had fallen on the battlefield. One must conclude that during the decisive phases of the battle Kellogg remained close to Custer, probably with the headquarters element of the regiment. His clothed appearance strongly suggests he was an early casualty of the battle. His body likely remained within range of the soldiers' carbines, which meant Indians had little time to mutilate him. With the battle still in progress, Indians bypassed Kellogg's body, which lay in an out-of-the-way place and was forgotten by the warriors and the women.

When one views the site of the Kellogg marker today on the east side of Custer Ridge, about 200 yards from the main battlefield monument, it is obvious it does not match Gibbon's route. That means Kellogg likely was neither killed nor buried there. If so, where did he fall? Few researchers have tackled that specific question. Vaughn's interpretation seemed suspect because he had disregarded the historical record too much in placing the reporter's death site too close to the southwest gate on the main Custer battlefield. Hixon gave the matter little attention. The most intriguing theory came from Charles Kuhlman, who in 1939 concluded Kellogg was one of seven men on top of Custer Hill, who played dead while the Indians to the west and southwest killed the men below them. When the Indians moved on to kill or plunder men elsewhere on the battlefield, these seven suddenly dashed down the hill hoping to escape to the river woods. Instead, all, including Kellogg, were killed along what is often referred to as the South Skirmish Line.[398] Kuhlman's theory is flawed in many respects. It seems incomprehensible that Kellogg, if among the last few men to be killed, would have remained clothed after the Indians killed him. Also, his body undoubtedly would have suffered greater violence than Gibbon's account revealed.

In the 1980s, researchers began looking at archeological evidence gathered during battlefield projects in 1984 and 1985 as well as long-disregarded Indian accounts and trying to relate the two. Leading this school of thought was Richard A. Fox, one of the archeologists for the first two battlefield digs. Developed over the years, his theories of the battle were published in his 1993 book, *Archaeology, History, and Custer's Last Battle*. Likewise, an article in the 1991 *Greasy Grass* magazine, "Gibbon's Route to Custer Hill," by Michael Moore and Michael Donahue, provided a framework for understanding the battle itself, and especially Kellogg's part.

According to traditional battle interpretations, the 7th Cavalry fought heroically until simply overwhelmed by the Indians' sheer numbers. Some students of the battle concluded Custer was killed during the cavalry's approach to the river crossing at Medicine Tail Coulee; if he had remained alive, the disaster never would have occurred. Others looked for scapegoats, often focusing on Reno for failing to sustain his attack against the village and fleeing to the bluffs. That freed hundreds of Indians to concentrate on the new threat posed by Custer. Benteen also has been criticized for his failure to obey Custer's recall order more promptly.

In dismissing what he labeled as the fatalistic themes of the past, Fox postulated a new approach based on the sudden disintegration of Custer's five companies as a cohesive force. Broadly, Custer sent forward his left wing, a two-company battalion under Capt. George Yates, toward the Little Big Horn River at the mouth of Medicine Tail Coulee while the right wing, a three-company battalion under Capt. Myles Keogh, remained on Luce Ridge some distance from the river. Subsequently, Yates was recalled and his men ascended a broad slope, called Deep Coulee or North Medicine Tail Coulee. At the top, at a place now designated Calhoun Hill, they rejoined the right wing, which had crossed Nye-Cartwright, or Blummer's, Ridge.

Fox believes the left wing of Companies E and F under Yates pushed ahead looking for an attack route. "The northern sojourn took the wing along the ridge — today known as Custer Ridge — between Calhoun and Custer hills, then westward into the valley, and finally to the banks of the Little Big Horn River. There, it seems, the officers found a suitable place to press an attack. Rather than attacking immediately, however, the wing returned to take up positions below and to the west of Custer Hill."[399] Custer likely accompanied the left wing. Kellogg would have, too.

Back in the Calhoun Hill area, light fighting occurred. Lt. James Calhoun's Company L held the Indians at bay, while Companies C and I remained in reserve. Indians infiltrated the coulees and ridges to the west and northwest, forcing the right wing's commander Keogh to deploy Company C against this mounting threat in an area Fox dubbed Calhoun Coulee. That proved disastrous. The Indians overwhelmed the company and sent survivors fleeing toward Calhoun Hill. Company L was unable to withstand the suddenly furious attacks by Indians from several directions. Panic spread from the Company C survivors to L's. North of Calhoun

Hill, Company I stood in reserve in a hollow between Custer Ridge and the first ridge east of it. Suddenly, panic-stricken men from the other two companies were running among them. The led horses were stampeded. Soon, the remaining men of the right wing fell under furious assaults by the Indians. Today's line of battlefield markers on the east slope of Custer Ridge provides stunning testimony to the sudden demise of Company I and members of C and L who made it that far. Fox states only about 20 of the 120 men in the three companies may have reached Custer Hill. This rout of the right wing forced the left wing of about 80 men to take up defensive positions on Custer Hill. The Indians surrounded the soldiers, who included Custer. As Fox states, "The famous 'last stand' had begun."[400]

Fox completes his development of the battle story by having Company E charge down Custer Hill to flush infiltrating Indians out of positions close to the embattled troopers. Just as with Company C's earlier charge, this one dissolved in panic. Many of the soldiers took refuge in Deep Ravine, where they were killed. The group on Custer Hill gradually dwindled, and at some point Custer was killed by bullets to the chest and left temple. Fox, who studied numerous Indian accounts, has the few men remaining on the hill flee toward their comrades, who may or may not have been alive in Deep Ravine. The battle ends at that point.

More important for consideration of Kellogg is Fox's lengthy chapter on the "Cemetery Ridge Episode." He credits the report of September 1877 by Lt. William Philo Clark as well as Cheyenne oral tradition for aiding in his theory that left wing soldiers made it into the Little Big Horn Valley at a ford north of the village. As part of his overall conclusion, Fox states, "Mark Kellogg, a civilian war correspondent with the expedition, very possibly died during the left wing trip to the river."[401]

As Fox notes, a number of men commented on the placement of Kellogg's body. For example, First Lt. Edward Mathey told researcher Walter M. Camp, "I buried Mark Kellogg's body on June 29. It was the last one buried and it lay near a ravine between Custer and the river."[402] Another officer, Second Lt. Richard E. Thompson, 6th Infantry, reported that Kellogg "lay 3/4 mile from Custer down near river on side hill about 100 yds from river."[403]

Private George W. Glenn also claimed to have seen the reporter's body when he accompanied Captain Benteen to the Custer field on June 27 and twice offered his views to Camp. In an undated letter, he wrote that the "first man were found on the ridge and on a littel nole were the Chief

Trumpeter with three airros in his head and one in his right shoulder the next were Keologg the New York Reporter a bout 50 yards of the Chief Trumpeter he only had airros in his Body[.][404] In a Jan. 22, 1914, interview with Camp, Glenn said: "When Benteen took Company H over the Custer Ridge on 27, he went up to the ridge via Crazy Horse gully. The body nearest the river was that of chief trumpeter Voss, and near to it was that of Kellogg, the newspaper reporter. Both of these bodies were within a stone's throw of the river. In Crazy Horse gully or washout there were bodies lying thick...."[405]

Glenn's account is the only one by someone who saw the field of combat that suggests how Kellogg was killed. However, Michael Moore and Michael Donahue in their 1991 *Greasy Grass* article expressed serious doubts about Glenn's tales, finding them largely inaccurate and inconsistent with other traditional accounts, notably Colonel Gibbon's and another by First Lt. James H. Bradley, 7th Infantry.[406] Bradley said: "The bodies were nearly all stripped, but it is an error to say that Kellogg, the correspondent, was the only one that had escaped this treatment. I saw several entirely clothed, half a dozen at least, who, with Kellogg, appeared to owe this immunity to the fact that they had fallen some distance from the field of battle, so that the Indians had not cared to go to them, or had overlooked them when the plundering took place."[407]

Some other accounts also differ significantly from Gibbon's. A July 8 *New York Herald* story of the battle said Kellogg was found on the skirmish line near Calhoun. The piece, written by Brisbin, was datelined "Custer's Battlefield, Little Horn, June 28, via Bismarck, D.T., July 6, 1876." Lounsberry likely sent it to the newspaper. June 28 was the day before Kellogg's body was reportedly found by Gibbon.[408]

First Sgt. John Ryan led a Company M detail that buried many of the Custer Hill dead, including brothers George and Tom Custer. He said nothing about Kellogg's burial site but offered other facts, some of which were inaccurate: "Custer's men were destitute of all clothing, with the exception of Mark Kellogg, the editor of the *Bismarck, Dakota, Tribune,* and he was not scalped. He carried a Spencer carbine with him, and rode a small mule. He wore a peculiar shaped boot, we knew him by that."[409] How and when Ryan came to see Kellogg's body are unclear, as he and his men were busy with the many dead on Custer Hill. His statement that the reporter was not scalped also runs counter to Gibbon's account.

However, Lt. Edward S. Godfrey, 7th Cavalry, seemed to agree with Ryan that the reporter may have died closer to Custer Hill: "Autie Reed

[Custer's nephew] and Bos [Boston Custer, Custer's other brother] lay 100 yards below the monument, and Kellogg lay between the monument and these two."[410] Another account similar to Ryan's and Godfrey's came from Pvt. William C. Slaper, Company M: "Boston Custer was found near the bodies of his two brothers. That of Mark Kellogg, the reporter for the *Bismarck Tribune* and *New York Herald*, who had accompanied the expedition, was close by. These bodies were on the line nearest to the river, making it appear that they were halted by an overwhelming force, which closed in on them so rapidly and in such superior numbers that they were given but little chance to put up a fight."[411]

Lounsberry wrote a long story about "The Correspondent Who Sacrificed His Life to Duty" that the *Herald* published July 10. He speculated that Kellogg, "being poorly mounted, it is possible he fell behind and did not go with Custer into the trap the Indians had prepared for him." More important, Lounsberry added, "He was shot in the side as if by an Indian in ambush, and fell about half a mile in the rear of Custer's column."[412] That reference is the only other one that indicates how Kellogg died.

According to Vaughn's article on Kellogg, he must have spent much time searching for the reporter's death site. But his views didn't consider the theory that Kellogg, fully clothed and barely touched, must have been an early casualty of the Indians' assaults and then forgotten. The key had to be Gibbon's account and matching its terrain details to today's landscape. Researchers Moore and Donahue studied Indian accounts, battlefield maps and aerial views to arrive at significant conclusions about where Gibbon crossed the Little Big Horn River and his path up to Custer Hill. In their article, "Gibbon's Route to Custer Hill," they concluded, "Located some 1,330 yards west of the Custer Hill position is a large cut in the bluffs overlooking the Little Big Horn River. Beyond this point to the west is the river bottom and the valley of the river, while to the east a small basin opens onto a grassy slope. It was undoubtedly here — within a stone's throw of the river — that Kellogg's body was found. Beyond this point, the basin breaks up into several ravines or small valleys, one of which leads up to the gently sloping ground, rising higher and higher, until it reaches the present national cemetery. The entire area is secluded and isolated from the rest of the battlefield."[412]

Today the Gibbon route, beginning at the present-day river, can be traced. The portion pertinent to Kellogg begins close to the modern course of the Little Big Horn by a shaded cut in the low bluffs. Nearby are the remnants of a gulch that Gibbon said he first checked for men of the 7th.

As one turns away from the gulch, a valley opens up into Gibbon's grassy slope. Gibbon's "valleys" clearly are what we call ravines, coulees and gullies today. Beyond the grassy slope lay the rolling landscape below and west of the ridge on which the Custer Battlefield National Cemetery rests. In their article, Donahue and Moore concluded, "Significantly [Gibbon] saw no evidence of burials in Deep Ravine, or elsewhere for that matter until he reached Custer Hill. Clearly, Gibbon crossed the river at a northern ford located near the June 29 camp, and approached the battlefield from the west, finding Kellogg's body in an isolated location near the river en route."[413]

The Kellogg site is beyond the protected area under National Park Service jurisdiction today and was not checked during the archeological surveys of 1984 and 1985. According to the article by Moore and Donahue, some artifacts, including a .50/70 cartridge case, a cavalry spur and a human leg bone have been uncovered in the area. A number of other artifacts were found inside the park fence, within 100 yards of the Kellogg area. None had any obvious tie to Kellogg. In November 1991, NPS archeologist Doug Scott and the battlefield's then-chief historian, Doug McChristian, studied the area, including using a metal detector in the depressed area just outside the park boundary fence and in the vicinity thought to fit the description of the Kellogg death site of 1876. Scott concluded, "The area has been heavily disturbed by gravel quarrying operations. It appears to have been scraped and gouged by heavy equipment. I doubt that the current topography can be correlated with the 1876 period...I cannot say this area was not the site, only that our limited reconnaissance did not yield any battle related items."[414]

Though no precise death site can be pinpointed today without artifactual evidence that links Kellogg to a specific location on the field, the studies by Fox, Moore and Donahue clearly offer the most compelling arguments for the general area. In Fox's book, an illustration shows a general representation of the wing movements and the soldiers' various positions from the Medicine Tail Coulee area to the point the left wing paused on Cemetery Ridge.[415] According to this map, the left wing, which would have included not only the headquarters staff with Custer but also the eager Kellogg, passed down the ridges and coulees to the right of today's battlefield visitors' center and cemetery. They maneuvered well down onto the valley floor north of the river and opposite a ford Fox labels as D1. The ford was pointed out to former battlefield historian Don Rickey by Cheyenne historian John Stands in Timber in 1956. The troops then headed

SANDY BARNARD

away from the river but did not retrace their own trail down from the high point of Custer Hill. Instead, they veered more south onto the rolling slopes on a path paralleling the river below the bluffs. In the vicinity of where Kellogg's body would be found, Fox labels a nearby ford as D_2. At that point the left wing soldiers turned toward Cemetery Ridge where they would pause for an estimated 20 to 30 minutes.

How did Kellogg come to be killed near the river? Indian accounts tell of firing at soldiers from the brush in the river bottoms near the fords. One can speculate that Kellogg, still mounted on his mule, was struck about this time. Perhaps he had been unable to control his mule and wandered away from the troops as they turned to go up the slope to the ridge. His fall might have gone unnoticed by the soldiers. Or, perhaps he fell too close to the heaviest Indian fire, and, wounded or dead, he could not be recovered by the retreating troops, who had no choice but to leave him. Conversely, his body may have remained under covering fire from the soldiers. One or more Indians may have risked their lives to lift his scalp and cut off his ear. Likely, they rifled his pockets, taking whatever of value he had. If he were wearing Lounsberry's bloodied Civil War belt, it, too, was seized. His notes were of no value and were tossed on the ground. His killers left his clothing and boots, suggesting again the soldiers' return fire put the warriors at risk.

At this point, according to Fox's theories, Custer's five companies may have remained intact, but disaster soon followed. As combat intensified higher on the ridges and Custer's units disintegrated, the warriors were drawn away from Kellogg. After the soldiers on the ridge were dead, the Indians neglected to return to resume their plunder of Kellogg's remains.

Today a marker to Kellogg rests on the east side of Custer Ridge. The original markers for the military victims were raised by an army detachment commanded by Capt. Owen Sweet in 1890. Maj. Samuel Burkhardt Jr., a lieutenant under Sweet in 1890, told Camp in 1913, "They found a stake marked Mark Kellogg on back side of ridge, where tombstone is now but put up no marker or tombstone at that time because none had been furnished."[416]

Mathey told Camp he had been sent to bury Kellogg on June 29 after everyone else had been buried.[417] If so, he is the only Little Big Horn participant to claim to have buried Kellogg, but he gave no indication of where he put the reporter. Inasmuch as the body was decomposing when

Gibbon ran across it, it's highly unlikely Mathey and his detail would have carted Kellogg three-quarters of a mile across rugged country on a hot June day to bury him on the far side of Custer Ridge. Surely Mathey buried the newsman where he fell near the river.

The army sent detachments to the field three times between 1877 and 1881 to police the field. In 1877, Custer and all but one of his identifiable officers were removed for burial at other locations. Custer was interred in the cemetery at West Point. The 1881 detail recovered as many remains as could be located after so much time and placed them in trenches at the base of a new stone monument erected on Custer Hill. No record indicates whether any of these details picked up Kellogg's remains or when the stake was erected for him in what is clearly the wrong location.

In a Nov. 24, 1912, letter, Sweet himself told Camp that Brisbin had "gathered up the notes and data found near and on the remains of Mark Kellogg." He added he deployed his company "in close skirmish order" and "repeatedly and daily crossed and recrossed the field in every direction as on the Reno Fields, searching every foot of ground for remains or part of remains." Camp responded on Jan. 7, 1913, by asking more questions about the Kellogg site. He also indicated he had met Mrs. Dunn two years earlier and she gave him a plug of tobacco from Kellogg's effects. Six days later, Sweet told him: "My means of [Kellogg's] identification was a board with his name on marking the spot. General Brisbin went to the spot and pointed out and explained what he remembered of the event, etc. I erected a new headstone or marker. It was different from the military markers, I remember. It was of the same style as the markers I erected for [civilians] Boston Custer and Autie Reed."[418]

How valid was Brisbin's advice to Sweet? In his 1890 newspaper report, Brisbin said, "In the evening an officer who had been over to Custer's battlefield came to me and said Kellogg, the *Herald* correspondent, was lying dead on the hillside, stripped of all his clothing except his boots and stockings."[419] That suggests Brisbin did not go to the Kellogg site while the body was still there, although he must have visited the battlefield at some point to gather information for his *Herald* account. Camp himself concluded, "The headstone for Mark Kellogg is on the wrong part of the battlefield on Custer Ridge, as attested by Colonel Mathey."[420]

No matter, the myth of Kellogg's burial site had been set. In 1896, the *New York Herald* paid for a marble marker to be installed in tribute to its dead correspondent, replacing the stick at the site.[421] In 1942, battlefield

Supt. E.S. Luce persuaded the *New York Herald-Tribune* and the *Bismarck Tribune* to share the costs of replacing the original stone. Luce told *Tribune* Editor Kenneth W. Simons, "This is the original stone and since its placement it is showing signs of wear, and, I may add, vandalism. It is badly chipped and cracked."[422] He indicated the original stood 42 inches high, 4 inches thick and 18 inches wide. The replacement stone was two inches shorter and two inches narrower. More important, the original wording was changed. It had read, "Sacred to the memory of Mark Kellogg, correspondent of the New York Herald who fell here with Gen'l. Custer June 25, 1876." The *Tribune* made sure it wasn't overlooked this time as the words "and reporter for the Bismarck Tribune" were added. In another letter to Simons, Luce reported the new stone was erected July 18, 1942, and apparently cost $46. He predicted the sandblasted letters would last 100 years.

Luce also asked about "Mark Kellogg material" the editor had told him at some point was in a storage vault at the newspaper. Simons said he would discuss the question of turning over material to Luce, but that apparently never occurred. In 1942, they may have been referring to the Kellogg diary that Mrs. Dunn's daughter had given the newspaper about two years earlier.

Luce figured in one more Kellogg tale. He told Vaughn that when he installed the replacement marker, he unearthed a "radius bone and an ulna bone, and several finger bones of the right hand" under the old marker base. He supposedly reburied them. He recalled hearing in Bismarck that Kellogg may have broken his right arm during the winter of 1875.[423] Thus, he theorized that he might have found Kellogg's remains at that site. For some reason he believed Kellogg had eaten his meals with Company F, which explained to him why the marker was placed in its incorrect location.

In May 1985, during an archeological project at the battlefield, world-famous forensic anthropologist Clyde Snow studied all the remains in hand, including those maintained in the National Park Service archives there. They included a right radius and a right ulna found in 1942 by Luce at the Kellogg marker. Apparently these had never been reburied, as Luce claimed. With this author present, Snow immediately debunked Luce's belief that the "Kellogg bones" showed any sign of fracture. Snow's findings were incorporated by archeologists Douglas Scott and Richard Fox into their book summarizing the digs of 1984 and 1985.[424] They concluded the individual stood about 5 feet, 7 inches. Based on measurement of Kellogg's clothing, that would be within the apparent range of height for the reporter. Also, according to Hopkins' genealogy of Kellogg and his family, "Colonel Lounsberry says of him: 'Mr. Kellogg was about 5 feet, 7 inches in height, weighing about 140, a bright active man'."[425] However, Scott and Fox placed the age range for the individual at between 18 and 35, much younger than Kellogg's age of 43 at the time of the battle.

The so-called Kellogg remains were included in a general reburial in the Custer Battlefield National Cemetery in June 1986. But the apparent clash between the historical record of the discovery of Kellogg's body after the battle and modern scientific study of the human bones Luce found at Kellogg's marker site remains unresolved. No matter how unlikely it may seem today, was Kellogg relocated for burial a considerable distance from where he fell? The question must remain open, at least until further archeological work can be conducted at the marker site. Scott indicated to the author in several conversations the Kellogg marker would likely undergo greater study during future archeological projects at Little Bighorn Battlefield National Monument.

Chapter 10
Aftermath of the Little Big Horn

Lounsberry clearly looms as the key figure in the maker of myths about his reporter Kellogg. To understand why, it's important to note the uneventful turns the colonel's life took in the 50 years he lived after the Little Big Horn. Excitement and success actually came early in life to Lounsberry, beginning with the Civil War. For example, early on the morning of April 2, 1865, Lounsberry, then a brevet major serving as the assistant adjutant general for the 2nd Brigade, 1st Division, 9th Army Corps, received orders from Col. Ralph Ely to form the 1st Michigan Sharpshooters and 2nd Michigan Infantry regiments "as quickly as possible, to throw out scouts and a heavy skirmish line and occupy the main rebel works" in front of the city of Petersburg, Va.[426] A Confederate deserter had revealed the enemy works were empty. Gen. Robert E. Lee, after 10 months of siege, had withdrawn the Army of Northern Virginia from Petersburg. At 3:10 a.m. Lounsberry rapidly pushed his men forward and occupied the main works. Ely reported the ground was unfavorable for such movement, "yet the flag of the 1st Michigan Sharpshooters was hoisted on the court-house at 4:28 a.m., and the flag of the 2nd Michigan on the custom-house a few moments later."

Ely cited Lounsberry's significant role in the capture of the city and his ability to seize the moment with dramatic pause: "At 4:25 a.m. Major Lounsberry was met in front of the court-house by three citizens bearing a flag of truce and a communication from the mayor and common council tendering the surrender of the town and requesting that persons and private property be respected. But the gallant old major [actually only 22 years old] could listen to no proposition until the 'old flag' was floating from the highest point of the courthouse steeple." The three men included Mayor W.W. Townes, who was assured by Lounsberry that the Michigan regiments and the Union Army of the Potomac "came in the name of liberty and in the defense of the right, and that they need have no fear, for all would be well with them so long as they remained at home and conducted themselves properly."

That had to be a heady moment for a 22-year-old man whose military career had begun not quite 48 months earlier when he enlisted as a private in Company I, 1st Michigan Volunteer Infantry. In July 1861, he was taken prisoner at the First Battle of Bull Run and was exchanged 11 months later. Rejoining the army as first sergeant of Company I, 20th Michigan Volunteer Infantry, he enjoyed considerable success, despite several serious wounds, and was discharged as a regimental commander with the brevet rank of colonel. Gen. Byron McCutcheon called him "the bravest soldier I ever knew."[427]

After the war his journalism career blossomed, leading by 1873 to his establishing the *Bismarck Tribune*. His journalistic success enabled him to forge significant political ties in Dakota Territory and nationally, and gave him hope that his ambitions for greater renown in politics might be realized. Actually, his political career may have peaked in 1876, when he was appointed postmaster in Bismarck. In 1884, he hoped for appointment as territorial governor, but the job went to a Chicago newspaperman, Gilbert A. Pierce. Lounsberry would live another 42 years, yet the best political plum he could gain was an appointment as a clerk in the General Land Office in Washington, D.C. Throughout the rest of his life the shadow of the Little Big Horn loomed ever larger. With his own ambitions never fully realized, Lounsberry was drawn to the great event in Bismarck's early history. With the passing years as a buffer against the violence that had claimed the life of his reporter Kellogg, Lounsberry grew wistful about what might have been, had he gone with Custer. It made for a good tale to share with his cronies and readers, even if more exaggeration than truth.

Lounsberry's selfishness with the story of the Little Big Horn denied Kellogg a stronger share of the glory he had earned with his blood on the battlefield. Lounsberry's pride in his secondary role was obvious almost from the moment the *Far West* steamed to the dock at Bismarck with its tragic news on the night of July 5. He was proud of his dual achievement in publishing the first full story about the battle in a special edition of his newspaper on July 6 and in burning up the telegraph lines to spread the story around the country. In 1894, he wrote, "I was the *Herald* correspondent and furnished them with the biggest scoop in the history of journalism, but suggested that they claim Kellogg as their correspondent, as he represented them through me, and they did, and paid his children $2,000.

"I was to have gone with Custer myself, but sudden illness in my family prevented. I would have been with Custer as Kellogg was but for that."[428] As noted earlier, that was just so much exaggeration.

At least in 1876, Lounsberry's newspaper acknowledged Kellogg's role and said nothing about his stand-in status for his editor. On July 12, 1876, he offered a reason why the Indians had barely touched Kellogg's body: "Perhaps as they had learned to respect the Great Chief, Custer, and for that reason did not mutilate his remains, they had in like manner learned to respect this humble shover of the lead pencil and to that fact may be attributed this result."[429] It's unlikely the Indians who killed Kellogg had any idea about the identity or the occupation of the man they shot off his mule.

In a separate article, Lounsberry offered similar sentiments: Kellogg "was energetic, intelligent, interesting, ready to endure any hardship, and that too without a murmur…. Mounted on a mule, with saddle bags loaded with pencil and paper, he looked odd, but he was the same true friend and live man that those who knew him best had ever found him to be. His body lay some distance from the main body of the troops; it was not stripped, and was not in any respect mutilated. Custer escaped mutilation because he was a great warrior, but even the Indians in their treatment of Kellogg acknowledged that in their estimation the pen was mightier than the sword. They treated Kellogg's body with greater consideration than was shown to that of Custer."[430]

Lounsberry's early praise of Kellogg appeared nationally, first in a detailed *New York Herald* story of July 10 and then elsewhere. In the *Herald*, Lounsberry wrote, "Kellogg gained a fine reputation for skill in his profession and was remarkable for courage and steadfastness." At another point, he claimed Kellogg "was one of the finest reporters in the land, and was among the first, if not the very first, sound telegraph operators in the country." Lounsberry repeated what a Terry aide had told him: "Kellogg was one among a thousand. He was ever on the alert, ever courteous, and took in the situation in a glance." Once again the colonel felt compelled to suggest the Indians knew the man on a mule, because of the *Herald's* exposes of the agency scandals. "As his wrappings indicated his profession, it is possible, and, indeed, probable, that to this fact may be attributed his escape from mutilation or other indignity."

Lounsberry concluded, "The newspaper fraternity loses one of its most worthy members, and the *Herald* one of its most valuable correspondents."[431] However, one of the *Herald's* competitors, the *New York Graphic* hooted at the notion the Indians spared Kellogg mutilation because of the *Herald's* stories. "Tally one for Buncombe!" it said.[432]

The same day the *Herald* expressed its own shared sentiments about Kellogg. "Every one among his civil and military companions liked and respected Mr. Kellogg.... There is a lesson which his death teaches. The army correspondent often holds the post of honor in journalism because he holds the post of danger. It is his duty and privilege to share the risks of battle, and for the sake of the pen to defy the dangers of the sword.... the correspondent must record the fight the moment it is fought, not wait for the slow official reports."

Yet, the newspaper editorial observed, "Glory came to Kellogg, as to all the others of that brave command, only by death.... He perished, like Custer and his brothers and all that gallant array, in the discharge of their duty, and no death could be nobler than that.... One more correspondent of the *Herald* has given his life to the dignity and honor of American Journalism."[433]

The next day the *New York Evening Post* followed with an even grander tribute to the fallen journalist: "If it is heroic to face danger and meet death calmly in the discharge of duty, then Mark Kellogg, the correspondent of the *New York Herald*, who died with Custer, was a hero. He was not a soldier, and had no soldier's laurels to win: but his duty as a correspondent was to go with Custer, and he went in pursuit of duty, not of honors. The danger was great to him as to any soldier in the column that he marched with, and he encountered it as coolly as they.... The brave civilian should not be forgotten while we honor the brave soldiers who fell in that great butchery on the banks of the Little Big Horn River. His courage and devotion reflect great honor upon civil life as theirs do upon the life of the soldier. His heroism is a credit to his profession as theirs is to theirs."[434]

On July 13, 1876, the *New York Daily Graphic*, a newspaper unique for its illustrations, published on page 86 an image of Mark Kellogg. It is similar to a Civil War era *carte de visite* photograph that has accompanied many articles about Kellogg. How the New York newspaper came up with the photograph so soon after news of his death is unknown. Inasmuch as Brick Pomeroy was publishing a newspaper, *Pomeroy's Democrat*, in the city, he may have given the photo to the *Graphic*.

SANDY BARNARD

An editor named McCreery for the *Dubuque (Iowa) Times* was a friend of Kellogg's. His remarks in tribute were picked up by a number of newspapers, including the *Council Bluffs Nonpareil*: "Mark was one of the most companionable of men, overflowing with wit, good nature and kindly feeling — a pleasant fellow in every sense of the word. We hope he has a good place where he has gone, for he was certainly deserving of it."[435]

Comments about Kellogg from the *Denver Daily Times* were picked up by Lounsberry on July 19, 1876: "Mark Kellogg was highly esteemed by all who knew him for his noble qualities of head and heart."[436] Like the Dunns, Lounsberry often maintained he knew little about Kellogg's family. Yet the article in the *Times* pointed out that his mother, Lorenda, was living with his sister, Mrs. Sydney Clinton, in Denver. "To them the news came with crushing force, particularly as it was the first information they had of his being with that command."

The July 19 story contained a series of puzzling comments by Lounsberry, who criticized larger papers, including the *Herald* for claiming Kellogg as their correspondent. He maintained he had offered Kellogg's services to other newspapers, but "neither [*Herald* and *Chicago Tribune*] had contributed one cent toward his expenses.... The entire expense of outfitting Kellogg was borne, and all arrangements for his work were made by the *Bismarck Tribune*."[437] Both, he complained, were willing to accept Kellogg's letters, "which were sent with our permission and passed through our hands to these journals."

In a later paragraph, Lounsberry asked, "Will not the wealthy journals who so gladly used Mark's work, and who are so anxious to claim him as their own, inaugurate some scheme for the relief of the two little ones left without father or mother...?" Whether the *New York Herald's* James Gordon Bennett heard Lounsberry's plea is unknown, but he contributed $500 to Kellogg's two daughters, according to a letter from Hannah Robinson, Kellogg's mother-in-law.[438] However, no evidence indicates Lounsberry himself ever contributed financially to the orphaned girls of his dead reporter. He inaccurately reported the amount sent by the *Herald* as $2,000, a figure often repeated in articles.

Given Lounsberry's references to Kellogg's family in these weeks, Dunn's inability to locate the reporter's survivors is equally baffling. Mrs. Dunn recalled her husband looked unsuccessfully for Kellogg's survivors: "His effects, satchel with all personal belonging together with his notes were sent to Mr. Dunn thinking that he would know where his people were — No trace could be found of any relatives."[439] Of significance is the letter written by Hannah Robinson to Dunn, dated March 4, 1877. She told Dunn that a Mr. Watson of La Crosse had recently met the druggist on the train. "Said you were a friend of Mark Kellogg, my son-in-law, and that you had in your possession his trunk & valise and whatever there is that he left, that you wished to send them to his little girls if you knew whose address to send them to, but I shall be very glad to have you do it, tho I don't suppose they are of much value, but they will be appreciated by the children in the future. He took to that country a file of democratic newspapers printed when Brick Pomeroy was proprietor of the paper. If you can find them anywhere, you will oblige me very much if you will send them as there is a man here that will pay the children well for them. They may be in his trunk."[440] She suggested Lounsberry might know where the trunk with the newspapers might be. Why they would have been so valuable in 1877 is unknown today.

She lamented Kellogg's passing. "Poor Mark. It is so sad to think of his senseless and terrible death among the Indians. I can hardly realize we shall never see him again. He has left two very nice little girls, aged 13 and 15. They have been with us now about 10 years and we are very much attached to them. The youngest Mattie is a fine musician, both good scholars. You have no doubt seen in the paper of Mr. Bennett's of the *Herald* donation to them of $500 which will be a great help to them in their education. We shall hope to hear from you soon."

In a postscript, she added, "Please send the trunk & things, whatever there is, to Mrs. Charles Robinson, La Crosse, Wis."

Inasmuch as Kellogg's diary and personal effects remained for many years in the Dunn family's possession, Dunn either never responded to her request or sent only some items, including possibly the trunk. Possibly Dunn was distracted about the time he received the letter. Mrs. Dunn's memoirs note that the family's original log drug store was destroyed by a fire March 17, 1877. Even so, Mrs. Dunn stated in 1938 to the WPA interviewer that she still possessed the original Kellogg diary. Perhaps she too had forgotten the Robinson letter, but her daughter still had it. About two years after her mother's death June 14, 1940, Doctor Quain donated the diary to the *Bismarck Tribune*.

However, Leonard Kellogg believed the mysterious silence of both Lounsberry and Dunn was intentional. He theorized the final pages of the diary might have contained unflattering details about the last days of the

SANDY BARNARD

campaign and Custer's actions, as the 7th Cavalry approached the Little Big Horn and its commander discounted the warnings of his scouts about the size of the Indian village he was planning to attack. Knowing the dead hero's reputation would surely suffer, both men, as war veterans themselves, might have thought it best to suppress Kellogg's potentially damaging information to prevent Custer's critics from further besmirching his memory. Thus, they decided it was best not to return the diary to the Kellogg girls in La Crosse.

Records provide little solid evidence of any such intention, just some tantalizing factual tidbits that intrigued Professor Kellogg. In 1896, Lounsberry wrote about Custer's final evening: "Custer occupied an inferior position until the night before the massacre when he was given orders to take his regiment and find but not engage the enemy. That night in joy he threw his arms around the neck of his favorite officer and said, 'Custer is himself again. Tomorrow we shall find and fight the Indians and whatever there is of glory in this campaign shall be for Custer and Custer's friends.' And so it was. He divided his friends from those who were not his warm supporters and only his friends went down to death with him."

Despite the statement's inaccuracies about when Custer received his orders, could it have some validity? The only way Lounsberry could have known about such comments would have been through Kellogg's diary or a final dispatch written en route to the Little Big Horn. As Professor Kellogg pointed out, not only were the final pages of the reporter's diary lost, but Lounsberry never printed Kellogg's final dispatch in its entirety.

Another possible hint was offered by Kellogg's former editor in La Crosse, Brick Pomeroy. Presumably in 1876 their relationship was anything but friendly because of the newspaper fiasco of 1868 in Council Bluffs. Yet, writing in his New York-based *Pomeroy's Democrat* newspaper on July 15, 1876, Pomeroy made what seems to be an outrageous claim: that Kellogg was also representing him on the Custer campaign: "Some weeks since he was engaged by us to accompany the expedition as a sub-rosa correspondent and gatherer of information for private use and for publication. Our latest advices from him was a letter anticipating disaster to the troops because of their ignorance of the method of warfare and their limited numbers."[441]

The motives of the always fiery, always political Pomeroy, who used the Custer affair for venomous attacks on Republican President Grant, are suspect. That Pomeroy would lie about his tie to Kellogg for political purposes would not be surprising. Moreover, consider the possibility if Kellogg and Pomeroy had reconciled by 1876. Kellogg, already writing for a number of newspapers, might have added Pomeroy's as one more outlet. If so, Pomeroy's comments would support Professor Kellogg's theory that Lounsberry, aided by Dunn, "covered up" what his correspondent wrote to protect Custer's reputation from further damage.

Another of Lounsberry's favorite post-Little Big Horn statements also may be weakened by closer analysis: His great battle scoop. In 1895, for example, he wrote that he was "the first to receive the news at Bismarck aside from those at the river landing, General Terry, Dr. Henry R. Porter and others first coming to his house and awakening him," after the boat's arrival at 11 p.m. July 5. But Terry remained out west on the campaign.[442]

Lounsberry next claimed he went with the military party out to Fort Lincoln to call on Mrs. Custer. As Lounsberry wrote, "When the words were uttered — 'Custer and all of his men are killed' — she screamed and fell. Words cannot picture the distress of that household, or the gloom that came upon that frontier fort." Undoubtedly, Lounsberry would have had a problem describing the situation. He wasn't at the fort. Instead, he was back in Bismarck preparing his special edition of July 6 and telegraphing the news to the *New York Herald*.

In this same 1895 article, Lounsberry, as on many other occasions, talked about how he had taken General Brisbin's notes, the notes of his reporter Mark Kellogg, and interviews with Terry, Terry's adjutant, Capt. Edward W. Smith, *Far West* Capt. Grant Marsh, scout Fred Girard, Dr. Porter and others, and prepared the huge story he sent to the *Herald*. He repeated the list of names in both his 1894 *Bismarck Tribune* article and his book, *Early History of North Dakota*, but in 1876 Terry and Girard were still in Montana at the time.[443] Both articles noted that the telegraph tolls cost $3,000. In 1894, he wrote, "I filed a copy of the new testament and directed certain chapters of that to be sent, if they run out of copy while I was preparing more, being determined to hold the wires against all other newspapers, in order that the *Herald* might have the greatest scoop on earth."

In 1911, Lounsberry was less dramatic in writing Walter Camp. Captain Smith, Doctor Porter, whom he described as "a warm personal friend," and the *Far West's* Captain, Grant Marsh, came to his office "on the arrival of the boat." The editor gathered as much information as he could to produce volumes of copy for the newspapers back east and for his own special edition on July 6. He seemed to suggest that any "interviews" with Terry had been done by others and the information was given to him. He concluded, "I do not believe that even the *Herald* ever realized the good work done by their actual correspondent, that is myself, on that occasion."[444]

John M. Carnahan, who knew Kellogg in La Crosse, and S.B. Rogers are credited as the diligent operators who kept the wire open for Lounsberry's transmission. However, shortly after Lounsberry's death in 1926, Carnahan debunked the colonel's role during that hectic 24-hour period in 1876. Writing on Oct. 17, 1926, from Missoula, Mont., to a Bismarck resident, William A. Falconer, he related the events of that night at the telegraph office.[445] The 10 x 17-foot telegraph office was 50 feet east of the railroad freight office. At 11 p.m. July 5, Smith, Porter and Marsh came to his office and awakened him. "They came in with a large suitcase filled with messages, newspaper specials and General Terry's official report." The line would be down until morning, so nothing could be done, except sort the material.

"On the morning of the 6th, I called up Fargo and told him to cut the wire through to St. Paul. He said, 'What's up?'

"I replied, 'Cut me through and listen.' He insisted and I said, "All the Custers are killed."

His letter makes it appear as if he stopped immediately for breakfast at the Capital Hotel, but 20 minutes later he was recalled to his telegraph key. "The first message I got was from James Gordon Bennett of the *New York Herald* asking for particulars. At 7 o'clock, I started in on General Terry's report."

About 10 a.m. the operators in St. Paul were being mobbed by reporters asking for more information. "Captain Smith was in the office and I asked him to make up a short Special that I might send to each paper who had special matter filed. He wrote about 250 words and I sent it with instructions to release to all at the same time."

Carnahan said he worked all day July 6 on Terry's report, then turned to private messages, which he finished about 5 a.m. the next day. After a few hours of sleep he began the special matter.

"Colonel Lounsberry had not got a word to the *Herald* up to 7 or 8 o'clock. The only thing the *Herald* had was my Special, written by Captain Smith, so you can see how absolutely absurd the Lounsberry story is." Carnahan told Falconer he worked on the material for 80 hours with only six hours sleep. Left unclear is why Carnahan waited so long to offer his spin on Lounsberry's claims for his efforts of July 6. Doctor Porter walked a middle ground between the accounts of the two men. He said Captain Smith and he hurried from the boat landing to Lounsberry's house and to Carnahan's. He credited Carnahan with spending 22 hours at his telegraph key, but was quiet about any role for Lounsberry.[446]

Lounsberry repeated his version for so long that it is welded tightly to history. In January 1934, the North Dakota Press Association selected Lounsberry for its Hall of Fame at the University of North Dakota at Grand Forks. In 1954, a plaque was installed on the spot in downtown Bismarck where Lounsberry supposedly dispatched his world-renown scoop. It was erected by Sigma Delta Chi, a professional journalism group now called the Society of Professional Journalists. At the time, his award was only the 10th to be erected. Other people who had been so honored included war correspondent Ernie Pyle, 18th century editor John Peter Zenger, famed publisher Joseph Pulitzer and Kansas grass-roots editor William Allen White.[447]

As time passed, the memory of Mark Kellogg's sacrifice at the Little Big Horn dimmed, but Mrs. Dunn, of all people, helped to keep it alive in one small way. According to her 1940 obituary, she had been involved in an effort to promote parks in Bismarck, including a park off the downtown named after Custer.[448] On May 17, 1921, 45 years after Kellogg headed off with the troops from Fort Lincoln, she arranged for a spruce tree to be planted in his honor in Custer Park.[449] On June 24, 1954, the Mineshoshe Chapter of the Daughters of the American Revolution honored Kellogg by laying a stone marker in the ground beneath the tree. The tree with its marker still stands in the park today[450]

SANDY BARNARD

Epilogue

As the *Denver Times* story of July 19, 1876, indicated, Kellogg's widely scattered family must have been stunned by Mark's death on the Little Big Horn. According to his papers at the University of Wyoming, J.W. Vaughn wrote numerous letters seeking to trace Kellogg's brothers and sisters, who by 1876 were scattered far from La Crosse. His article on Kellogg includes additional information on a number of family members. Crucial are the direct descendants of Kellogg, beginning with his two daughters. His death especially had to be a shock to the girls, Cora Sue, only 14, and Mattie Grace, 12. Their mother had been buried in Oak Grove Cemetery in La Crosse in 1867, and a new inscription was carved on the monument over her grave: "Mark H. Kellogg. Was killed with General Custer in battle with the Indians on the Little Big Horn June 25, 1876. Aged 44 years." His age was incorrect. The family's sadness deepened the next year when on Oct. 1, their grandfather, Charles R. Robinson, died.[451]

According to city directories for Bridgeport, Conn., by 1879 or 1880, Hannah Robinson had moved the two girls and herself from La Crosse to Bridgeport, Conn., to settle in with the family of William Disbrow, an insurance agent whose relationship to the Robinsons is unclear.[452] By 1885, Mattie's name began appearing, giving her occupation as an artist. Cora Sue was never listed. Hannah continued to be listed through 1891. She died March 21, 1891, at age 76 and was buried in Lot 78, Section 78, in Bridgeport's Mountain Grove Cemetery.

Now on her own, Mattie was listed in 1892 as a music teacher. On Dec. 21, 1892, Mattie, 29, married 25-year-old Dr. Franklin S. Temple, the son of Lyman Wesley Temple and Katherine Augusta Temple. According to Vaughn, he had recently graduated from the Albany Medical College of Union University in Albany, N.Y. Nine months later, Sept. 12, 1893, Mark Kellogg's grandson, Franklin Lyman Temple, was born in Boston. Vaughn states that the Temple family lived in Los Angeles and

Syracuse, N.Y. However, on June 1, 1917, Mattie Grace died at age 52 of nephritis in Lowell, Mass.[453] She was buried next to her grandmother in Bridgeport in unmarked graves. Nearby are large monuments over the graves of legendary showman P.T. Barnum and Tom Thumb.[454] Dr. Temple, according to Vaughn, lived until Dec. 7, 1956, when he died at age 90 in Derry, N.H.

In 1918, Mattie's son Frank married Elizabeth L.J. Imberger, and they had a daughter, Winifred Virginia Temple, in February 1920. Winifred, now Winifred Stewart, recalls her mother saying "Mattie was the nicest person. There was not a woman on earth better than Mattie."[455]

Frank Temple provided Vaughn with a photo of a reporter at work during the Modoc War of 1873. His mother apparently believed the person in the photo was her father, Mark Kellogg, but the historical record clearly shows Kellogg was in Minnesota and North Dakota that year. Vaughn also traced Mattie's sister, Cora Sue, who may have been in Bridgeport through the date of her sister's wedding. He found that she worked as a dental assistant from 1893 to 1900 in Denver, where she likely had extended family. At some point she left there and married Edward Allison Ulrey, a mining man from Cincinnati, Ohio. She was about 37 and he was 53 and had a daughter by a previous marriage. Cora apparently lived in Salt Lake City, Utah, from 1903 until her death Dec. 6, 1938. She apparently maintained her ties with her sister's son back east in Massachusetts. Winifred Stewart recalls that her father and Cora corresponded, but she has none of their letters. She remembers hearing that Cora ran a silver mine after her husband died in 1918. Vaughn stated that Cora lived at the Plandome Hotel in Salt Lake City for the last 20 years of her life and may have worked there as a desk clerk. According to Vaughn's sources, Cora was "close-mouthed" and said nothing about her background. Such comments helped Vaughn to conclude she inherited that tendency from her equally close-mouthed father who had failed to tell Lounsberry and Dunn about his own background.

Vaughn relied extensively on Frank Temple, who died in 1962, for much of his information. From him, he learned that Mattie also had said little about her own father. Thus, Winifred Stewart, who lives in Chico, Calif., today, and her own sons, Richard and Ronald Balch, were unaware of their connection to Mark Kellogg and the Little Big Horn. In a letter, Rick Balch wrote, "Our kinship with Mark Kellogg came as a surprise to us. I had known that my great-grandmother, Mattie Grace, was a Kellogg, but that was as much as I knew about her family."[456]

In another letter, Rick Balch outlined the family's line to the present-day.[457] In 1936, his grandmother, Elizabeth, died, and Frank Temple married Florence Kingsley in 1937. Winifred Temple married Walter George Balch in October 1942. Their older son, Richard (Rick) Stuart Balch, was born in May 1947 in Cambridge, Mass. Their younger son, Ronald Lee Balch, was born in December 1949 in Orange, Calif. Their sons live today in Chico, Calif. In July 1972, Winifred married Dr. Al David Stewart

The activities of Rick and Ron Balch are quite interesting, considering their great-grandmother Mattie Grace's own background. Rick is an artist and Ron is a musician. However, the line of descendants of Mark Kellogg hasn't stopped with them. Rick is unmarried, but brother Ron and his wife Gloria have two daughters, Jennifer Lynn Balch, born February 1981, and Stefanie Michelle Balch, born January 1983. The two girls are the great-great-great granddaughters of frontier journalist Mark H. Kellogg and his wife, Martha Robinson Kellogg.

Through the years Kellogg often had been dismissed as "mysterious" and "aloof," traits that some researchers felt might have extended through the family line. However, that is not the case with the living descendants of Kellogg. As Rick Balch wrote, "From what I have read, I would agree with you that the full story has yet to be told." His mother, his brother and he all expressed their interest and desire, as Rick said, in "bringing greater clarity and completeness to the telling of that story."

SANDY BARNARD

While on the 1876 campaign, Bismarck Tribune reporter Mark H. Kellogg wrote four columns that were published by the newspaper. They are reproduced here. His original spelling, grammar and punctuation have been retained for the most part, except where confusion might arise. Brackets have been used to indicate omissions that were the result of illegible microfilm copies.

KELLOGG COLUMN NO. 1
PUBLISHED MAY 17, 1876

TERRY'S EXPEDITION

Off for the Big Horn — Master of Troops — Strength of the Expedition — Notes, News and Jottings.

Special Correspondent of the Bismarck Tribune.

In Camp, May 14th 1876- Your correspondent joined the expedition Sunday and went into camp. At that time the order for march was given for five o'clock Monday morning; but owing to the severity of the storm of Sunday evening, the order was countermanded, and the expedition will not move until Wednesday morning. The appearance of the camp is very inspiriting [sic], and brings vividly to mind days agone, during the "late unpleasantness," when grim visaged war stalked boldly over the land. Located three miles below Fort Lincoln on a beautiful table of land, level as a floor, and on the banks of the Missouri on the east, with a range of coteaus on the west at a distance of two miles; overlooking a panoramic view that is peculiarly attractive. Officers and men are in the best of health and spirits, not withstanding the depressing effects of the weather, and eager to move. So far as I have as yet ascertained the outfitting is complete in detail as well as in the aggregate.

ROSTER
IN COMMAND

Gen. Alfred H. Terry

STAFF

Capt. E. W. Smith, Adjutant General.

Capt. O. E. Michales, Ordinance Corps.

Asst. Surgeon J. W. Williams, Medical Director.

Lt. H.J. Nolan QM.

Lt. R.A. Thompson, ACS.

Lt. Edward Maguire, Engineer Officer.

Acting assistant surgeons, Ashton, Porter and Woolsey.

7TH CAVALRY

Lt. Col. Geo. A. Custer, Commanding.

Lt. W.W. Cook[e], Adjutant.

Lt. H.J. Nowlan, Q.M.

Maj. M.A. Reno, Com'd'g Right Wing.

Capt. F.W. Benteen, Com'd'g Left Wing.

"	M.W. Keogh,	"	1st Battalion.
"	G.W. Yates,	"	2d	"
"	T.B. Weir,	"	3d	"
"	T.H. French,	"	4th	"

Capt. M. Moylan, commanding Co A; Capt. T. W. Custer, com'd'g Co C; Capt. T.M. McDougall, com'd'g Co B; 1st Lt. E.S. Godfrey, com'd'g Co K; Lt. A.E. Smith, c'm Co E; Lt. D. McIntosh, c'm Co G; Lt. E.O. Mathey, com'd'g Co M; Lt. J. Calhoun, com'd'g Co K; Lt. Gibson, com'd'g Co H; Lt. J.E. Porter, com'd'g Co I; Lt. DeRudio, Co A; Lt. B.H. Hodgson, com'd'g Co B; Lt. W.S. Edgerly, com'd'g Co D; Lt. G.D. Wallace, com'd'g Co G. Lt. C.A. Varnum; Lt. H.M. Harrington, Co G; Lt. R.R. Nave, Co K; Lt. J.G. Sturgis, attached to Co E; Lt. W.V.W. Riley, Co F.

17TH INFANTRY

Capt. L.H. Sanger Commanding Battalion.

Capt. Malcolm McArthur, com'd'g Co C; Lt. Josiah Chance, com'd'g Co G; Lts Frank Garretty and J. Nickerson Co C; Lt. H.P. Walker Co G.

6TH INFANTRY

Capt. S. Baker, com'd'g Co B; Lt. John Carland

20TH INFANTRY

Lt. Low com'd'g Detachment; Lt. F.X. McKinzie.

INDIAN SCOUTS

Lt. G.D. Wallace, com'd'g; Fred Girard, Interpreter.

BATTERY

Consisting of four one inch and two 2 and 1/2 inch Gatling Guns, Lt. Low, commanding.

THE HEADQUARTERS GUARDS.

Consist of one company of the 6th Infantry, and are commanded by Capt. S. Baker.

THE TRAIN

Chas Brown, Chief Wagonmaster, J.C. Waggoner Chief Packer, J.M. Ayers Chief Herder.

STRENGTH OF COMMAND.

1 General officer, 8 staff officers to the commanding General, 27 officers of the 7th cav., 3 officers with the Gatling Battery, 8 officers of inft, 4 Acting Asst. Surgeons. Total, 50 officers.

750 men of the 7th cavalry, 32 men with the Gatling Battery, 128 Infantry, 1 Commissary Sergeant, 2 Hospital Stewards 45 Indian Scouts. Total number of enlisted men, 968.

CIVILIAN EMPLOYEES.

1 clerk, 3 guides, 2 interpreters, 1 master mechanic, 2 blacksmiths, 2 wheel wright, 1 chief packer, 9 assistant packer, 1 master of transportation, 5 assistant wagon masters, 162 civilian teamsters. Total, 190. Grand total 1,207.

ANIMALS

752 mules, 33 Q M horses, 695 Govt. horses, 26 battery horses, 95 pack horses, 74 hired horses. Total, 1,674.

All of the 7th Cavalry are connected with the expedition, including the three companies lately arrived from the south.

Gen. Terry proposes to carry an ample supply of provisions with the marching column to provide against the possible failure of the supply boats to reach Glendive Creek, the position for the proposed depot of supplies on the Yellowstone. All available means of transportation is required for transporting, and its organization has required much attention of the officers.

Gen. Terry [   ] that the

LINE OF MARCH

will follow Gen. Stanley's trail of 1873. The hostile Indians are in camp on the Little Missouri; Big Horn and Powder rivers. The expedition will make a stand at the [   ] crossing on the Gen. Stanley Trail. Gen. Gibbons' command are marching east from Ft. Ellis with two hundred cavalry. Gen. Terry sent orders Sunday via Ft. Ellis, to Gen. Gibbons to move down the Yellowstone to Stanley's stockade, above Glendive Creek — If possible to cross over to attack the Indians at the mouth of the Powder river.

PERSONAL

Gen. Alfred H. Terry is arranging for the campaign with all of his well known executive ability brought into play. His courteous manner and kindly tones win fast the affections of the men in his command. Nothing seems to escape his notice, not even the smallest detail, and I am safe in stating that no expedition of the Government has ever excelled in preparation, and careful detail, the one now about the move.

Gen. Geo. A. Custer, dressed in a dashing suit of buckskin, is prominent everywhere. Here, there, flitting to and fro, in his quick eager way, taking in everything connected with his command, as well as generally, with the keen, incisive manner for which he is so well known. The General is full of perfect readiness for a fray with the hostile red devils, and woe to the body of scalplifters that comes within reach of himself and brave companions in arms.

Fearing to intrude too much upon your space at the time, I will omit further personal mention in this; but shall have occasion from time to time to make mention of the many gentlemanly officers and others connected with the expedition, as we move along.

JOTTINGS

I have visited every department and every position of the camp, and find everywhere perfect preparation, order and system. Everything is moving along like clockwork. The citizen teamsters, and other citizens connected, have "accepted the situation," are ready and anxious to move.

This morning some ambulance mules were missing. The scouts took the trail, and, after an hour or so, came upon them, securely fastened to trees in the dense forests about two miles south east of the camp, and brought them in. The thieves supposed the expedition would move daybreak this morning; that there would not be time to hunt for lost stock, and after the soldiers were away they could take their mules in any direction they chose. It was a cunning scheme, but fell through.

We will break camp at three a.m. Wednesday, and move at 5 a.m., weather permitting; and now that all is ready everyone is anxious to start to be rid of the ennui of camp life.

And now, at this writing, two p.m., May 15th, the elements promise pouring rains, which may defer the proposed moving on the morning of the 17th. This day's delay has allowed time for a fuller preparation, if that was necessary or possible; and if anything is left undone it will be something beyond the comprehension of men whose experience and judgment have prepared in general and detail so completely that nothing seems remaining undone. During a short

INTERVIEW

held with Gen. Terry, to-day, he informed me that there was to be no child's play as regards the Indians. They must be taught that the Government was not to be trifled with, and such measures would be taken as would learn the Indians to feel and recognize that there existed in the land an arm and power which they must obey.

FRONTIER.

(The expedition moved this morning at 5 a.m the band playing Garry Owen and the Girl I Left Behind Me as they disappeared in the distance.— Ed.)

KELLOGG COLUMN NO. 2,
PUBLISHED MAY 24, 1876

BIG HORN EXPEDITION.

Tents Struck — Order of March — Custer is the Front — Terry's Characteristics and Expectations — Camp on the Heart — Paying off, &C.

Special Correspondence Bismarck Tribune,

Camp of Terry's Expedition, Heart River, May 17, 1876, — At 3 a. m. this morning

REVILES [SIC]

sounded shrill and sharp through Gen. Terry's camp two miles south of Fort A. Lincoln and an hour later tents were struck, and at five a.m. the column formed preliminary to the march. Taking up the line of march the column moved Northwards through the late camp, and out over the coteaus. Two miles west of Fort A. Lincoln a halt was made a line in the following

MARCHING ORDER

was made: [sic]

Gen. Custer, with two companies of cavalry and forty scouts, filed in ahead, Charley Reynolds, chief scout, and F. F. Girard, Interpreter, accompanying. Gen. A.H. Terry and staff and the 7th cavalry band followed and in the order named the remainder of the expedition: Seventh Cavalry, Artillery, Ambulances, Forage Wagons, with Infantry interspersed here and there, and in the rear and on the flanks of the column a detachment of cavalry was deployed as skirmishers, the cavalry and infantry marching in two columns. This was the order of march for the day, and will continue to be the order until circumstances demand a change.

It was a cheering and

BRILLIANT SIGHT

I witnessed from the highest peaked coteau west of Fort Lincoln, within a few miles where your reporter took a stand. Foggy and damp though the morning, yet the inspiriting [sic] strains of martial music floated through the air.

The roads being heavy, and the wheeling difficult, the column moved slow and halted frequently, yet at 3 p. m. the main column reached the camp ground we now occupy which Gen. Custer, who had arrived three hours ahead of us, had chosen. It is a delightful spot for a camp situated on the borders of the limpid waters of the Big Heart. The ground selected, a basin of 1,000 or 1,200 acres, is as level as a barn floor with coteaus surrounding it on all sides. Clear and sweet water is abundant and grass and timber plenty. The scouts were stationed on the highest peaks for observation, and the fighting material of the column placed in position to be ready at any moment to ward off or attack an enemy. The

INCIDENT

of to-day, with me, has been the antics of Waggoner's pack mules. Some of them are fresh in the work, and, mule like, after becoming wearied with their load, commenced bucking and kicking to rid themselves of it. It would make a stoic show his molars to see "them devilish critters" cut up. However, Waggoner and his assistants brought them to time and into camp in good order.

A wagon tongue or two was broken but they were quickly replaced, but no accidents worthy of notice has occurred thus far. The

PAYMASTER

is paying off the troops, this p.m., and the "boys" will have a "stake" in their pockets for a much longer period than they usually keep one there, and yet they are not happy, but think constantly of the girl left behind or other pleasures.

It is understood that the column will take up its line of march early in the morning, and move towards where dwells the hostile red man.

GENERAL A.H. TERRY

is in excellent health and spirits, and hopes the Indians will gain sufficient courage to make a stand at or before we reach the Yellowstone River. His equable temper and genial manner show that the responsibilities resting on him, although weighty, wear him not at all.

All of our military acquaintance start out fresh, hopeful and chuck full of energy for a melee with the "noble red man" (?) [Kellogg's punctuation]. There has been great cheerfulness exhibited by the rank and file during all of the preparation for this expedition, and now that camp with its ennui is left behind, everybody is supremely happy. At least so appears the social atmosphere.

As usual on occasions of this kind

GEN. CUSTER

is full of life and spirit, the same true soldier, exhibiting the dashing bravery of a man who knows no fear, true to the life in him. His energy is unbounded. Fatigue leaves no traces on him, and whatever care possesses him is bidden within his inner self. His men respect him, and will dare to do brave things under his leadership.

The weather is delightful, the scenery and surroundings ditto, so your correspondent is just at this time fully contested with his lot, although it be for the [   ] in the "tented field."

I dare not intrude on your space to the extent I would wish, and conclude by thanking all of the officers of the expedition, I have come in contact with, for the uniform kindness. While the omission of names at

MARK KELLOGG   171

this time is necessary yet I am none the less grateful to them all.

FRONTIER.

(The expedition camped Saturday evening on the big Muddy, fifty miles from Bismarck, having marched 13 miles the first day; ten and five-eighths the second day; 14 miles on the 3d; and nine and one-third miles on Saturday. Indians for the first time were seen on Saturday evening, being a few evidently hostile just at sunset on the bluffs in front of the camp. A severe hail storm passed over the column on Thursday and another on Friday making everybody uncomfortable; on Thursday one of the artillery teams ran away but were sufficiently amused after hauling a Gatling gun about two miles on a dead run. Gen. Custer led the advance alone with two companies of cavalry until Saturday when Gen. Terry joined him. Revilee [sic] uniformly sounds at 3 a.m., the command marching at 5, camping usually about 3 p.m., marching as will be seen from 10 to 15 miles per day. A base of supplies has already been established on the Yellowstone where the command will, probably be heard from via one of the boats operating on the Yellowstone. Gen. Terry was informed by carrier of the trouble on the Fort Pierre route to the Black Hills, and will, no doubt take proper action to protect the whites.—Ed. Tribune.)

KELLOGG COLUMN NO. 3

PUBLISHED JUNE 14, 1876

BIG HORN EXPEDITION

A readable letter from the Bismarck Tribune's Special Correspondent—Progress of the Expedition—Notes, Reflections and Incidents.

Special Correspondence Bismarck TRIBUNE

In the field, near Rosebud Buttes, D.T., May 29, 1876 — I wrote you from the Big Muddy in the 20th ult. We have been marching steadily since slowly making our way to the

HOME OF THE HOSTILES.

We're now within three days march of the Yellowstone, about 160 miles from Bismarck. The

BAD LANDS

of the Little Missouri have been passed and the grazing lands beyond reached.

SANDY BARNARD

NO INDIANS

have been seen since my last report though Gen. Custer and a few scouts when out hunting one morning came suddenly upon a blazing campfire which had been abandoned but a few minutes before. The General does not get frightened but in this case he deemed discretion the better part of valor and got not "near the hearts of the people" as the politician would say, but near to the sabers of the gallant 7th. Aside from this no fresh traces of them have been seen, and no trouble is anticipated with them until the buffalo range, west of the Yellowstone, is reached. Opinions as to whether we will meet them in force are varied.

GEN. TERRY

keeps a close tongue and his opinions seldom become public property. He holds his command in hand, however, as if he expected attack, and is ever prepared for it. Gen. Terry, through his watchfulness and care of his officers and men, through his kind words and acts has become endeared to all in the command, and the men will stand by him to a man as they ever have by the more

DASHING CUSTER

who, as the men say, may be seen

HELL WHOOPING

over the prairie at almost any time of the day. Free from the responsibility of command, all of his energies may be employed in the work assigned him, ever in the saddle, only when eating, sleeping or writing, he is generally on the flank, or far in advance of the column with a few trusty scouts, making observations of the country, on the alert for signs of Indians, with which he is as familiar as a white man can be, and occasionally hunting for pastime. Gen. Terry always leads the advance of the column; Custer is with him when not on the "scoot" as the boys have come to call it.

So far no

ACCIDENTS

to speak of have occurred. Two mules have been killed by order being no further use to the command. A private in company I, 7th cavalry was

BITTEN BY A RATTLESNAKE

but immediate remedies were applied and the man is getting on nicely. Aside from the usual surgical operations, cutting, and sucking the wound, &c. Doctors Williams and Porter administered

TWENTY SIX OUNCES OF WHISKEY.

MARK KELLOGG

Twenty-four had been guzzled without effect on the man or the poison which the whiskey was intended to counteract. But the last two ounces weakened both. The man lay in a drunken stupor for several hours but the snake poison was killed and, as stated, the man is slowly recovering. During the time the remedy was being administered many amusing remarks were passed among the lookers on. Some of them would like a bite themselves; others wished for a preventative which all expressed admiration for the

CURATIVE POWERS

of whiskey straight.

At this writing only three men are in the ambulance; one from an accidental shot to the heel. The officers are

ALL WELL.

Game was found in abundance until the Little Missouri was reached. On the 21st the Indian scouts brought in seven antelope besides many others which were killed by hunting parties. One day

CHAS REYNOLDS,

chief scout of the expedition killed three and fourteen in all were brought in. A few elk have been seen and Gen. Custer killed one lynx. Antelope were in sight most of the time until the Little Missouri was reached.

The country for the first few days of our march resembles very much that about Fort Lincoln, with which your readers are generally familiar. Hills, valleys, and streams, a good soil with a liberal amount of wood and water, generally suited for farming purposes [sic], are the principle characteristics. The grazing is first class and the country is a most excellent one for stock growing. This is shown by the abundance of game which now abounds and the traces of columns of buffalo which in former times roamed over these prairies. The bee, the buffalo and the Indian are ever crowded ahead as civilization advances and, with the expedition for the survey of the North Pacific near the line of which our course has run, the buffalo have gone. The Indian must soon follow. The chiefs want the country and the Great Spirit has decreed that the red man must pass on. The Indians have a secret of

GEOGRAPHY

of their own which is familiar to the leading ones. All of the

ANCIENT LANDMARKS,

or rather those which have become distinguished are carefully noted and ever after remembered. The names are generally exceedingly appro-

SANDY BARNARD

priate. For instance in this region we have Rattlesnake Den, Wolf Den, Maiden's Breasts, Rosebud Buttes, Young Man's Buttes and

LOST WATER BUTTE.

From the side of the latter bursts a stream of water of probably sixty inches which after running on the surface for about one hundred yards, disappears in the earth. Hence its name.

Near this Butte, some years ago, a small body of Arickarees had a fight with a considerable number of Sioux. Three of the former and five of the latter were killed. The balance of the Rees escaped during the night. It does the soul of

BLOODY KNIFE,

one of the scouts of the expedition, good, to tell of the bloody battles which have been fought on the ground west and south of Berthold. The Rees some years ago were the proudest and bravest so they were the strongest in numbers of any of the Indian tribes. They claimed to be the first people. The Grosventres (or Big Bellies) were a race which followed them, and the Mandans were so limited in numbers that they only occupied the bluffs; but these

PRIMITIVE CAMPS

filled and occupied the land. All was well with them until the white man crowded the Sioux on them from far off Minnesota, and introduced among them small-pox and other terrible diseases, which have reduced them in numbers until a few families only are left of this once mighty people. Ever friendly to the whites they have been ever on the

WAR PATH

with the Sioux until the treaty of 1875, made with the Sioux of Fort Lincoln, when they agreed to bury the hatchet and smoke the

PIPE OF PEACE.

The Indian, however, is not noted for his steadfastness or his strict adherence to treaty obligations, hence a few Sioux scalps have dangled from the belt of the Ree warrior, even since this famous treaty.

The Indian scouts have great respect for the

LONG HAIRED CHIEF,

as they call Gen. Custer, though he long since abandoned those golden ringlets, and now wears a

FIGHTING CUT,

as all good soldiers should, and he has no difficulty obtaining information from them. They admire his dashing ways and respect him as a man and respect his position, hence any information they are able to impart is carried directly to him. Indeed the General is so familiar with [   ] that he can talk with them by signs almost as readily and understandingly as the interpreter, while he has picked up quite a smattering of Indian. Near Young Mens Butte

A LONELY GRAVE

was found with the head-board bearing the name, rank, &c., " Sergt. Stempker, Co. L., 7th Cavalry, Aug. 26, 1873." So, you will observe, the gallant 7th has been this way before. This brave fellow died here surrounded only by his brave comrades, hundreds, perhaps thousands of miles from mother or sister, or the home of his childhood. Life is beset with hidden footfalls. When we least expect it death approaches. The sensitive mind always becomes sad when in the presence of death but to meet with the dead on the western plains has a peculiar effect. The churchyard where sleep our friends and relatives may be passed without serious thought. But here death with his grim visage stares at us from unexpected places forcing an entire change in the channel of our thoughts. Shall we leave beneath the sod of the almost limitless prairies the forms of any of those now with us, who are so full of life and hope? We shall see.

I said we met fresh traces of Indians once only. Once we saw two

EVIDENTLY HOSTILE

Indians gazing from the distance at the expedition. Evidently they are seeking information. They disappeared and were seen no more. The

INDIAN RUNNER

is an institution of the plains. The manner in which they get over the ground is simply wonderful. These Indians were probably sent by the hostile chief to learn as to the progress the expedition was making, and to gain information as to its character. Satisfying themselves they will return at the rate of one hundred miles per day, without food or water, or sleep, and without excessive fatigue, Indian and pony will fly over the prairies like the wind, with occasional rests of a few minutes to give the pony a chance to graze while the rider nods, the runners will rush along for three days, making as many hundred miles. To us the Indians are constantly informed of the

MOVEMENT OF THE TROOPS,

so if they purpose giving battle they will certainly be prepared to do it.
As we move westward the

GRAZING IMPROVES

and here in the Little Missouri valley the season is at least a month in
advance of the season on the Missouri. This would be a splendid grazing
region were the water good. The grass is heavy and nutritious, but the
water is too strongly impregnated with alkali.

MILLIONS OF LOCUSTS

are just now making their appearance in this region. Too young to fly
or do much harm, in few days, should the winds favor them, they may
sweep down upon the defenseless agriculturists on the border doing untold damage. Fortunately the season is, and has been, a wet one, and the
growth of the pests has been held in check while the rank growth of vegetation has satisfied them on the ground where they were produced.

On the 26th scouts reached us from Fort Lincoln bring late papers
announcing

CABINET CHANGES.

Comment is unnecessary. No one expected Don Cameron to be Secretary of War and of course all were surprised. The appointment, however, it
was conceded might prove a good one. The

PROMISCUOUS FIRING

at game has long since stopped and occasionally the boys fret at not
being permitted to take advantage of some splendid shot. Discipline, however, is necessary, and none realize this more fully than the privates in the
command. The dreaded bad land or

MAUVAIS DE TERRE

were struck on the 27th. We camped that night at their entrance on the
head of Davis Creek. Grass high and luxuriant, wood in abundance, water
very slightly alkaline. Our camp for the night was a peculiar as well as a
picturesque one; occupying the head of the narrow valley from east to
west, and occupying a length of half a mile; surrounded by every conceivable shaped buttes. With pickets stationed on the towering peaks, the Indian scouts, standing out in bold relief against the sky, straight and un-
movable as statues of stone, to our vision; the long rows of tents, and
white wagons creating a scene so vividly beautiful as to impress the beholder during life. The column has hardened to the work, and endures the
working finely. Little or no illness, the men were in good spirits and the

animals in good heart. Sweet strains of music broke out on the still air from the 7th Cavalry Band which morn and eve affords us a rich treat. Before us lay the wonderful Bad Lands of Dakota, which Sully said looked like hell with the fires out. Here they are not wide in extent — about five miles — but they grow in width until near the mouth of the stream they average many miles — at Buford fifty miles.

It is a

COMMON ERROR

to presume that all of Dakota is one vast plain — or field of bad lands, when, in fact, there is not a foot of bad lands east of the Missouri in that Territory and none west, except along the valleys of certain streams. They produce no vegetation and are as well defined in the beginning and ending as a plowed "land" on the prairie. I mounted one of the highest cone shaped Buttes and from its peak looked over a sea, as it were, of ridges of broken-topped, square topped, cone-topped buttes, the cone-shape predominating, the majority of which are reddened to a bright red brick color, from the action of great heat at some time in the unwritten, and probably unknown period of the past. The whole rock formation is moltened and fused as if it had been in the intense heat of a furnace for years.

Our march on the 29th was up through the valley of Davis Creek crossing it six times, each crossing requiring a bridge. Our camp that evening was a very attractive one; situated on a level basin on which is growing the gramma grasses in profusion. On the west the waters of the Little Missouri are flowing swiftly along, and on its banks stands a growth of large timber, mostly cottonwood. Underneath is a heavy under growth; principally of bullberry, plum, wild cherry, currants, &c, all of which are all in full bloom, making the air redolent with fragrance. The water of the Little Missouri is unexpectedly low and clear.

It was with feelings of regret that I left the valley of Davis Creek and the Bad Lands behind, and I discovered that many are of the same mind. The beautiful scenery, grim, rough, and broken though it is, has more attractions, creates fewer emotions, entrances the senses, awe inspires, and bewilders the beholder who observes to the full more than pen can picture or artist can paint. This natural highway created by the Great Architect is one of those delightful spots which are found here and there all over the great West. The only lack for the most perfect stock raising pastures is that of water, which at the western end of the valley, it is strongly impregnated with alkali, as to be entirely unfit for use. The grasses are extremely insuriant

SANDY BARNARD

to growth, and the valley is locked in by ranges of buttes that secures perfect security from the bitter winter winds of the raw plains of either side.

The citizens of Bismarck with the expedition are in robust health. Their stock keep up well and appear to be improving. No accident of any note has occurred to any of their outfits and their loads are becoming lighter daily.

Gen. Custer, with a battalion of cavalry (and 12 scouts with Lieut. Varnum at their head) was ordered to scout up the Little Missouri River, this morning, and accordingly Gen. Custer, with his outfit left camp at 5 a. m. to-day, and returned a few minutes ago. He reports having ridden 45 miles to-day, crossing the Little Missouri 34 times, passed Rosebud Butte at a distance of three miles from camp. The valley of the river averages a mile in width, level, and plenty of grass. Saw no signs of Indians, other than those of camps, of a year ago. Saw no game, and there is no subsistence for Indians. Gen. Custer states himself and party had a pleasant ride, moving along rapidly, and halting only sufficient long enough to breath their horses. Each company carried their own rations and Waggoner, with five mules packed accompanied the reconnaissance.

We will move over the Little Missouri to-morrow and camp near the stream on the opposite side. The camp to-day has been quiet. Firing for promiscuous purposes is forbidden, and fishing has been the chief amusement of the day. As I write a big thunder shower is approaching from the west which looks ugly.

FRONTIER

KELLOGG COLUMN NO. 4
PUBLISHED JUNE 21, 1876

BIG HORN EXPEDITION

Arrival at Mouth of Powder River — Junction with Gen. Gibbon's Command- Localities of Indians — Probabilities of the War, Disposition of Troops, &c. — Death of Sergeant Fox — The Bad Lands — Incident, Personals, &c., &c.

Special Correspondence Bismarck Tribune

MARK KELLOGG   179

CAMP OF TERRY'S EXPEDITION, NEAR MOUTH OF POWDER RIVER, JUNE 12, 1876. — Since I last wrote you two weeks have passed. How they have been spent I will presently show. We reached

POWDER RIVER

June 6th. Gen. Terry took the Far West and proceeded up the Yellowstone 35 miles met Gen. Gibbon's command. The cavalry of this command were ordered back to the mouth of the Rosebud near which several hundred lodges of Indians were reported. The programme for the future is given below.

GEN. GIBBON

has had no general engagement with the Indians but the Indians were uncomfortable near for some time and three men were killed in sight of camp. They were short of supplies for some days but were relieved from Fort Ellis.

THE TROOPS

are so thoroughly organized that if the Indians can be found they will be taught a lesson that will be a lasting one to them. It is believed they

INTEND TO FIGHT

but they are no match for the force sent against them. But I can best give the record of our march in the shape of

NOTES FROM MY DIARY,

which will be found below:

June 10. — Gen. Terry, with two companies of cavalry returned from a trip to the mouth of the Powder River at 10 p.m. last night in a pelting rain. The trip was very unpleasant.

Gen. Terry, who went up on the Far West, found Gen. Gibbon and his troops 35 miles up the Yellowstone river from the mouth of the Powder river in camp, not being able to cross on account of high water. The Yellowstone is booming high and has a current of 8 miles per hour. The steamer was 8 1/2 hours making the trip up and an hour and fifty minutes running down. The Powder river is rising rapidly, and a route down its valley is impracticable for the wagon train, and the cavalry are out seeking a route over the table land.

The programme fixed upon today is first. Taking the supposition that if the Indians have moved southward, that Gen. Crook will meet and look after them. Gen. Gibbon's four companies of cavalry were ordered to, and will arrive at the mouth of the Rosebud tonight to prevent the crossing of

SANDY BARNARD

Indians at that point if any should attempt it. Major Reno, with a battalion of cavalry, and 12 days rations, and one Gatling gun is ordered to march up the Powder river to its forks, then to push across the country to the head waters of the Mispah river, down the stream to its mouth, then on across to a fork of the Tongue river, down its course to the main stream of that river, where he will meet Gen. Terry and balance of the command, who will move down the Powder river to its mouth and be conveyed from there by steamer to and up the Tongue river until Maj. Reno is met when Gen. Custer will outfit nine cavalry companies and with pack mules for transportation, will rampage all over the country, taking in the Rosebud and the Big Horn rivers, valleys and ranges. Gen. Custer declined to take command of the scout of which Maj. Reno is now at the head of, not believing that any Indians would be met with in that direction. His opinion is that they are in bulk in the vicinity of the Rosebud range.

By Odometer measurement the column has marched a distance from Fort. A. Lincoln to where in struck the Powder river, of 293 1/2 miles.

June 11. — Camp broke up at an early hour this morning and marched until 6 p. m. over a rough route, a portion of the way, on the

YELLOWSTONE

river banks a short distance below the mouth of the Powder river, and opposite the mouth of Custer Creek. To day Charley Reynolds and your corespondent have been ranging among the butte formation, hunting some, and secured large deer; game very scarce. There is not much difficulty in moving around in the

BAD LAND

country if mounted on an active mule, the deep canons can all be headed off and the coteau ranges, and many of the buttes can be moved on and down the sides of; but in many instances it is well enough to dismount in descents. It would be impossible to move wagons over or across such a formation.

The present camp will be used as the expedition

SUPPLY DEPOT

for a while at least. I found on arrival here Col. Moore, the commander at Ft. Buford, with 8 companies of infantry in camp. The Colonel will remain in command of the depot when the commander of the expedition moves on which will make it exceedingly agreeable for those who remain behind, for Col. Moore is a very frank, kind, manly gentleman, whom everybody likes that comes in contact with him.

The valley of the Yellowstone here is about three miles wide, but little timber growing on its banks. The valley is lined in either side by ranges of ugly looking bottom of the bad land formation. Capt. J.W. Smith has made a townsite claim here, has two large tents erected, and therein stored eight or ten thousand dollars worth of goods, which the soldiery are eagerly purchasing. It is an amusing scene to see the bardy fellows in great crowds struggling for a place at the improvised counter, behind which are several employees dealing out with rapidity the many wares called for by the impatient purchasers. We have had very heavy rains of late which has made marching troublesome, and caused delays; but to-morrow the steamer will leave us and then we cut loose entirely from civilization and make war to create peace. It will be some time before I will have an opportunity to reach the TRIBUNE again; but in the meantime I will keep a faithful record of events and occurrences.

June 12. — An unexpected experience greeted me to day on the shape of a steamboat trip down the Yellowstone river. The steamer went down to bring up the remainder of the supplies at the stockade on the mouth of Glendive Creek. Capt. Marsh extended me a courteous invitation to "go along" and I accepted cheerfully. The run, eighty-six miles in distance, was made in exactly three hours, an average of over 28 miles per hour. That's no "fish story." Colonel, but a fact, and I think this proves the Far West a clipper to "go along." This steamer has been very busy since she came into the Yellowstone river, having made a full trip from its mouth to Tongue river, a distance of 400 miles, thence down to Glendive Creek, 116 miles, a run back to mouth of Powder river, 86 miles, and today from the latter stream to Glendive again, and will return to depot to morrow. The navigation of the Yellowstone is vastly superior to that of the Missouri river; its banks do not wash at all, and are gravel as well as its bed. Thus no bars are formed, and no change of channel occurs. Capt. Marsh states that navigation is excellent at a much lower stage than at present as far up as "Pompey's Pillar," which is a distance of 460 miles from the junction with the Missouri, and 60 miles above the mouth of the Big Horn. The valley of the Yellowstone is of level and slightly rolling prairie formation with but little timber, for a distance of about a hundred miles above Glendive creek, below which point, and above the distance named, there is an abundance of timber, chiefly Cottonwood. The grasses are of luxuriant growth and quality. At an occasional point along the stream the bad land formation juts down to the banks, and once in a while the formation

SANDY BARNARD

reaches some miles as a bank of the river both on the Montana as well as the Dakota sides. Were it not for the existence of a few cains of rapids that occur, and which a small outlay of money would soon remedy, that is no doubt a steamer the size of the Far West could navigate without hindrances at any stage of water usual to the stream [   ] we ran swiftly down, [   ] ducks on the shore, and [   ] other small game [   ] Strates of lignite [   ] in thin veins and of [   ]. The climate seems very [   ] of Bismarck, somewhat [   ] believe. Vegetation is of [   ] growth here that there [   ] in the future, life may be [   ] this valley will be people. Unique people who will [   ] if nothing more. I am placed under obligations for favors kindly granted by Capt. Grant Marsh and   [   ] Burleigh, clerk of steamer.

The early morning of May 31st, is a dark gloomy, misty, threatening one, yet the march was resumed at the hour of 8 a.m. at which time the clouds lifted and the weather became more pleasant. The scouting of the Little Missouri River, 106 miles west of Fort Lincoln, on our [   ] beyond the [   ] heavy, and the trail passed over a very broken country; up, up, and down, down, circuitously and zig zaggy through all the day, and until we reached camp at 5 p.m., having marched thirteen miles, and going down Whistler's trail into a pretty valley, affording all the conveniences for a good camp.

In the early part of to-day Charlie Reynolds, and your correspondent, took a quiet scout all by ourselves, some few miles from the left flankers we struggled up the precipitous sides of a very prominent point which, from its appearances, we named the

RATTLESNAKE BUTTE.

Leading our animals along gently after having arrived at its top we looked around and viewed one of the handsomest panoramic views it has been my lot to witness. In all directions, as far as the vision could reach, was to be seen the irregular butte formation of inconceivable as well as conceivable shapes; their clay colored and deep brick red tops, clothed on their sides a portion of the way from their base to the apex created a contrast that was at best fascinating and bewildering, About eight or ten miles in the northeasterly direction, clearly defined was the far reaching apex of Rose Bud Butte, more to the left came strongly in view the Sentinel Buttes, and here and there glimpses of portions of the beautiful little valley of the Little Missouri River, with its bordered banks of bright hued grass green, and heavy timbered darker green colors, flashing in sunlight like some Eden spot. After gazing awhile with a long drawn breath we turned our attention to something more material, and were shortly rewarded by a discovery of four Rocky Mountain sheep, commonly called by mountaineers,

BIG HORNS

which were quietly grazing on the sweet gramma grass of the hillside, unaware of the fate in store for them. Quick as thought, bang, bang, and two of them were stricken down by leaden messengers from our trusty rifles; two sprang away; but only a moment eroded after the first firing before the sharp report from Reynold's rifle sounded out clear and bugle like on the air, and a third fell a victim to the unerring aim of our trusty guide. It was but a short time until we had our animals packed with this choice mountain delicacy, when we wended our way toward the column which had, in the meantime, gone into camp four miles away from us. How we successfully reached the base of that butte with our animals, is yet a mystery to me, so steep, and so crooked and rough was the pathway. After a single misstep by our horses our mangled remains might have been found in the deep valley below, hundreds of feet.

Today the country was so rough in formation that the mounted commanders of the Infantry were forced to walk as they flanked along in the march. While trudging along up and down, and over the ugly formations, Major John Carland discovered an indenture in a butte well shaped, and about six feet deep. At its bottom he found a deposit of clear crystal like ice, of which he received a supply for himself and friends who enjoyed at least one drink of ice water in the Bad Lands. The Major says there was never anything so delicious; the day was hot and the "tramp, tramp" tedious and tiresome, and this unexpected relief was like nectar on parched lips, burning throats, and feverish stomachs.

June 1st. — Rousing from sleep at 4 a.m. thrown open the front of the tent, and lo! and behold! the ground was all

COVERED WITH SNOW,

and cold, cutting blasts of northwest wind shivered my physical frame, and sent my mental caliber down to many degrees below zero. Two or three inches of snow lying on the ground, and the great flakes falling like fury. The blankets looked tempting, and experience taught that there would be no "onward march" that day, so into the arms of morpheus I [   ] plunged, and there stayed until hunger drove me out. All day long the whited flakes came pelting down, all the night following [   ] but

184   SANDY BARNARD

little cessation, and through the day of June 2d this winter reminder kept up its tone. No movement of the column. The camp was in perfect quiet, uninterrupted except by a trumpet call or the braying or whimpering of the four footed animals picketed on the plain, and unprotected from severe punishment caused by this unexpected gift from Sir John [   ] place. The storm while [   ] caused no suffering [   ] the morning of June 3rd [   ]in the calm of an [   ]a cloudless sky and [   ] sun whose warm rays soon melted the snowy covering and [   ] of the [   ] the march on May [   ] burning briskly gave an appearance of having been on fire for a considerable period of time.

The weather through today, June 3d, has been cool, with a fresh northwest wind blowing which dried the mud rapidly.

The column moved more rapidly today, having marched twenty-five miles and went into camp on Beaver Creek, which is a very pretty, clear watered, swift running stream, wending its course through a very attractive little valley. Grass is more luxuriant than before, and there is sufficient wood for camping purposes, dotted here and there with green colored buttes of various forms. Speaking of the

BAD LANDS,

I believe that no man possess the genius or nobility to so pen picture, or paint picture the scenery that meets one gaze on passing through this ugly, and at the same time beautiful and singularly fascinating region, as to give more than a faint conception and slight idea to the reader or beholder. I climbed, with considerable labor, to the tops of some of the most elevated buttes, and from there viewed the country. In all directions were seen the same everlasting formations. The sides of many of the buttes described in my last, for the first fourteen mules distance, are covered with a luxuriant growth of the bench or gramma grass, interspersed with small bench growth of cactus of various kinds, and a growth of pink, blue, white lilac and yellow colored flowers; one species of which, of the [   ] exhaled a [   ] delicate perfume. All the rest, while beautiful in color, and delicate in texture, give no fragrance, and are

LIKE A [   ]

without heart.

A large majority of those buttes have a deepish brick red color, created from being burned by an intense heat, others have the common clay-like appearance, and they are so mixed up as to create a pleasant contrast. On the very tops of some of these buttes lie loosely, and others firmly fixed in the soil, a conglomerate mass of rock of various species, all fused into one common mass, a portion which resembles melted glass, another that of molten iron, yet another that of burned brick, with a deposit of mica and pyrites of iron fused in, the whole forming a serious study for the scientist. The scenery in the Bad Lands, that possesses the most picturesque and the most attractive, is that portion lying near the Power River. The formations are more grotesque, more forcible, grander, and a considerable growth of spruce and cedar trees exist on the ranges, but the marching is more tedious, because of the rough formation; grasses are hardly seen, naught but sage brush, cactus, prairie dog villages and rattlesnakes are produced as one reaches the head of this region that

HIS SATANIC MAJESTY

must have had supervision of during its creation.

Owing to information brought to the command from Gen. Gibbon, who reported, under date of May 24th, the intelligence reaching Gen. Terry, seven days thereafter, that he, Gibbon, with his command was in camp on the Rose Bud River, then 150 miles from us, on half rations; that he had ordered supplies from Fort Ellis, which he expected to arrive on June 1st; that small bands of hostiles were frequently seen. Gen. Terry changed his line of march, and we left the Stanley trail at O'Fallon's Creek, and marched in due course toward Powder River. For the first two days after the column followed strictly the guidance of the chief guide, Reynolds. On the evening of the second day it was decided that Gen. Custer, accompanied by Col. Weir's company of Cavalry should scout and find a trail leading into the Powder River valley, the company to be used as videttes to point out the way to the column following. Your correspondent had the pleasure of accompanying the scouting party, and writes, from personal observation, what he knows to be a fact. At 5 a.m. the scouting party started, Gen. Custer in the lead as usual. We found the route broken, rough and circuitous. Like a great serpent, the body moved zig zagging, turning and twisting, leaving guides for the column at prominent points until at last they were placed at distances five, ten, twenty and thirty rods apart, so tortuous was the winding way. Gen. Custer stated [   ]. Terry that he would secure a favorable trail and water his horses in the waters of the Powder River at 5 p.m. that day; and right nobly did he fulfill his promise. Riding like the wind, at a break neck pace, where a misstep of his true footed animal would have precipitated himself and gallant rider down hundreds of feet into yawning depths below. Nothing daunted him, on he goes, never

SANDY BARNARD

tiring, his boundless energy and will overcoming all seeming obstacles, and after a hard ride of fifty miles reached the

POWDER RIVER,

the heart of the Indian home, at half past three, having secured a feasible trail, and fulfilled his promise to Gen. Terry, tarrying only thirty minutes in the time stated. The route was marched over during the day by the main column and the rear came into camp at 5:30 p.m. of that day, having marched a distance of 32 miles, over a country in all appearances, impossible to cross, marching up steep sided buttes, ever cone like formations, traveling for a mile or more on a narrow line called a "Hog's Back," a line of only sufficient width to permit the passing over of one army wagon, the oldest being at a precipices angle, whose angle lay hundreds of feet below, still this invincible band moved on, and on, undaunted by the gigantic prospects, and finally, and on good marching time for a body like this, with its 160 laden wagons, reached camp without accident, fatigued, but in good heart and spirits; joyful because of having accomplished a remarkable feat. There is established another route, another trail, across a section of country which heretofore has been supposed to present but one feasible route, and geographer will hereafter note

TERRY'S TRAIL

across the Bad Lands, as he makes up his atlas and maps.

Today, June 9th, the main body is lying in camp. Busy preparations are going forward organizing for a cavalry scout in full force, the rations and forage to be transported on Waggoner's pack mules; and now

THE REAL WORK

of the campaign commences, and a vigorous pursuit of the hostile tribes will be made, and they are to be taught that the army has a strong arm, which when it reaches out teaches all belligerents and murderous, massacring devils, like the hostiles of the northwest, that they must respect the government that feeds and cloths them, and be governed by the laws enacted for the purpose. No more marauding, roving, scalp lifting raids will be tolerated, and this lesson will be taught to all those who disobey the laws of the land.

GEN. TERRY,

accompanied by two companies of cavalry, left camp on the afternoon of June 6th for the mouth of Powder River to meet the Far West which was lying there awaiting orders. He took the Far West, and on the 9th proceeded up the Yellowstone to meet Gen. Gibbons.

Among other curious things connected with the

EXPEDITION

are the names of the Indian scouts, some of the principle [sic] ones being: "Ne-al-ri pat Running Bull," Na-ca-ba-ban, The Lucky," "Hocus-ta-rix, Bob Tail Bull," and "Hoo-nanch, Soldier," &c.

These same Indians have a somewhat facetious naming for such individuals as attract their attention; as for instance, they name Gen. Terry, "One-Star," his epaulets showing his rank by the one star in the center of the bars; Adgt. Smith they name "The Man That Always Looks Mad;" Chief Engineer Maguire is called "Big Belly," because of his obesity; Capt. Gibbs of the staff is styled, "Man With Lump-on-His-Back," owing to a stoop of his shoulders; Major Hughes, staff officer, is yclept "Slim Man," and Capt. Michiales, ordinance officer, they speak of as "Four Eyes," for the reason that he wears spectacles and carries a gold glass, and so they go on, applying names frequently that seems to them fitting, but which are out of place here. Now let me say a word or two for the

SEVENTH CAVALRY

whose acts, demeanor and habits I have closely watched. I am speaking of the private solid now. As a body they are fine appearing, strong quick, athletic fellows, always cheerfully ready to obey the order of command, whether it is for mount, picket duty, pioneer labor, or police work. The bulk of the work at the crossing of streams, or while moving over rough country falls upon them, and it's a real pleasure to see the handiness with which they handle the pick and spade and throw the dirt. Sharp, quick work soon bridges a previous impassable crossing, or levels down sidling banks. They are all splendidly mounted and equipped, undoubtedly better than any other cavalry regiment in the United States service, and they devote most of their spare time in attention to the steeds that carry them. Take them all in all they comprise just such a regiment as one would choose as an escort through the country of a foe, or where it was positive hard fighting would occur. Gen. Custer and the officers of his command have reason to feel proud of the brave, well drilled, fully disciplined men of this command, and if any doubt the respect or affection they have for their commander let him or them cast an insinuation against "Leather Breeches," as they jocularly style their General, and receive a broken head for his or their pains.

On this bright beautiful morning of June 11th I am informed that the present opportunity for mailing will close at noon of today, as the steamer

188   SANDY BARNARD

will depart at that time.

No incident of import has occurred since the 8th inst. The column made a splendid move on June 7th, moving a distance of thirty-five miles over the most stubborn, ugly formed country it has yet contended with. The scenery, as approached from the east, nearing Powder and the Yellowstone Rivers, increases easily in attractiveness. The formations are more irregular and possess the advantage of shrubbery, and a good sized growth of spruce add very much to the beauty of the scenery. One point in this day's march I wish to note, and I regret very much the falling rain prevented an opportunity to gain even an [   ] sketch. Passing along on the very ridge, "Hog's Back," of one of the highest elevations of this section, attention was drawn to a work that nature's elements had made not only beautiful in the extreme, but very peculiarly. Sitting on a level jutting of rock and earth, containing several acres, that sprang abruptly out of from the perpendicular side of a butte, whose top was hundreds of feet above, were the perfect pictures of old ruins, shaped as are the walls of many of the old ruins of the World. Running close to the seeming like parapet, on which these formations were situated, was a deep yawning chasm, looking as if designed for a moat. Surrounding all were the precipious and curiously formed butte, whose sides were covered with luxurious growing grasses. It was a picture to leave lasting impressions in the beholder, and one that man can but feebly picture, such a gloriously beautiful spot as repays for all the trouble and hardship endured in reaching it.

The column, with the exception of six companies of cavalry, which are on a ten days scout in search of the hostiles, are today in camp on the banks of the Yellowstone River and Custer Creek, which is to be the depot of supplies, for the present at least. The march from the camp on Powder River, twenty-four miles in distance, was a hard one, over a dry rough country, and a well soaked soil, caused by heavy rain falls of the past few days. From this point will radiate the cavalry

IN FORCE,

and is the general impression that the hostiles will be found in the course of ten days.

[Column was unsigned]

SANDY BARNARD

After Mark Kellogg's death, the New York Herald published his last letter to the newspaper. It had been written June 21, four days before his death.

****

MARK KELLOGG COLUMN

NEW YORK HERALD

JULY 11, 1876

****

MR. KELLOGG'S LAST LETTER

The following private letter and hurried correspondence for publication from the pen of our slaughtered correspondent, Mark Kellogg, will be read with painful interest. We give them both just as written, in order to enable our readers to see the last written messages from our gallant correspondent in all their simplicity and force:—

THE PRIVATE LETTER

IN CAMP ON YELLOWSTONE

JUNE 21, 1876

TO THE EDITOR OF THE HERALD:—

Enclosed please find manuscript, which I have been forced to write very hurriedly, owing to the want of time given me for the purpose. My last was badly demoralized from wetting, as then briefly explained, and I have feared it would not prove acceptable on that account. The officers of the expedition have written generally to their friends to watch for the HERALD, as they know I am to record their deeds. I will endeavor to give you interesting letters as we go along. I have the liberty of the entire column, headquarters and all, and will get down to bottom facts in all matters connected with the expedition. Very truly yours

M.H. KELLOGG

THE LETTER FOR PUBLICATION

The following letter for publication was written by Mr. Kellogg four days before the daring charge of Custer, in which the latter and all of his followers, including our correspondent, lost their lives:—

YELLOWSTONE RIVER
MOUTH ROSEBUD RIVER, JUNE 21, 1876

From June 12, the date of my last communication, until June 19, the only occurrences of General Terry's command were the establishment of a supply depot at the mouth of the Powder River and making the steamer Far West a moving base of supplies, having on board thirty days' rations and forage; the movement of the steamer to the mouth of the Tongue River with the headquarters command on board and the march of General Custer from the mouth of Powder River to the mouth of Tongue River, an estimated distance of forty-five miles, moving up the valley of the Yellowstone River. During the trip no incident occurred except a display of

SHARP RIFLE FIRING

on the part of General Custer who brought down an antelope at 400 yards and neatly shot off the heads of several sage hens. The country north of Powder River, for a distance of twelve to fifteen miles, is very poor, low and causing hard marching, with a soil producing no grasses, only sage brush and cactus. En route, on the 15th, the column passed through an abandoned Indian camp, apparently less than a year old. It had been a large camp, being two miles or more in length, and must have contained 1,200 or 1,500 lodges. Game was very scarce, and no buffalo at all were seen.

THE YELLOWSTONE RIVER

is looming high, and its current is so swift, eddying and whirling as to create a seething sound like that of soft wind rustling in the tall grass. Its color resembles yellowish clay at this point. It is cool and pleasant to the taste, and is a larger body of water than that of the Missouri River above its mouth, but very much superior for purposes of steamboat navigation. The waters of the Tongue River are of a deepish red color, running swiftly, and not very palatable to the taste.

A STARTLING STORY

On the 19th of June General Custer, with six companies of cavalry, crossed the Tongue River, about three miles from its mouth, by fording, and marched to a point about nine miles above where Major Reno, with six companies of the Seventh Cavalry, were in camp, having returned from the scout he was ordered upon; but for some cause unknown to your correspondent, Major Reno was unfortunate enough not only to exceed but to disobey the orders and instructions of General Terry, a copy of which is subjoined, viz:—

EXTRACT OF ORDER.
HEADQUARTERS DEPARTMENT OF DAKOTA
IN THE FIELD, CAMP ON POWDER RIVER, M.T.,

JUNE 10, 1876

Field Special Orders, No. 2.

2. Major M.A. Reno, Seventh Cavalry, with six companies (right wing) of his regiment and one gun from the Gatling battery, will proceed at the earliest practicable moment to make a reconnaissance of the Powder River from the present camp to the mouth of the Little Powder. From the last named point he will cross to the head waters of Mizpah Creek, and descend that creek to its junction with Powder River. Thence he will cross to Pumpkin Creek and Tongue River, and descended the Tongue to its junction with the Yellowstone, where he may expect to meet the remaining companies of the Seventh Cavalry and supplies of subsistence and forage.

Major Reno's command will be supplied with subsistence for twelve days, and with forage for the same period at the rate of two pounds of grain per day for each animal.

The guide Mitch Bouyer and eight Indian scouts, to be detailed by Lieutenant Colonel Custer, will report to Major Reno, for duty with this column.

Acting Assistant Surgeon H.R. Porter is detailed for duty with Major Reno. By command of Brigadier General Terry.

EDW. SMITH, Captain Eighteenth Infantry,

Acting Assistant Adjutant General

MAJOR RENO'S ERROR

Major Reno made an error in that he crossed, going a due south course, from the forks of the Powder River, where he found a fresh hostile trail. General Terry had planned to have Major Reno return to the column, marching down the valley of the Tongue River; and after he had formed the junction General Custer was to organize his regiment for a scout up the valley of the tongue, thence across to the Rosebud, striking near its head;

thence down that valley toward General Terry, who would in the mean-time move by steamer to the mouth of the Rosebud, join General Gibbon's command, transfer it across the Yellowstone; then, at the head of Gibbon's cavalry, march up that valley until he met and joined General Custer. The plan was an excellent one, and but for the unfortunate movement of Major Reno the main force of the Indians, numbering 1,500, would have been bagged. As it is,

A NEW CAMPAIGN IS ORGANIZED

and tomorrow, June 22, General Custer, with twelve cavalry compa-nies, will scout from its mouth up the valley of the Rosebud until he reaches the fresh trail discovered by Major Reno, and move on that trail with all the rapidity possible in order to overhaul the Indians, whom it has been ascertained are hunting buffalo and making daily and leisurely short marches. In the meantime General Terry will move on the steamer to the mouth of the Big Horn River, scouting Pumpkin Creek en route, with General Gibbon's cavalry as well as infantry, which are marching toward the Big Horn on the Yellowstone. This part of the command will march up the Big Horn Valley in order to intercept the Indians if they should attempt to escape from General Custer down that avenue. The hope is now strong, and I believe, well founded, that this band of ugly customers, known as

SITTING BULL'S BAND

will be "gobbled" and dealt with as they deserve. General Custer's command made a rapid march from Tongue River to the Rosebud, over some portion of which the route covered was

THE MAUVAISES TERRE

in its ugliest forms; up and down ascents and descents so abrupt as to appear impassable for locomotion, circuiting and twisting hither and thither—now along a narrow defile, then through a deep, abrupt canyon, in which the sun's rays created a warm, still atmosphere that caused pant-ing breaths and reeking perspiration. However, the sharp quick march of the cavalry kept pace with the steamer which was running up the Yellowstone. Frequently by us in the rear the light-colored buckskin suit on the person of General Custer would be seen, followed closely by the head of the column, as he and they climbed the heights from out the wind-ing, yawning abysses below.

THE LAND IMPROVED

As we proceed further up the valley of the Yellowstone River its at-tractions become more marked, more defined and more beautiful. Vegeta-

SANDY BARNARD

tion increases in size, in the grasses as well as in the timber. Beautiful little islands are frequently seen, covered to their very edges with a thick growth of trees, whose vivid green foliage hides the branches that reach far outward over the yellowish waters flowing swiftly beneath. The banks of the river are abrupt, the channel unchanging, the bod [sic] of which is composed of gravel and its depth sufficient at its usual low stage to allow light draught steamers to navigate its length from its emptying into the Missouri River to the mouth of the Big Horn, a distance of nearly 600 miles. I write of this stream as I see it, for the purpose of informing the thousands of readers of the HERALD of the magnitude and facilities it affords for commercial purposes in the near future, when its beautiful valley shall have become populated, of a stream that has an appearance upon the maps of being only a mere creek. A valley of your own "away down East" is merely the area of a race track compared with the valleys of the far West. Here they range from thirty to five hundred miles in length, ranging in width from one to fifteen. The upper portion of the Yellowstone Valley, that is to say, the upper half of the valley, is superior to the balance in all respects — for grass and timer, not only in quantity, but in quality; for richness of soil; for health and climate; for its abundance of game, its quantities of fish and other things besides.

CHARACTER OF GENERAL TERRY

Brigadier General A.H. Terry, in command of this expedition, I find to be my ideal of a commanding general — large brained, sagacious, far reaching, cool under all circumstances and with rare executive abilities. He is besides genial, courteous, frank and manly. So far as he is concerned, I contend that his planning has been of the finest character, and unless his subordinates frustrate them by overt acts of their own, must be successful. He has won the hearts of all who have come to know him and he is highly regarded by the entire command. Of his staff, while it might seem invidious in me to mention singly, still it is my privilege to say that I find them all kind, courteous, high-toned gentlemen, all of whom fill creditably and well the requisites of their various positions. And now a word for

THE MOST PECULIAR GENIUS IN THE ARMY,

a man of strong impulses, of great hearted friendships and bitter enmities, of quick nervous temperament, undaunted courage, will and determination; a man possessing electric mental capacity and of iron frame and constitution; a brave, faithful, gallant soldier, who has warm friends and

MARK KELLOGG   195

bitter enemies; the hardest rider, the greatest pusher, with the most untiring vigilance, overcoming seeming impossibilities and with an ambition to succeed in all things he undertakes; a man to do right, as he construes the right in every case; one respected and beloved by his followers, who would freely follow him into the "jaws of hell." Of Lieutenant Colonel G.A. Custer I am now writing. The pen picture is true to the life, and is drawn not only from actual observation, but from an experience that cannot mislead me.

THE OFFICERS OF THE GALLANT SEVENTH

The officers of the several companies of the Seventh Cavalry, so far as my acquaintance extends, are as brave and gallant a lot of men as ever drew a sword in their country's cause. I can say as much for the infantry. Brave and true-hearted every one of them. In my opinion, based upon an experience and familiarity with the army and its men for years, I believe I am safe in saying that the present expedition under the command of General Terry is made up from among the best of the American service, the Seventh and Second cavalry and the Sixth, Seventeenth, Twentieth and Seventh infantry.

OTHER DISTINGUISHED OFFICERS

My acquaintance with General Gibbon and General Brisbin is limited, but I hear them highly spoken of on all hands. Their record in days gone by bears me out in stating that they occupy positions to which they are eminently fitted, and their commands are made up of the same fearless fellows as compose the Seventh Cavalry.

INDIAN BRAVADO.

General Gibbon and command departed from Fort Ellis, Montana, Territory, on April 1, pursuant to orders, and marched to a point designated on the Yellowstone, where they have been held in check and prevented from crossing by the extreme high water and rapid current of that stream. While lying in camp not far from the mouth of the Rosebud, during the past four weeks they have been frequently annoyed by bravado demonstrations of the hostile Indians on the heights opposite them, who would dash up on their ponies, laugh in derision, about, whoop and cavort around, like so many gymnasts, and then ride off at a gallop with a war whoop. All this had to be submitted to, for it was simply impossible to cross the boiling, seething, roaring stream that intervened without hazarding valuable lives.

SANDY BARNARD

FIRST ACCOUNT OF THE CUSTER MASSACRE

TRIBUNE EXTRA.

Price 25 Cents. BISMARCK, D. T., JULY 6, 1876.

MASSACRED

GEN. CUSTER AND 261 MEN THE VICTIMS.

NO OFFICER OR MAN OF 5 COMPANIES LEFT TO TELL THE TALE.

3 Days Desperate Fighting by Maj. Reno and the Remainder of the Seventh.

Full Details of the Battle.

LIST OF KILLED AND WOUNDED.

THE BISMARCK TRIBUNE'S SPECIAL CORRESPONDENT SLAIN.

Squaws Mutilate and Rob the Dead

Victims Captured Alive Tortured in a Most Fiendish Manner.

What Will Congress Do About It?

Shall This Be the Beginning of the End?

It will be remembered the the Bismarck Tribune sent a special correspondent with Gen. Terry, who was the only professional correspondent with the expedition. Kellogg's last words to the writer were: "We leave the Rosebud tomorrow and by the time this reaches you we will have

MET AND FOUGHT.

the red devils, with what result remains to be seen. I go with Custer and will be at the death." How true! On the morning of the 22d Gen. Custer took up the line of march for the trail of the Indians, reported by Reno on the Rosebud. Gen. Terry, apprehending danger, urged Custer to take additional men, but Custer having full confidence in his men and in their ability to cope with the Indians in whatever force he might meet them, declined the proffered assistance and marched with his regiment alone. He was instructed to strike the trail of the Indians, to follow it until he discovered their position, and report by courier to Gen. Terry whowould reach the mouth of Little Horn by the evening of the 26th, when he would act in concert with Custer in the final wiping out. At four o'clock, the afternoon of the 24th, Custer scouts reported the location of a village recently deserted, whereupon Custer went intocamp, marching again at 11 p. m., continuing the march until daylight, when he again went into camp for coffee. Custer was then fifteen miles from the village located on the Little Horn, one of the branches of the Big Horn, twenty miles above its mouth, which could be seen from the top of the divide, and after lunch General Custer pushed on. The Indians by this time had discovered his approach and soon were seen mounting in great haste, riding here and there, it was presumed in full retreat. This idea was strengthened by finding a freshly abandoned Indian camp with a deserted tepee, in which one of their dead had been left, about six miles from where the battle took place. Custer with his usual vigor pushed on making seventy-eight miles without sleep, and attacked the village near its foot with companies C, E, F, I, and L, of the seventh cavalry. Reno having in the mean time attacked it at itshead with three companies of cavalry which, being surrounded, after a desperate hand to hand conflict, in which many were killed and wounded, cut their way to a bluff about three hundred feet high, where they were reinforced by four companies of cavalry under Col. Benteen. In gaining this position Col. Reno had to recross the Little Horn, and at the ford the hottest fight occurred. It was here where Lieutenants McIntosh, Hodgson and Dr. DeWolf fell; where Charley Reynolds fell in a hand to hand conflict with a dozen or more Sioux, emptying several chambers of his revolver, each time bringing a red-skin before he was brought down—shot through the heart. It was here Bloody Knife surrendered his spirit to the one who gave it, fighting the natural and hereditary foes of his tribe, as well as the foes of the whites.

The Sioux dashed up beside the soldiers in some instances knocking them from their horses and killing them at their pleasure. This was the case with Lt. McIntosh, who was unarmed except with a saber. He was pulled from his horse, tortured and finally murdered at the pleasure of the red devils. It was here that Fred Girard was separated from the command and lay all night with the screeching fiends dealing death and destruction to his comrades within a few feet of him, and, but time will not permit us to relate the story, through some means succeeded in saving his fine black stallion in which he took so much pride. The ford was crossed and the summit of the bluffs, having, Col. Smith says, the steepest sides that he ever saw ascended by a horse or mule, reached, though the ascent was made under a galling fire.

The companies engaged in this affair were those of Captain Boylan, French and McIntosh. Col. Reno had gone ahead with these companies in obedience to the order of Gen. Custer, fighting most gallantly, driving back repeatedly the Indians who charged in their front, but the fire from the bluff being so galling, forced the movement heretofore alluded to. Signals were given and soon Benteen with the four companies in reserve came up in time to save Reno from the fate with which Custer about this time met. The Indians charged the hill time and again but were each time repulsed with heavy slaughter by its gallant defenders. Soon, however, they reached bluffs higher than those occupied by Reno; and opened a destructive fire from points beyond the reach of cavalry carbines. Nothing being heard from Custer, Col. Weir was ordered to push his command along the bank of the river in the direction he was supposed to be, but he was soon driven back, retiring with difficulty. About this time the Indians received strong reinforcements, and litterally swarmed the hill sides and on the plains, coming so near at times that stones were thrown into the ranks of Col. Reno's command by those unarmed or out of amunition. Charge after charge in quick succession, the fight being sometimes almost hand to hand. But they drew off finally, taking to the hills and ravines. Col. Benteen charged a large party in a ravine, driving them from it in confusion. They evidently trusted in their numbers and did not look for so bold a movement. They were within range of the corral and wounded several packers, J. C. Wagoner, among the number, in the head, while many horses and mules were killed. Near 12 o'clock the fight closed, and the men worked all night strengthening their breastworks, using knives, tin cups and plates, in place of spades and picks, taking up the fight again in the morning. In the afternoon of the second day the desire for water became almost intolerable. The wounded were begging piteously for it; the tongues of the men were swollen and their lips parched, and from lack of rest they were almost exhausted. So a bold attempt was made for water. Men volunteered to go with canteens and camp kettles, though to go was almost certain death. The attempt succeeded though in making it one man was killed and several wounded. The men were relieved, and that night the animals were watered. The fight closed at dark, opening again next morning, and continuing until the afternoon of the 27th. Meantime the men become more and more exhausted and all wondered what had become of Custer. A panic all at once was created among the Indians and they stampeded, from the hills and from the valleys, and the village was soon deserted except for the dead. Reno and his brave band felt that succor was nigh Gen. Terry came in sight, and strong men wept upon each others necks, but no word was had from Custer. Hand shaking and congratulations were scarcely over when Lt. Bradley reported that he had found Custer dead, with one hundred and ninty cavalry men. Imagine the effect. Words cannot picture the feeling of these, his comrades and soldiers. Gen. Terry sought the spot and found it to be too true. Of those brave men who followed Custer, all perished: no one lives to tell the story of the battle. Those deployed as skirmishers, lay as they fell, shot down from every side, having been entirely surrounded in an open plain. The men in the companies fell in platoons, and like those on the skirmish line, lay as they fell, with their officers behind them in there proper positions. General Custer, who was shot through the head and body, seemed to have been among the last to fall, and around and near him lay the bodies of Col. Tom and Boston, his brothers, Col. Calhoun, his brother-in-law, and his nephew young Reed, who insisted on accompaning the expedition for pleasure, Col. Cook and the members of the non-commissioned staff all dead—all striped of their clothing and many of them with bodies terribly mutilated. The squaws seem to have passed over the field and crushed the skulls of the wounded and dying with stones and clubs. The heads of some were severed from the body, the privates of some were cut off, while others bore traces of torture, arrows having been shot into their private parts while yet living, or other means of torture adopted. The officers who fell were as follows: Gen. G. A. Custer, Cols. Geo. Yates, Miles Keogh, James Calhoun W. W. Cook, Capts. McIntosh, A. E. Smith, Lieutenants Riley, Critenden, Sturgis, Harrington, Hodgson and Porter, Asst Surgeon De Wolf. The only citizens killed were Boston Custer, Mr. Reed, Charles Reynolds, Isiah, the interperter from Ft. Rice and Mark Kellogg, the latter the Tribune correspondent. The body of Kellogg alone remained unstriped of its clothing, and was not mutilated. Perhaps as they had learned to respect the Great Chief, Custer, and for that reason did not mutilate his remains they had in like manner learned to respect this humble shover of the lead pencil and to that fact may be attributed this result. The wounded were sent to the rear some fourteen miles on horse litters striking the Far West sixty odd miles up the Big Horn which point they left on Monday at noon reaching Bismark nine hundred miles distant at 10 p. m.

The burial of the dead was sad work but they were all decently interred. Many could not be recognized: among the latter class were some of the officers. This work being done the command wended its way back to the base where Gen. Terry, awaits supplies and approval of his plans for the future campaign.

The men are worn out with marching and fighting, and are almost wholly destitute of clothing.

The Indians numbered at least eighteen hundred lodges in their permanent camp, while those who fought Crook seems to have joined them, making their effective fighting force nearly four thousand. These were led by chiefs carrying flags of various colors, nine of whom were found in a burial tent on the field of battle. Many other dead were found on the field, and near it ten squaws at one point in the ravine—evidently the work of Ree or Crow scouts.

The Indian dead were great in number, as they were constantly assaulting an inferior force. The camp had the appearance of being abandoned in haste. The most georgeous ornaments were found on the bodies of the dead chiefs, and hundreds of finely dressed and painted robes and skins were thrown about the camp. The Indians were certainly severely punished.

We said of those who went into battle with Custer none are living—one Crow scout hid himself in the field, and witnessed and survived the battle. His story is plausable, and is accepted, but we have not room for it now. The names of the wounded are as follows:

LIST OF WOUNDED.

Private Davis Corey, Co. I, 7th Cav., right hip; Patrick McDonnall, D, left leg; Sergt. John Paul, H, back; Priv. Michael C. Madden, K, right leg; Wm. George, H, left side, died July 3d, at 4 a. m.; 1st Sergt. Wm. Heyn, A, left knee; Priv. John McVay, C, hips; Patrick Curcoran, K, right shoulder; Max Wilke, K, left foot; Alfred Whitaker, C, right elbow; Peter Thompson, C, right hand; Jacob Deal, A, face; J. H. Meyer, M, back; Roman Rutler, M, right shoulder; Daniel Newell, M, left thigh; Jas. Muller, H, right thigh; Elijah T. Strounde, A, right leg; Sergt. Patrick Carey, M, right hip; Privt. James E. Benett, C, body, died July 5th, at 3 o'clock; Francis Reeves, A, left side and body; James Wilbur, M, left leg; Jasper Marshall, L, left foot; Sergt. James T. Riley, E, back and left leg; Privt. John J. Phillips, H, face and both hands; Samuel Severn, H, both thighs; Frank Bruun, M, face and left thigh; Corpl. Alex B. Bishop, H, right arm; Privt James Foster, A, right arm; W. E. Harris, M, left breast; Chas. H. Bishop, H, right arm; Fred Homsted, A, left wrist; Sergt Chas. White, M, right arm; Privt Thos. P. Varner, M, right ear; Chas. Campbell, C, right shoulder; John Cooper, H, right elbow; John McGuire C, right arm; Henry Black, H, right hand; Daniel McWilliams, H, right leg.

An Indian scout, name unknown, left off at Birthold: Sergt M. Riley, Co. I, 7th Infantry, left off at Buford, Consumption; Privt David Ackison, Co. E, 7th cav., left off, July 4th, at Buford, Constipation.

The total number of killed was two hundred and sixty one; wounded 52. Thirty-eight of the wounded were brought down on the Far West; three of them died en route. The remainder are cared for at the field hospital.

De Rudio had a narrow escape, and his escape is attributed to the noise of beavers, jumping into the river during the engagement. De Rudio followed them, got out of sight, and after hiding for twelve hours or more finally reached the command in safety.

The body of Lt Hodgson did not fall into the hands of the Indians; that of Lt. McIntosh did, and was badly mutilated. McIntosh, though a half-breed, was a gentleman of culture and esteemed by all who knew him. He leaves a family at Lincoln, as does Gen. Custer, Cols. Calhoun, Yates, Capt. Smith, and Lt. Porter. The unhappy Mrs. Calhoun, loses a husband, three brothers and a nephew. Lt. Harrington also had a family, but no trace of his remains was found. We are indebted to Col. Smith for the following full list of the dead; to Dr. Porter for the list of wounded, which is also ful:

KILLED.

Field and staff, George A. Custer, Brevt. Major General.

W. W. Cook, Brevt. Lt-Colonel.

Lord, Asst. Surgeon, J. M. DeWolf, Acting Asst. Surgeon.

N. C. Staff, W. W. Sharrow, Surg Major.

Henry Voss, Chief Insptr.

Co.	Name	Rank
A	Henry Dallans	Corp.
"	G. K. King	"
"	J. E. Armstrong	Privt
"	James Drinaw	"
"	Wm. Moody	"
"	R. Rowlins	"
"	James McDonald	"
"	John Sullivan	"
"	Thos. P. Switzer	"
B	Benj. Hodgson	2d Lieut
"	Richard Doran	Privt
"	George Mask	"
C	T. W. Custer	Brevt Lt-Col
"	H. M. Harrington	2d Lt

The body of Lt. Harrington was not found, but it is reasonably certain that he was killed.

Co.	Name	Rank
"	Edwin Baba	1st Sergt
"	Finley	Sergt
"	Finkle	"
"	French	Corpl
"	Foley	"
"	Ryan	"
"	Allen	Privt
"	Criddle	"
"	King	"
"	Bucknell	"
"	Eisman	"
"	Engle	"
"	Brightfield	"
"	Fanand	"
"	Griffin	"
"	Hamel	"
"	Hattisoll	"
"	Kingsouts	"
"	Lewis	"
"	Mayer	"
"	Mayer	"
"	Phillips	"
"	Russell	"
"	Rix	"
"	Ranter	"
"	Short	"
"	Shea	"
"	Shade	"
"	Stuart	"
"	St. John	"
"	Thadius	"
"	Van Allen	"
"	Warren	"
"	Windham	"
"	Wright	"
D	Vincent Charley	Farrier
"	Patrick Golden	Privt
"	Edward Hansen	"
E	A. E. Smith	Brevt Capt
"	E. Sturgis	2d Lt

The body of Lt. Sturgis was not found, but it is reasonably certain he was killed.

Co.	Name	Rank
"	F. Hohmeyer	1st Sergt
"	Egnen	Sergt
"	James	"
"	Hagan	Corp
L	James Calhoun	1st Lt
"	Miller	Privt
"	Tweed	"
"	Vetter	"
"	Cashan	"
"	Kiefer	"
"	Andrews	"
"	Crisfield	"
"	Harnington	"
"	Haugge	"
"	Kavaugh	"
"	Lobering	"
"	Mahoney	"
"	Schmidt	"
"	Lunon	"
"	Semenson	"
"	Riebold	"
"	O'Connell	"
"	J. J. Crittenden	20th Inf
"	Butler	1st Sergt
"	Warren	"
"	Harrison	Corpl
"	Gilbert	"
"	Seiller	"
"	Walsh	Teptr
"	Adams	Privt
"	Assdely	"
"	Burke	"
"	Cheever	"
	McGue	"
"	McCarthy	"
"	Dugan	"
"	Maxwell	"
"	Scott	"
"	Babcock	"
"	Perkins	"
"	Tarbox	"
"	Dye	"
"	Tessier	"
"	Galvin	"
"	Graham	"
"	Hamilton	"
"	Rodgers	"
"	Snow	"
"	Hughes	"
K	D. Whitney	1st Sergt
"	Hughes	Sergt
"	J. J. Callahan	Corpl
"	Julius Helmer	Trptr
"	Eli U. T. Clair	Privt
I	M. W. Keogh	Col

" J. E. Porter—the body of Lt. Porter was not found, but it is reasonably certain he was killed.

Co.	Name	Rank
"	F. E. Varden	1st Sergt
"	J. Bartard	"
"	John Wild	Corpl
"	G. C. Morris	"
"	S. T. Staples	"
"	J. M. Gucker	Trptr
"	J. Patton	"
"	H. A. Bailey	Blacksmith
"	J. E. Broadhurst	Privt
"	J. Barry	"
"	J. Conners	"
"	T. P. Downing	"
"	Mason	"
	Blorm	"
"	Meyer	"
"	McElroy	Trptr
"	Mooney	"
"	Baker	Privt
"	Boyle	"
"	Bauth	"
"	Conner	"
"	Darling	"
"	Davis	"
"	Farrell	"
"	Hiley	"
"	Huber	"
"	Hime	"
"	Henderson	"
"	Henderson	"
"	Leddiston	"
"	O'Conner	"
"	Rood	"
"	Reese	"
"	Smith 1st	"
"	Smith 2nd	"
"	Smith 3rd	"
"	Stella	"
"	Stafford	"
"	Schoole	"
"	Smallwood	"
"	Tarr	"
"	Vaugant	"
"	Walker	"
"	Bragew	"
"	Knight	"
F	G. W. Yates	Capt
"	W. Van Rieley	2d Lt
"	Kenney	1st Sergt
"	Nursey	Sergt
"	Vickory	"
"	Wilkinson	"
"	Coleman	Capt
"	Ferman	"
"	Briody	"
"	Brandon	Farrier
	Manning	Blacksmith
"	Atchison	Privt
"	Brown 1st	"
"	Brown 2nd	"
"	Bruce	"
"	Brady	"
"	Burnham	"
"	Cather	"
"	Carney	"
"	Dohman	"
"	Donnelly	"
"	Gardiner	"
	Hammon	"
"	Kline	"
"	Krianth	"
"	Luman	"
"	Losse	"
"	Milton Jas	"
"	Madson	"
"	Monroe	"
"	Ruddew	"
"	Omeling	"
"	Siefous	"
"	Sanders	"
"	Wanew	"
	Way	"
"	Lerock	"
"	Kidey	"
"	E. C. Driscoll	"
"	D. C. Gillette	"
"	C. H. Gross	"
"	F. P. Holcomb	"
	M. E. Horn	"
"	Adam Hitlsmer	"
"	P. Killey	"
"	Fred Lehman	"
"	Henry Lehman	"
"	E. P. Lloyd	"
"	A. Mcirhargey	"
"	J. Mitchell	"
"	J. Noshang	"
"	J. O'Bryan	"
"	J. Parker	"
"	F. J. Pitter	"
"	Geo. Post	"
"	Jas. Quinn	"
"	Wm. Reed	"
"	J. W. Rossberg	"
"	D. L. Lymons	"
"	J. E. Troy	"
"	Chas. Van Bramer	"
"	W. B. Whaley	"
G	Daniel McIntosh	1st Lt
"	Edward Botzer	Sergt
"	M. Considine	"
"	Jas Martin	Capt
"	Otto Hageman	"
"	Benj. Wells	Farrier
"	Henry Dose	Trptr
"	Crawford Selby	Saddler
"	Benj. F. Rodgers	Privt
"	Andrew J. Moore	"
"	Jno. J. McGinniss	"
"	Edward Stanley	"
"	Henry Seafferman	"
"	John Papp	"
H	Geo Lee	Corpl
"	Julian D. Jones	Privt
	Thos. E. Meador	"
M	Miles F. O'Hara	Sergt
"	Henry M. Scollier	Corpl
"	Fred Stringer	"
"	Henry Gordon	Privt
"	H. Klotzbursher	"
"	G. Lawrence	"
"	W. D. Meyer	"
"	G. F. Smith	"
"	D. Somers	"
"	J. Tanner	"
	H. Tenley	"
"	H. C. Voyt	"
	Boston Custer	Civilian
	Arthur Reed	"
	Mark Kellogg	"
	Chas. Reynolds	"
	Frank C. Mann	"

INDIAN SCOUTS.

Bloody Knife

Bobtailed Bull,

Stab,

Total number of Commissioned officers killed	14
Actg asst Surg.	1
Enlisted men	237
Civilians	5
Indian Scouts	3

Courtesy *The Bismarck Tribune*

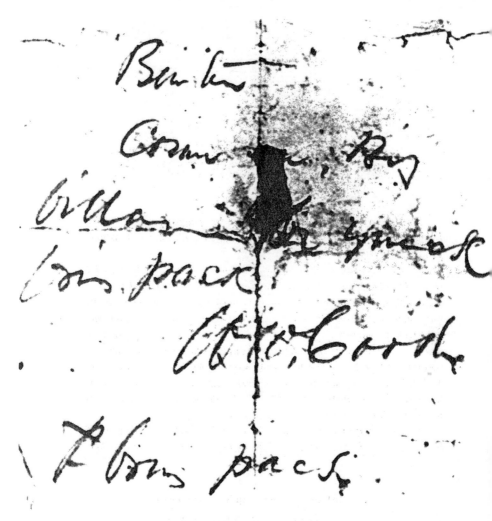

Perhaps concerned that Pvt. John Martini, an Italian immigrant, would garble Custer's order to Capt. Frederick Benteen, Lt. W.W. Cooke hastily scrawled this note for Martini to hand to Benteen. It was the last message from Custer's doomed command. It reads: "Benteen. Come on. Big Village. Be quick. Bring packs. P.S. Bring Pack. W.W. Cooke."

Courtesy The Bismarck Tribune

MARK KELLOGG'S DIARY

The diary of Mark Kellogg, a newspaper correspondent for the Bismarck Tribune, is a most valuable document concerning the Big Horn-Yellowstone Expedition of 1876.

The diary consists of 37 sheets of copy paper, measuring 3 3/4 x 18 1/4 inches, folded to form a note book 3-3/4 x 9 inches. The size of the sheets vary somewhat, edges of paper are ragged and torn and some sheets are badly water stained. Page one of the diary commences in the center of the book and the pages are numbered from 1 to 42, but an error in numbering was made and as a result there are two pages numbered 6, 7 and 28. Pages 19 and 20, covering parts of Kellogg's entries from May 28 and 29, are missing. All of Kellogg's entries are made in pencil and are clearly legible except the sheets which have been stained or marked by water. The diary is now in the collections of the State Historical Society of North Dakota.

Kellogg's diary as here printed has been carefully copied from the original notes. The corrections or changes made by Kellogg are given exactly as written.

[Matter printed in italic was deleted by
Kellogg in the original journal]
•••••••••

Broke camp May 17th Early morning foggy, heavy roads. Formed in marching order 2 miles West Ft. L. Camped at 3. P. M on the Big Heart *[13 miles out]*. 13.2 miles travelled. Splendid camp, wood, grass & water plenty.

May 18th Revielle 3. A M Under march 5. P.M. Halted at noon on Sweet Brier—10-5/8 miles travelled. Slight rains near camp, heavy rains all around. In camp at 4 P.M. Custer in person suffusing [with ?] energy.

May 19th Revielle 3. A.M. Broke camp 5. A.M. and under way. Passed through Prairie Dog villages saw some Antelope and Reynolds, the guide, shot one. Custer, pioneering ahead with scouts & two Co's. Cs *[Custer]* with them all day. Quite a novel excitement. Rains of last night makes taveling heavy for forage and camp teams. Took lunch today noon hard tack & bacon. Greyhounds after Jack Rabbit. Rabbit won the race. Terrific hail & rain storm as went into camp, cold, etc. Last of teams in at dark roads growing heavier. Scout reached us this A. M. with mail & news of B. Hillers being massacred. Traveled 14 miles. Grazing very light, wood scarce & Game 5 miles away.

May 20th—Reveille at 5. A.M. Broke camp at 8. Marched four miles to crossing of [word not deciphered] the Muddy, found little trouble at this crossing & wood was procured for tonight & tomorrow mornings uses. Gen. Terry in advance as well as Gen. Custer this A. M. Teams standing the rough, heavy work well Arty *[artillery]* team stampeded, ran mile, broken pole only damage. March 9.2 miles. Went into camp W. side of Big Muddy on heights. Slight showers through P.M. & roads soft, but Big Muddy was an easy crossing, grazing better, weather raw with West wind.

May 21. Reveille 3. A.M. Broke Camp 6. A.M. Weather misty, dark, heavy clouds threatening rain. Indian scouts brought in 7 Antelope. At noon the clouds broke, arose & Passed away leaving a clear sky & strong West wind. Column moving along nicely. Antelope more plenty. Several been killed through the day. Went into camp at 5 P.M. Marched 13.3 miles. Terry & Custer to the front, Roads better, getting West of the water shed. 1 mule shot diseased with Glanders. 1 mule left behind, played out. Plenty water no wood had to haul as come on. 3 Invalids in ambulance one from accidental shot in the heels. On the South nearly all day very rough, cone formation *[Mauvais]* first appearance of Mauvais de terre, *[Bad Lands]*. General Country rolling but many high buttes with peculiar names given by Indians viz. Rattlesnake Den, Wolfs Den Cherry Ridge Maidens Breasts. *[Veteniary]* U S A Vetsinary surgeon—Dr. C. A. Stein duties begin when get into camp. Reynolds, our guide out at 2 A.M. found an excellent route. Struck Stanley trail at noon today, left it *[Tuesday]* Friday last.

May 22d Column took line of March at 5 A.M. Weather clear, cool, pleasant. Getting beyond Watershed, roads harder, drier Was at front with Gen Terry & Custer all day; but little scouting done today. The guide Reynolds, & Blood Knife ahead. Plenty of Antelope seen today. Reynolds,

200   SANDY BARNARD

killed 3, & 14 in all were brought in. Struck Custers return Black Hills trail of 74 at 10. A M. Marched 15.4 miles today, crossed the Thin Faced Creek, a tributary of Knife River at 12:15 P.M. and went into camp *[near the Young Mans Buttes.]* A wagon upset today and the driver was injured considerably. The country is dry here, no rain here since prairie fires of *[two]* 2 weeks ago; but grazing is best we have had. Sufficient water, but not plenty & poor quality. An abundance of timber. Health of column continues good. Found first Grouse, & plenty here. Some Curlew, & large *[flo]* flocks of Jack Snipe.

May 23d—Broke camp at 5 A.M. Weather cool clear, Southerly winds. Marched 8 miles and went into camp at Young Mens Buttes. Plenty timber best grazing we have had, & a spring of clear, cold water. Gen C— While *[run]* Chasing Elk ahead of Advance, & when very near an Elk came onto *[a freshly]* fresh burning camp fire left by hostiles. He about faced & returned to column. First Elk seen, Antelope plenty. Arickarees some years ago had fight on & about Young Mens Buttes. We are camped within 40 miles of Berthold North course. Scouts say could reach in one day easy on ponies Abt 10 miles W. is Lost Waters Butte Stream water 16 to 18 inches diameter rushes out of side of Butte. Makes considerable stream & disappears after running 100 yards. Gen C- visits Scouts much at home amongst them. Cause of short march today to give stock chance to rest, have long march tomorrow. Sergt Stempker, Co. L 7th buried at this point Aug 26th 1873. head board undisturbed. Just at dusk Indians seen about 3 miles away, moving along on top of Coteau.

May 24th Camp broken and under March at usual hour. Weather clear cool, bright. Antelope plenty. Gen C. Capt Tom C. & party miles away on right flank hunting. nearly most of day killed Elk & Lynx. Crossed line of survey of N.P.R.R at 9. A.M. Travelled on Custers return Yellowstone trail of 73 today. Reached camp on fork of Big Heart at 3. P.M. travelled 19 1/8 miles, roads hard, dry, crossings easy. Health of column continues good. Most beautiful and convenient camp yet struck. Plenty wood, excellent grazing. Stream clear. Cool & swift running plenty small fish. Men bathing. Gen Terry, continually in the advance. 1st issue rations. Face of Country past 2 days high rolling prairie very beautiful in its green carpet. On cut bank of stream opposite camp is a plainly defined strata of lignite 5 to 6 ft in depth. Large pieces of lignite in bed of river all along drifted in.

May 25th Broke camp 5 A.M. Marched 19.4 miles 15.4 miles out had to use bridge at a drain crossing. Went into camp on tributary of

N. of B Heart since left Ca Big Heart at 3. P.M. Plenty grass, water & wood. Grazing improving rapidly. Grass here evidently 2 or 3 weeks in advance of that on Mo. River. Weather beautiful. Country passed over today very handsome. *[Gen Terry in advance at head]* 4 men on sick list. Only 2 *[Govt]* mules played out as yet, both Govt. Stock generally improving. *[Since we]* Past 3 days discovered the grass containing millions of *[infinitesimally]* infintisimal sized *[of]* locusts. Too small to hurt grass now.

    May 26th Broke camp 5.30 A.M. crossed run on bridge. Marched 4.2 miles to another feeder of Big Heart, put in bridge, thence to another feeder of Big Heart, going into camp at 2:30 P.M. marching 12 4/10 miles. Scouts from Lincoln on road at 3. A.M. with a mail. Weather hot and dry, first day of real heat yet experienced. Good grass, and water, no wood. Marched over considerable cactus growth today & some red gravel beds seen, first indications of approach to Bad Lands. Gen Custer, pioneering at front all day. Lays all the camps, & attends in person to much of detail of march. *[Energy un]* Antelope plenty, no signs of other game - No Indian signs for past three days. Mail brought news by telegraph to Gen Terry, of Cabinet changes. Some astonishment expressed because of appointment of Don. Cameron, as Secy of War. Hardly expected in military circles. Past 2 days we have marched between the Stanley trail west of 73. It is an excellent route thus far. Sent. Should properly be called Terrys Trail.

    May 27th Broke camp at 5. A.M. Weather clear and warm with pleasant wind from west. Gentle rain last night makes *[trav]* marching very pleasant. Marched 10 miles, and struck entrance of Bad Lands & went into camp, *[grass]* on a *[feeder]* the head of Davis Creek. Grass excellent. Water slightly alkalied. Valley narrow, camp stretches out lengthwise & *it* is the most picturesque imaginable. red, cone topped Buttes in all directions. Column enduring march finely. Men and stock hardening & improving. Band plays on set out for march and during evening daily. Actual distances marched today 17 1/2 miles. Owing to having crossed Stanleys trail at some point where it was obliterated the column marched about 3 miles too far South, and now it was that Gen Custers fine memory came into play. What is known as Sentinel Buttes, anglicized, by the Indians as "Two Buttes Facing Each Other" which are seen approaching the Bad Lands from the Eastward, & were pronounced so at once and emphatically by Gen Custer. Scouts were sent Northward and in the course of an hour found the trail. A counter march was ordered and the column about faced and were soon on the trail and winding *[their]* way down the sides of a

               SANDY BARNARD

steep Butte whose base is at the East entrance to the Bad Lands. Gen Custer and a few scouts made a march down the valley from camp an hour or so after reaching camp & found the route very feasible only as regarded the crossings. Gen Terry issued orders for 3 Co's Cav. to advance in morning armed with picks & shovels.

May 28th Broke camp 5. A.M. Pioneers ahead. Marched today 7 3/4 miles. Made 8 crossings of Davis Creek & went into camp at 12:30. Creek very tortuous, crossing deep. Made ascent of highest Buttes, viewed surrounding country a sea of cone & ugly formation. *[Expecte]* Grass excellent, water alkalied plenty wood. Expected reach Little Mo. this evening; but found pranks. [?] Waters unexpectedly quite clear in L. Mo. & very low. Will probabably lay here one or two days. as a considerable work corduroying, &c is necessary to make crossing feasible. Man rattlesnake bitten yesterday all right. Says whiskey is a "big thing." Anticipated Indian trouble in bad lands, or going up defile and Butte. west of Mo L. *[Mo]*, but no signs of their being in this vicinity.

May 30th Main column lie in camp today, Gen Custer, with battallion and Lt. Varnum with 12 scouts moved out of camp at 5 A.M. on a reconnoitering & scouting expedition. Expected in tonight. No incident today. Considerable quanty fish caught in L. Mo, such as Skip Jacks Graylings, and a few Silver Cat. No shooting allowed today. Gen Custer & battallion returned 6. P M scouted 45 miles up L. Mo Valley. Its average mile wide, good grass. crossed stream 34 times. No Indian signs except those a year old. 5 pack mules along with forage. Heavey shower early part of night.

May 31st Early morning gloomy, dark, misty threatening rain. Broke camp 8. A.M. clouds lifted and Weather pleasanter, Crossing of L. Mo, not bad, hauling heavy, and beyond westward the trail was over very broken country up, up & down, down, zig zagging up the high steep Buttes. Trail very tortuous clear through to tonights camp which was reached at 2. P.M, after a march of 12 9/10 miles. *[Reynolds]* going down a steep Butte on Whistlers "cut off" into valley where camped. Sufficient wood, & water. Grass very fine. latter of poor quality. Reynolds, & I off on a scout miles away from head of column, shot 3 Rocky Mountain sheep, dressed them, packed on our horses and tramped over 4 miles into camp. Went down very long steep Buttes, twisted down clay formations where if have stumbled would have gone down pricipice hundreds of feet. Men & stock all right. Had splendid panoramic view from Battlement Butte. *[about 8 miles]* in all directions. Red topped to North more than any other direction.

Rose Bud Butte on L. Mo. about 8 or 10 miles, in S. E. direction. 12 miles fr Camp. Saw column winding its way along. Carland found while "marching on" well shaped hole with ice in it, hot day, very refreshing. Commenced pouring rain at 7 P.M.

June 1st Reveille at 3 A.M, looked out found 2 inches on ground & snowing hard. Has snowed nearly all day. Have not moved. 7 P.M. snowing harder than ever wind blowing fr N.W. growing colder. Stock feeling the storm Very dull in camp, some card playing, no incident wood plenty, & fires kept burning all around, but few Sibley stoves, at Hd Qrs & 3 or 4 officers tent. Yesterday 8 miles W. L. Mo. camp. Saw a coal strata on fire, looked like whole side mountain on fire vein about 4 ft thick. Lignite cropping out all along.

June 2d Layed in camp all day, weather cold, snowing at intervals all day, very disagreeable. During P.M. forage and supply wagons hauled across crossing & up hill to start in early morning. Gen Terry impatient of delay. Will try to reach Beaver Creek tomorrow.

June 3d Camp broke & column in motion 5. A M Weather clear, & cold raw N.W. wind. Marched 25 miles camped on Beaver Creek, beautiful stream & valley. Grass *[sward]* luxuriant, wood sufficient. 10 AM 2 whites & 1 Ind. scouts *[from Gibbons command]* met head column. *[Gib]* with despatches from Gibbons command. *[They left]* on Rose Bud, between Powder & B. Horn. They left camp on 24th Gibbons command on half rations expected supplies from Ft Ellis June 1st 3 soldiers & 1 citizen while hunting killed by hostiles. Saw 20 to 50 in bands frequently through the day. Antelope plenty today. This camp is 35 miles from Yellowstone via Stanleys route to stockade. Gen T- will change course of march, & go direct to Gibbons command on the RoseBud. Str Josephine md 2d trip to stockade left her cargo and left the river. Str Star of the West at stockade at 10 A M

June 2d Will stay there until this column reaches unless otherwise ordered. 7 P.M. Weather warmer, clear, & no wind. Country passed over today except 1st 6 miles, handsome grass par excellence, splendid grass for stock but think of 8 inches of snow on ground June 2d. Snow fell to foot or more depth on Y. Stone, drifts 3 ft deep. same storm & time. Scouts had trouble find or keep trail.

June 4th Under march 5. A.M. Weather clear, cool, pleasant marching marched 18 miles camped on Stanleys return trail of 72 on his camping grounds on Beaver Creek grass plenty not so good as has been

SANDY BARNARD

water clear, cold, & swift running wood plenty. Indian signs week old saw today. Antelope plentier than at anytime on this march. Terry tired out, took ambulance 4 miles from camp 1 of Clarks teams played out. The roads good but country very rolling. "Vet" said to Recruit climb our hill, when on top see another. *[his experience]* - "Boys." Joshing "Capt Michailes" - chf ordnance, Indians call him "4 eyed battle ass" - Health of colunm good. Carland & Chance hunting. Dismounted to shoot Antelope, Horses ran away, in rear & flank of column, exhausted themselves chasing stock then gave $5.00 each to have horses caught. Chance shot 1 Antelope. Passed through P. Dog Village today.

June 5th Broke camp usual time Marched mostly a South Course 10.4 miles, struck Stanleys return 72 trail again descended into Bad Lands crossed Cabine Creek at 11. A M, Marched 20.2 miles & camped, grass fair, water ditto, no wood, used dried sagebrush for cooking. Worse road have had & worst country. Chief products sagebrush, cactus & rattlesnakes. Antelope very plenty. No Indian signs today. Been ahead with Reynolds. Killed 2 Black tailed deer & 2 Antelope. Tonights camp on open plains. Hd Qrs on hill top, handsome and convenient camp, but for lack of wood. 2 mules died last night. Saw 1st Buf. signs today, tracks fresh, since snow.

June 6th Broke camp and under march at 4.30 A.M. Weather clear, cool. breezy. March 10.4 miles to near head O. Fallons Creek crossed, and marched 22.3 miles where we crossed fork again and went into camp at 4.45 P.M. *[having marched 6 miles]* Had some difficulty in finding crossing Country along creek flat, very broken, and soil soft. Are making new trail entirely. Marching been generally excellent today. Reynolds guiding discretionanly - Timber heavy all cottonwood, plenty fair water, grazing not good. Sage brush & cactus principal growth today. First Buffalo Killed today. Two privates Troop H, out hunting yesterday not returning last night, fears they had been captured by hostiles; but they reached column about 10 A.M. all night got lost, & belated in bad land region, which we are yet in. Priv. McWilliams Troop H, accidentally shot himself with a revolver today; ball took effect calf leg ran down tendon, and lodged just under skin top of foot, flesh wound lay him up a month. marched through Prairie dog village containing 700 or 800 acres. Little fellows surprised & barked top of voices. *[Saw while with advance today deserted wood hovel, evidently put together without use of axe. Rough, dry logs piled together with broken limbs and sticks placed in then mudded. A mere hovel. Some white men wintered there evidences of horse, & well beaten path in front extending some distance each side of structure.]* Saw 1st wind puff today.

June 7th Under March 4:45: A.M. Weather misty, clouds heavy threatening rain. Marched today 32 miles & camped on Powder River. *[Cavalry]* Gen Custer, at 3.30. Gen T. and head of column 5. P.M. & the rear of Col. at 8. P.M. Terribly rough country. Gen C- with Col Weirs troops, used as videttes, scouted ahead & succeeded finding a passable *[trav]* route over a country would seem impractical, up, up, down, down, zig zag, twisting turning &c Gen C. rode 50 miles, fresh when arrived. Told Terry last eve, would succeed finding trail & water horse in P. River. 3. P.M. today, succeeded at 3.30 P.M. Most attractive scenery yet. Spruce & Cedar on Buttes, marched on "hogs back" highest Buttes in country for mile or two, if teams went either side roll down hundreds feet. Only *[trail]* route could be *[found]* made in this direction. Saw, what seemed like Ancient ruins. Buffalo seen today, none taken, order no firing. This camp excellent, wood, water, grass plenty. Timber all Cottonwood of smallish or medium size. Every one tired out, & stock completely so. Several mules & few horses *[played]* dropped out *[today]* of teams today. Some breakage to wagons slight damages. Remarkable march. We are 26 miles in direct line from camp on Fallon Creek last night. Have marched thus far 32.3 miles. Its 20 miles from here to mouth P. River. Fish

June 8th In camp all day. Gen. Terry, with 2 Co's Cav, left after noon for mouth Powder River intercept steamer. Preparations being made for an 8 days Cavalry Scout in full force. Waggoners pack train carrying forage, and *[rations]*. field rations. Indians Killed a buffalo today & had a pow-wow over it. Yesterdays march hard on stock; but a 2 days halt here will recuperate them. The scouts sent last night by Gen. T. to mouth of P. Riv. returned today, bringing letter mail Str Far West brought up. Report scouts from Gibbon, which met this column some days ago & were sent back with despatches, were unable to go to Gibbon, driven back to stockade by hostiles. They saw 4 Sioux, who ran away when seeing them. Hostiles probably, near mouth P. Riv, & in neighborhood Tongue Riv.

[May 9th] The returned scouts killed buffalo enroute, & had pow-wow over it 1st one killed.

[May] June 9th Lay in camp today. Scouts came in from mouth P. River, with mail brought up by Str Far West & information Gen. T. gone up Y. Riv. 30 miles on Str meet Gibbon who marching down Y. River valley from Junction with Terry. Organization for scouting completed & only awaits Gen T. return. It is probable the bulk hostiles on Tongue Riv. & between tr. & Powder Riv. Scouts saw 4 mounted Sioux who ran when saw Scouts .

Entries in the diary after June 9 are missing from the notebook. But it is possible to supplement them with the dispatches which he sent back to the *Tribune* up to June 24. His last dispatch, written on that date, contains these strangely prophetic words:

"We leave the Rosebud tomorrow and by the time this reaches you we will have met the red devils, with what results remains to be seen. I go with Custer and will be at the death."

[Additional notes found in Kellogg's Notebook]

"Bloody Knife, Nes i ri pat
Running Bull, Ho-cus-pa-cut-rer, Wa-ca-ta-hau. The Lucky
Ha Cus p Hucus-ta-nix. Bob Tail Bull Hoo-nanch. Soldier
Gen Terry, One Star - Adjt. Smith
Man that always looks Mad.
Capt Maguire Big Belly, Lt Gibbs Lump on his Back,
Capt Hughes Slim Man, Capt Michiales, Four Eyes
Gen Custer, "Long "Hair" ed
Chief & Hard Back Sides -
Lt Varn Col Cook, Handsome Man,
Nowlan, Man that Swings.
Lt Varnum

DETAILS	
Mules	*752*
Q.M. Horses	*32*
Gov. "	*695*
Batty. "	*26*
Pvt. horses	*95*
Hired	*74*
Total	*1674*

SANDY BARNARD

ENDNOTES

[1] *Bismarck Tribune*, July 6, 1876, p. 1. The phrase "at the death" was commonly used in that period to mean "in battle." Thus, Kellogg was unlikely predicting his own death.

[2] Oliver Knight, *Following the Indian Wars, The Story of the Newspaper Correspondents Among the Indian Campaigners* (Norman: University of Oklahoma Press, 1960), p. 203.

[3] Oliver Gramling *AP, The Story of News* (New York: Farrar and Rinehart Inc., 1940), p. 87.

[4] John C. Hixon, "Custer's 'Mysterious' Mr. Kellogg," *North Dakota History*, July 1950, pp. 145-163.

[5] J.W. Vaughn, "The Mark H. Kellogg Story," *The Westerners New York Posse Brand Book* (New York: The Westerners New York Posse, 1961), Vol. 7, No. 4 (1961), pp. 73-91.

[6] Lewis O. Saum, "Colonel Custer's Copperhead: The Mysterious Mark Kellogg," *Montana The Magazine of Western History* (Helena: Montana Historical Society, 1978), Vol. 28, pp. 12-25.

[7] *Brainerd Tribune*, Oct. 19, 1872, p. 1; *Brainerd Tribune*, Nov. 23, 1872. p. 1.

[8] *Brainerd Daily Dispatch*, May 20, 1971, Centennial Edition, n.p.

[9] *St. Paul Daily Pioneer*, July 7, 1876, p. 4. The author also located a number of news briefs from Brainerd and Bismarck that did not carry the Frontier reference but appeared to have been written by Kellogg. In addition, a number of other columns, written under different pen names from many locales in Minnesota, were likely written by Kellogg.

[10] See Michael Moore and Michael Donahue, "Gibbon's Route to Custer Hill," *Greasy Grass* (Hardin, Mont.: Custer Battlefield Historical & Museum Association, 1991), Vol. 7, pp. 22-32.

[11] Dunn was born Christmas Day, 1839, in Lawrenceburg, Ind. In the 1850s, he lived in Indianapolis. He attended Indiana University in 1856 and fought with the Union Army in the Civil War. In the early 1870s, he

lived first in Brainerd, Minn., working as a druggist, before moving in mid-1872 to Edwinton, D.T., later renamed as Bismarck.

[12] *Bismarck Daily Tribune*, June 29, 1895, p. 3.

[13] A number of fine works exist on the background of the 1876 campaign. See Robert M. Utley, *Cavalier in Buckskin* (Norman: University of Oklahoma Press, 1988); Richard Allan Fox, *Archaeology, History, and Custer's Last Battle* (Norman: University of Oklahoma Press, 1993); John S. Gray, *Centennial Campaign* (Ft. Collins, Colo.: The Old Army Press, 1976); and Jerome A. Greene, *Battles and Skirmishes of the Great Sioux War, 1876-1877* (Norman: University of Oklahoma Press, 1993).

[14] For more details on the day-to-day activities of the various columns throughout the campaign, see the following books by James Willert: *Little Big Horn Diary: Chronicles of the 1876 Indian War* (La Mirada, Calif.: James Willert Publisher, 1982) and *March of the Columns, A Chronicle of the 1876 Indian War, June 27-September 16* (El Segundo, Calif.: Upton and Sons, 1994).

[15] *Bismarck Tribune*, Sept. 27, 1876, p. 1.

[16] Christina Dunn Miscellaneous Papers, Fannie Dunn Quain Collection, State Historical Society of North Dakota.

[17] Timothy Hopkins, *The Kelloggs in the Old World and the New* (San Francisco: Sunset Press and Photo Engraving Co., 1903). Photocopies of pertinent pages provided to the author by Leonard F. Kellogg without page numbers. All Kellogg genealogy is from this source, except where noted.

[18] Vaughn, "The Mark H. Kellogg Story," pp. 73-91.

[19] Vaughn, "The Mark H. Kellogg Story," p. 73.

[20] The author and the late Professor Leonard F. Kellogg, a collateral descendant of Mark Kellogg, exchanged numerous letters before his death in 1990. He determined that Vaughn erred in his interpretation of some of the family's genealogy, which he corrected.

[21] Enos's father was Jabez (1734-1791 — Mark's great-grandfather), who served with the militia during the early Indian wars and later fought in the 1776 Battle of Bunker Hill in the American Revolution. Jabez's father was Joseph Kellogg (1685-? — Mark's great-great-grandfather), who was born in Hadley, Mass. Mark's great-great-great-grandfather was John Kellogg (1656-?) of Farmington, Conn., and Hadley, Mass. John's father (Mark's great-great-great-great-grandfather) was Lt. Joseph Kellogg (dates unknown), who was one of three brothers who immigrated to the Boston area in the mid-1600s. He

reportedly married twice and within both marriages had 20 children. He likely was the actual "Prodigious Progenitor" referred to by Vaughn. Joseph was the son of Martin Kellogg of Great Leighs and Braintree, England, and his father was the aforementioned Phillippe Kellogg.

[22] Vaughn, "The Mark H. Kellogg Story," p. 74.

[23] *Waukegan Weekly Gazette*, Oct. 9, 1850, p. 1.

[24] *Waukegan Weekly Gazette*, March 15, 1851, p. 4.

[25] *Waukegan Weekly Gazette*, July 8, 1876, p. 2.

[26] *Waukegan Weekly Gazette*, July 15, 1876, p. 2. The author of the item could not be identified, either from the Waukegan or Dubuque account.

[27] Albert H. Sanford and H.J. Hirshheimer, *A History of La Crosse, Wisconsin 1841-1900* (La Crosse: La Crosse County Historical Society, 1951), p. 9. Much of what follows on the town's history is taken from Sanford and Hirshheimer as well as *History of La Crosse County, Wisconsin* (La Crosse: La Crosse Area Society for Historic Preservation, 1977).

[28] *History of La Crosse County, Wisconsin*, p. 386.

[29] *History of La Crosse County, Wisconsin*, p. 514.

[30] *History of La Crosse County, Wisconsin*, p. 514.

[31] *A History of La Crosse, Wisconsin 1841-1900*, p. 30.

[32] *History of La Crosse County, Wisconsin*, p. 448.

[33] *A History of La Crosse, Wisconsin 1841-1900*, p. 34.

[34] Les Crocker and Caroline B. Heisler, *The Kellogg House* (unpublished manuscript, University of Wisconsin at La Crosse, Area Research Center Files, 1977), p. 1.

[35] *History of La Crosse County, Wisconsin*, p. 408.

[36] *La Crosse Republican-Leader*, Aug. 27, 1871.

[37] *La Crosse County Historical Sketches* (La Crosse, Wis.: La Crosse County Historical Society, 1940), p. 9.

[38] Vaughn, "The Mark H. Kellogg Story," p. 74.

[39] *La Crosse Chronicle*, Jan. 27, 1892, p. 1.

[40] *History of La Crosse County, Wisconsin*, p. 393-394.

[41] *History of La Crosse County, Wisconsin*, p. 394.

[42] *History of La Crosse County, Wisconsin*, p. 394.

[43] *History of La Crosse County, Wisconsin*, p. 401.

[44] *History of La Crosse County, Wisconsin*, p. 402.

[45] Vaughn, in his "Mark Kellogg Story," inaccurately stated the fire occurred in 1867, p. 74.

[46] Crocker and Heisler, *The Kellogg House*, p. 7.

[47] *History of La Crosse County, Wisconsin*, p. 405-406.

[48] *La Crosse Republican-Leader*, July 4, 1876, p. 3.

[49] *History of La Crosse County, Wisconsin*, p. 477-478.

[50] Letter to author from Leonard F. Kellogg, Oct. 11, 1982.

[51] *La Crosse Cross Daily Union*, Oct. 24, 1859, p. 4.

[52] *La Crosse Daily Union*, Nov. 11, 1859. p. 1.

[53] *La Crosse Union and Daily Democrat,* Dec. 20, 1859, p. 1.

[54] *La Crosse Union and Daily Democrat*, Dec. 25, 1859, p. 1.

[55] *La Crosse Union and Daily Democrat*, Dec. 28, 1859, p. 1.

[56] *La Crosse Republican*, Jan. 19, 1860, p. 1.

[57] *La Crosse Union and Daily Democrat*, Feb. 21, 1860, p. 1.

[58] *La Crosse Union and Democrat*, March 8, 1860, p. 1.

[59] *La Crosse Union and Democrat*, March 11, 1860, p. 1.

[60] *La Crosse Union and Democrat*, March 10, 1860, p. 1.

[61] *La Crosse Union and Democrat*, April 16, 1860, p. 1.

[62] Author's interview with Ed Hill, fall 1981, and on subsequent occasions.

[63] *La Crosse Union and Democrat*, May 5, 1860, p. 1.

[64] *La Crosse Tri-Weekly Democrat*, Feb. 19, 1862, p. 2.

[65] Saum, "Colonel Custer's Copperhead," p. 14.

[66] *La Crosse Union and Democrat*, May 15, 1860, p. 1.

[67] Sanford and Hirshheimer, *A History of La Crosse*, p. 107.

[68] *La Crosse Weekly Democrat*, June 6, 1860, p. 2.

[69] *La Crosse Tri-Weekly Union and Democrat*, June 27, 1860, p. 1.

[70] *La Crosse Tri-Weekly Union and Democrat*, Oct. 24, 1860, p. 1.

[71] *La Crosse Tri-Weekly Union and Democrat*, Nov. 12, 1860, p. 1.

[72] *La Crosse Tri-Weekly Union and Democrat*, Nov. 28, 1860, p. 4.

[73] *La Crosse Democrat*, Dec. 3, 1860, p. 2.

[74] *La Crosse Democrat*, Dec. 3, 1860, p. 4.

[75] *History of La Crosse County, Wisconsin*, p. 498.

[76] *La Crosse Tri-Weekly Union and Democrat*, Jan. 11, 1861, p. 1.

[77] *La Crosse Tri-Weekly Union and Democrat*, Jan. 18, 1861, p. 1.

[78] *La Crosse Tri-Weekly Union and Democrat*, March 4, 1861, p. 1.

SANDY BARNARD

[79] *La Crosse Tri-Weekly Union and Democrat*, March 8, 1861, p. 1.

[80] *La Crosse Tri-Weekly Union and Democrat*, March 6, 1861, p. 1.

[81] *La Crosse Tri-Weekly Union and Democrat*, March 15, 1861, p. 1.

[82] *La Crosse Tri-Weekly Union and Democrat*, April 24, 1861, p. 1.

[83] *La Crosse Tri-Weekly Union and Democrat*, April 26, 1861, p. 1.

[84] *La Crosse Tri-Weekly Union and Democrat*, May 20, 1861, p. 2.

[85] A search of the National Archives revealed no military or pension records for Kellogg. In addition, no known account from this period reveals any remarks by Kellogg about Custer.

[86] *La Crosse Weekly Democrat*, Dec. 20, 1861, p. 1, 4.

[87] *La Crosse Tri-Weekly Democrat*, Feb. 5, 1862, p. 1.

[88] *La Crosse Tri-Weekly Democrat*, Feb. 19, 1862, p. 1.

[89] *La Crosse Tri-Weekly Democrat*, April 18, 1862, p. 1.

[90] *La Crosse Tri-Weekly Democrat*, May 21, 1862, p. 1.

[91] *La Crosse Tri-Weekly Democrat*, Aug. 19, 1862, p. 2.

[92] *La Crosse Democrat*, Sept. 9, 1862, p. 4.

[93] *La Crosse Democrat*, Sept. 23, 1862, p. 4.

[94] *La Crosse Weekly Democrat*, Sept. 30, 1862, p. 3.

[95] *La Crosse Weekly Democrat*, Oct. 7, 1862, p. 1.

[96] *La Crosse Weekly Democrat*, Oct. 14, 1862, p. 3

[97] *La Crosse Democrat*, Oct. 21, 1862, p. 1.

[98] *La Crosse Democrat*, Oct. 21, 1862, p. 1.

[99] *La Crosse Weekly Democrat*, Oct. 28, 1862, p. 3. According to a June 29, 1976, memorandum by Ed Hill of the University of Wisconsin at La Crosse Area Research Center, in the museum building of the La Crosse County Historical Society, there is an ad for the *Daily Democrat*. Included are actual photographs, taken by H. C. Heath, of Pomeroy and Kellogg. Kellogg is described as a bookkeeper for the Democrat for that year (1863).

[100] *La Crosse Weekly Democrat*, Dec. 2, 1862, p. 1.

[101] *La Crosse Weekly Democrat*, Feb. 3, 1863, p. 3.

[102] *La Crosse Weekly Democrat*, March 31, 1863, p. 1.

[103] *La Crosse Weekly Democrat*, June 2, 1863, p. 1.

[104] *La Crosse Weekly Democrat*, March 31, 1863, p. 1.

[105] *La Crosse Weekly Democrat*, April 7, 1863, p. 1.

[106] *La Crosse Weekly Democrat*, April 20, 1863, p. 1.

[107] *La Crosse Weekly Democrat*, April 20, 1863, p. 1.

[108] *La Crosse Daily Democrat*, July 3, 1863, p. 1. Whatever became of this box is unknown. Given the inscription, which would be a direct sign of Kellogg's ownership, it no doubt would be quite valuable today.

[109] *La Crosse Daily Democrat*, July 25, 1863, p. 1.

[110] Hopkins, *Kelloggs*, p. 1028.

[111] *La Crosse Weekly Republican*, Sept. 30, 1863, p. 1.

[112] *La Crosse Weekly Republican*, Sept. 30, 1863, p. 1.

[113] *La Crosse Weekly Democrat*, Nov. 17, 1863, p. 1.

[114] *La Crosse Daily Democrat*, Nov. 16, 1863, p. 1.

[115] *La Crosse Daily Democrat*, Nov. 16, 1863, p. 1.

[116] *La Crosse Daily Democrat*, Nov. 17, 1863, p. 1.

[117] *La Crosse Weekly Democrat*, Dec. 4, 1863, p. 3.

[118] *La Crosse Weekly Democrat*, Jan. 26, 1864, p. 4.

[119] *La Crosse Weekly Democrat*, June 14, 1864, p. 3.

[120] *La Crosse Weekly Democrat*, June 21, 1864, p. 1.

[121] *La Crosse Weekly Democrat*, June 21, 1864, p. 1.

[122] *La Crosse Weekly Democrat*, July 5, 1864, p. 3.

[123] *La Crosse Weekly Democrat*, July 12, 1864, p. 3.

[124] *La Crosse Weekly Democrat*, Oct. 17, 1864, p. 1.

[125] *La Crosse Weekly Democrat*, Sept. 19, 1864, p. 3.

[126] *La Crosse Weekly Democrat*, March 20, 1865, p. 1.

[127] *La Crosse Weekly Democrat*, March 27, 1865, p. 1. It appeared on March 27, but was written March 22.

[128] *La Crosse Weekly Democrat*, March 27, 1865, p. 1.

[129] *La Crosse Daily Republican*, April 15, 1865, p. 1.

[130] *La Crosse Weekly Democrat*, April 17, 1865, p. 1.

[131] *La Crosse Weekly Democrat*, June 5, 1865, p. 1.

[132] *La Crosse Weekly Democrat*, June 12, 1865, p. 1.

[133] *La Crosse Weekly Democrat*, Sept. 11, 1865, p. 1.

[134] *La Crosse Daily Democrat*, Sept. 14, 1865, p. 1.

[135] *La Crosse Daily Democrat*, Sept. 18, 1865, p. 1.

[136] *La Crosse Weekly Democrat*, Oct. 2, 1865, p. 1.

[137] *La Crosse Weekly Democrat*, Dec. 4, 1865, p. 1.

[138] *History of La Crosse County*, p. 674.

[139] *La Crosse Daily Democrat*, Dec. 29, 1865, p. 1.

[140] *La Crosse Daily Democrat*, Dec. 29, 1865, p. 1.

[141] *La Crosse Daily Democrat*, Dec. 30, 1865, p. 1.

[142] *La Crosse Weekly Democrat*, Jan. 15, 1866, p. 1.

[143] A. *Bailey's La Crosse Directory for 1866-1867* (La Crosse, Wis.: A. Bailey, Publisher, 1866), p. 55. Given the copyright date, likely the book was compiled in early to mid-1866 but was expected to serve the full year 1866-1867

[144] *La Crosse Daily Republican*, Dec. 8, 1866, p. 1.

[145] *La Crosse Daily Democrat*, Jan. 12, 1867, p. 4.

[146] Letter to author from Arthur N. McBain Jr., Grand Chapter of Royal Arch Masons, La Crosse, Wis., Feb. 14, 1983.

[147] James Anderson, secretary for Aurora Lodge No. 100, Brainerd, Minn., provided a 1948 history of the lodge, *Charter Members of Aurora Lodge No. 100*, written by Carl Zapffe. This incident is reported on pp. 42 and 43. The information was obtained from Frontier Lodge No. 45 in La Crosse sometime before.

[148] *La Crosse Daily Democrat*, Feb. 4, 1867, p. 1.

[149] Professor Leonard Kellogg studied the *Democrat's* local news columns during this period and believed they reflect Kellogg's writing hand. Author's correspondence with Leonard F. Kellogg, 1981-1990.

[150] *La Crosse Daily Democrat*, Feb. 26, 1867, p. 1.

[151] *La Crosse Daily Republican*, April 1, 1867, p. 1.

[152] *La Crosse Daily Democrat*, April 1, 1867, p. 1.

[153] *La Crosse Daily Democrat*, April 1, 1867, p. 4.

[154] *La Crosse Daily Republican*, April 3, 1867, p. 1.

[155] *La Crosse Daily Democrat*, May 18, 1867, p. 1. The *La Crosse Daily Republican* published a similar obituary notice on p. 1 that day.

[156] *La Crosse Daily Republican* , May 18, 1867, p. 1.

[157] Bill O'Neal, "Sixguns on the Diamond," *Old West*, Summer 1983, p. 10

[158] O'Neal, "Sixguns," p. 11.

[159] Sanford and Hirshheimer, *History of La Crosse, Wisconsin - 1841-1900*, p. 220.

[160] Sanford and Hirshheimer, *History of La Crosse, Wisconsin - 1841-1900*, p. 220-221

[161] *La Crosse Daily Democrat*, April 11, 1867, p. 4.

[162] *La Crosse Daily Democrat*, April 18, 1867, p. 4.

[163] *La Crosse Daily Democrat*, May 4 , 1867, p. 4.

[164] *La Crosse Daily Democrat*, May 18, 1867, p. 1.

[165] *La Crosse Daily Democrat,* June 4, 1867, p. 4. The *Republican* carried a similar notice on its p. 1.

[166] *La Crosse Daily Democrat,* June 5, 1867, p. 4.

[167] *La Crosse Daily Democrat,* June 17, 1867, p. 4.

[168] *La Crosse Daily Democrat,* June 15, 1867, p. 4.

[169] *La Crosse Daily Democrat,* June 21, 1867, p. 4.

[170] *La Crosse Daily Democrat,* June 22, 1867, p. 4.

[171] *La Crosse Daily Democrat,* July 1, 1867, p. 4.

[172] Researcher James Brust informed the author in February 1995 that he had located a post-Little Big Horn reference to Kellogg in the July 8, 1876, issue of the *Red River Star*, published in Moorhead, Minn. It noted that Kellogg was well-known along the Northern Pacific Railroad as a newspaper correspondent "under the non (sic) de plume of 'Pioneer'."

[173] *La Crosse Daily Democrat,* Jan. 2, 1867, p. 1.

[174] *La Crosse Daily Democrat,* Oct. 7, 1867, p. 2.

[175] *Omaha, Neb., Daily Herald*, May 6, 1868, p. 2. The paper welcomed the new Council Bluffs paper, noting its first issue appeared "Sunday morning last." That would have been Sunday May 3, 1868.

[176] See Saum, "Colonel Custer's Copperhead, The 'Mysterious' Mark Kellogg," p. 12-25. Saum theorizes that Kellogg was much more of an active Copperhead than previously believed. He offers substantial insight into Pomeroy and related political figures who shared, more or less, his views.

[177] *Council Bluffs Democrat*, Aug. 20, 1868, p. 2. That would have placed his arrival in town sometime during October 1867.

[178] *Council Bluffs Democrat*, Aug. 20, 1868, p. 2.

[179] Author's correspondence and interviews with Leonard F. Kellogg, 1981-1990.

[180] Saum, "Colonel Custer's Copperhead," p. 17.

[181] Saum, "Colonel Custer's Copperhead," p. 20.

[182] *Omaha, Neb., Daily Herald*, May 6, 1868, p. 2.

[183] *Omaha, Neb., Daily Herald*, May 6, 1868, p. 2.

[184] *Council Bluffs Democrat,* May 16, 1868, p. 4.

[185] Kellogg lived at the Pacific Hotel during this period. Bushnell's *Business and Resident Directory of Council Bluffs, July 1st, 1868* (Council Bluffs, Iowa: Nonpareil Printing Company), p. 67. This may have been a reprint inasmuch as its title page bears the date 1898 under the printing company's name.

[186] *Council Bluffs Democrat,* May 26, 1868, p. 2.

[187] *Council Bluffs Democrat,* June 3, 1868, p. 4.

[188] *Council Bluffs Democrat,* July 25, 1868, p. 4.

[189] *Council Bluffs Democrat,* Aug. 20, 1868, p. 2.

[190] Henry Mendelson, "A Half Century of Journalism in Council Bluffs from 1849 to 1900," unpublished typescript in Council Bluffs Library, p. 86. The document appears to have been a master's thesis for a graduate student at Creighton University in 1935.

[191] *La Crosse Daily Democrat,* Jan. 6, 1869. p. 1.

[192] *La Crosse Daily Democrat,* Jan. 6, 1869. p. 1.

[193] Saum, "Colonel Custer's Copperhead," p. 22.

[194] J.M. Wolfe, *Council Bluffs Directory for 1869-70* (Council Bluffs, Iowa: Evening Bugle Book and Job Printing House, 1869), p. 79.

[195] Saum, "Colonel Custer's Copperhead," p. 19.

[196] *La Crosse City Directory and Business Advertiser for 1870-71* (La Crosse, Wis.: Democrat Book and Job Printing Office, 1870), p. 73, p. 104.

[197] *St. Paul Pioneer-Press,* Jan. 22, 1876, p. 4.

[198] Charles R. Wood, *The Northern Pacific, Main Street of the Northwest* (Seattle, Wash.: Superior Publishing Co., 1968), p. 9.

[199] Wood, *Northern Pacific,* p. 18.

[200] Wood, *Northern Pacific,* p. 20.

[201] *La Crosse Republican and Leader,* Oct. 8, 1871, p. 4.

[202] *La Crosse Republican and Leader,* Aug. 16, 1871, p. 2.

[203] *Bismarck, N.D., Tribune,* May 5, 1875, p. 4.

[204] *Bismarck, N.D., Tribune,* Sept. 11, 1917, p. 4.

[205] *Brainerd, Minn. Tribune,* July 31, 1872, p. 1. A news brief notes that a Mr. Clapp has taken over the Brainerd Drug Store.

[206] *La Crosse Republican and Leader,* Nov. 25, 1871, p. 2.

[207] *St. Paul Daily Pioneer,* July 12, 1872, p. 3.

[208] *St. Paul Daily Pioneer,* July 27, 1872, p. 2.

[209] *St. Paul Daily Pioneer,* Aug. 1, 1872, p. 2.

[210] *St. Paul Daily Pioneer,* Aug. 2, 1872, p. 2.

[211] *Brainerd Tribune,* Aug. 31, 1872, p. 1.

[212] Hopkins, *The Kelloggs,* p. 1028.

[213] *Brainerd Tribune,* July 15, 1876, p. 1.

[214] *Brainerd Daily Dispatch*, Aug. 17, 1918, p. 4.

[215] *St. Paul Pioneer*, Aug. 24, 1872, p. 2.

[216] *Brainerd Tribune*, Aug. 24, 1872, p. 1.

[217] *Brainerd Tribune*, Aug. 24, 1872, p. 1. Reference provided by James Brust.

[218] *St. Paul Pioneer*, Aug. 25, 1872, p. 2.

[219] *Duluth, Minn., Tribune,* Aug. 25, 1872, p. 3.

[220] *Brainerd Tribune*, Aug. 31, 1872, p. 1.

[221] *St. Paul Pioneer*, Sept. 12, 1872, p. 2.

[222] *Duluth, Minn., Tribune,* Sept. 19, 1872, p. 1.

[223] *Brainerd Tribune*, Oct. 5, 1872, p. 1.

[224] *St. Paul Pioneer*, Sept. 27, 1872, p. 2.

[225] "Brainerd of '70s Called 'Roaring Camp of Vice'," *Brainerd Daily Dispatch*, Unnumbered section and page, Centennial Edition, May 20, 1971.

[226] *Brainerd Tribune*, Oct. 26, 1872, p. 1.

[227] *Brainerd Tribune*, Oct. 5, 1872, p. 1.

[228] *St. Paul Pioneer*, March 19, 1873, p. 2.

[229] *Brainerd Tribune*, Nov. 9, 1872, p. 1.

[230] *St. Paul Pioneer*, Nov. 14, 1872, p. 2.

[231] *Brainerd Tribune*, Nov. 16, 1872, p. 1.

[232] *Brainerd Tribune*, Dec. 7, 1872, p. 1.

[233] *Duluth Tribune*, Nov. 14, 1872, p. 1.

[234] *Duluth Tribune,* Nov. 16, 1872, p. 2.

[235] Zapffe, *Charter Members of Aurora Lodge No. 100*, p. 27, 29.

[236] *Brainerd Tribune*, Oct. 19, 1872, p. 1.

[237] *Brainerd Tribune*, Nov. 23, 1872, p. 1.

[238] *Brainerd Tribune*, Feb. 8, 1873, p. 4.

[239] Zapffe, *Charter Members of Aurora Lodge No. 100,* p. 43.

[240] Letter to Author, Harvey R. Hansen, May 16, 1983.

[241] *St. Paul Pioneer*, Jan. 29, 1873, p. 2.

[242] Wood, *The Northern Pacific*, p. 21-22.

[243] Carl Zapffe, *Seventy-five Year, Aurora Lodge No. 100, Brainerd, Minnesota, 1872-1947* (Brainerd: Aurora Lodge No. 100, 1947), p. 8.

[244] *St. Paul Pioneer*, Feb. 12, 1873, p. 2.

[245] *St. Paul Pioneer*, Feb. 16, 1873, p. 3.

[246] *St. Paul Pioneer*, Feb. 25, 1873, p. 2.

[247] St. Paul Pioneer, March 5, 1873, p. 2.

[248] St. Paul Pioneer, March 19, 1873, p. 2.

[249] St. Paul Pioneer, March 20, 1873, p. 2.

[250] St. Paul Pioneer, April 3, 1873, p. 2.

[251] St. Paul Pioneer, April 15, 1873, p. 2.

[252] See George F. Bird and Edwin J. Taylor Jr., Part I, *History of the City of Bismarck, North Dakota, The First 100 Years, 1872-1972* (Bismarck: Bismarck Centennial Association, 1972). The book notes that the Whistler Expedition of 1871 involving Rosser comprised 500 soldiers, 50 Indian scouts and 100 wagons. The 1872 expedition, again involving Rosser, was led by Gen. David Stanley and left Fort Rice, Dakota Territory, July 21, 1872. If Kellogg accompanied either, it likely was the 1871 expedition.

[253] St. Paul Pioneer, May 1, 1873, p. 3.

[254] St. Paul Pioneer, May 13, 1873, p. 2.

[255] St. Paul Pioneer, May 16, 1873, p. 2.

[256] Bird and Taylor, *History of the City of Bismarck,* p. 5.

[257] Marshall H. Jewell, *Jewell's First Annual Directory of the City of Bismarck,* (Bismarck, 1879), p. 10.

[258] Bird and Taylor, *History of the City of Bismarck,* p. 17-18. The authors claim that Dunn established his Pioneer Drug Store in May 1872. Jewell's Directory gives the same date, p. 15.

[259] Bird and Taylor, *History of the City of Bismarck,* p. 21.

[260] Bird and Taylor, *History of the City of Bismarck,* p. 21. In their respective works, the authors (p. 25) and Jewell (p. 14) state the town's name was changed to honor Germany's "Iron Chancellor," Prince Otto von Bismarck, in an attempt to entice German aid in financing the railroad.

[261] Jewell, *Jewell's Directory,* p. 22. See also Elwyn B. Robinson, *History of North Dakota* (Lincoln, Neb.: University of Nebraska Press, 1982), p. 316.

[262] Frank E. Vyzralek, "Clement A. Lounsberry, Journalist & Historian," *Plains Talk,* Summer 1971, p. 3.

[263] St. Paul Pioneer, June 6, 1873, p. 2.

[264] St. Paul Pioneer, June 2, 1873, p. 1.

[265] St. Paul Pioneer, June 22, 1873, p. 2. Inasmuch as he claimed that he knew the location where Rosser was halted in 1872, that raises the possibility he accompanied that year's expedition, although the timing of his writings would seem to preclude that. See note 250.

[266] *St. Paul Pioneer*, July 8, 1873, p. 3.

[267] *Bismarck Tribune*, July 11, 1873, p. 1.

[268] Clement A. Lounsberry, "In Ye Olden Time," *Bismarck Daily Tribune*, July 6, 1895, p. 4.

[269] *Bismarck Tribune*, July 11, 1873, p. 1.

[270] *Bismarck Tribune*, July 23, 1873, p. 2.

[271] *Bismarck Tribune*, July 23, 1873, p. 4.

[272] *St. Paul Pioneer*, July 24, 1873, p. 2.

[273] *St. Paul Pioneer*, Aug. 2, 1873, p. 1.

[274] *Bismarck Tribune*, Aug. 6, 1873, p. 4.

[275] *Bismarck Tribune*, Aug. 13, 1873, p. 1.

[276] *Bismarck Tribune*, Aug. 27, 1873, p. 2.

[277] *Brainerd Tribune*, Oct. 4, 1873, p. 1.

[278] Vaughn, "The Mark H. Kellogg Story," p. 85; Hixon, "Custer's 'Mysterious' Mr. Kellogg," p. 149.

[279] *St. Paul Pioneer*, Nov. 16, 1873, p. 2.

[280] B.F. Slaughter papers, State Historical Society of North Dakota.

[281] "Tribune Founded by Col. Lounsberry as Weekly, July 11, 1873, Chronicled Stirring Drama of Pioneer Days," *Bismarck Tribune Jubilee Edition*, July 11, 1923.

[282] O'Neil himself would come to a violent end the next year when he was shot to death. *Bismarck Tribune*, Dec. 16, 1874, p. 4.

[283] *St. Paul Pioneer*, Nov. 21, 1873, p. 2.

[284] *St. Paul Pioneer*, Jan. 28, 1874, p. 2.

[285] *St. Paul Pioneer*, Feb. 6, 1874, p. 2.

[286] *St. Paul Pioneer*, March 19, 1874, p. 2. This column was actually written almost a month earlier on Feb. 23.

[287] *St. Paul Pioneer*, March 28, 1874, p. 2.

[288] *Bismarck Tribune*, April 15, 1874, p. 5.

[289] *Bismarck Tribune*, April 15, 1874, p. 4.

[290] *St. Paul Pioneer*, April 23, 1874, p. 2. According to the *Bismarck Tribune* of May 27, 1874, the Burleigh County Pioneers included some 75 people who promised to promote the social, business and agricultural interests of Bismarck and its vicinity.

[291] *Bismarck Tribune*, May 6, 1874, p. 3.

[292] *St. Paul Pioneer*, June 5, 1874, p. 2.

[293] Vaughn, "Mark H. Kellogg Story," p. 85-86.

[294] Joseph Henry Taylor, *Frontier and Indian Life and Kaleidoscopic Lives* (Valley City, N.D.: Washburn's 50th Anniversary Committee, 1932), p. 114-116.

[295] *Bismarck Tribune*, Aug. 19, 1874, p. 3.

[296] *Bismarck Tribune*, Oct. 14, 1874, p. 2.

[297] St. Paul Pioneer, Dec. 27, 1874, p. 2.

[298] See Robert M. Utley, *Cavalier in Buckskin* (Norman: University of Oklahoma Press, 1988), p. 151-153.

[299] Utley, *Cavalier*, p. 153.

[300] *New York Herald*, July 9, 1876, p. 4.

[301] Hixon, "Custer's 'Mysterious' Mr. Kellogg," p. 150.

[302] *St. Paul Pioneer*, Dec. 27, 1874, p. 2.

[303] *St. Paul Pioneer*, March 27, 1875, p. 2.

[304] *St. Paul Daily Pioneer-Press*, July 30, 1875, p. 2.

[305] *St. Paul Daily Pioneer-Press*, Aug. 18, 1875, p. 2.

[306] *St. Paul Pioneer*, March 27, 1875, p. 2.

[307] *Bismarck Tribune*, April 7, 1875. p. 2.

[308] *St. Paul Pioneer-Press*, April 25, 1875, n.p.

[309] *Bismarck Tribune*, April 21, 1875. p. 1.

[310] *St. Paul Pioneer-Press*, June 25, 1875, p. 2.

[311] *Fargo Record*, May 1896, p. 20.

[312] *Bismarck Tribune*, Sept. 6, 1875. p. 2.

[313] *Bismarck Tribune*, Aug. 25, 1875. p. 2.

[314] *Bismarck Tribune*, Oct. 13, 1875. p. 2; *Bismarck Tribune*, Dec. 22, 1875. p. 8.

[315] *Bismarck Tribune*, Nov. 3, 1875. p. 1.

[316] *Bismarck Tribune*, Oct. 20, 1875. p. 3.

[317] *St. Paul Pioneer-Press*, Jan. 22, 1876, p. 4.

[318] *St. Paul Pioneer-Press*, Feb. 10, 1876, p. 4.

[319] Clement A. Lounsberry, *Early History of North Dakota*, p. 315.

[320] Lounsberry, *Fargo Record*, May 1896, p. 20.

[321] Lounsberry, *Fargo Record*, January 1897, p. 2

[322] Lounsberry, *Bismarck Tribune*, June 23, 1875, p. 1.

[323] Lounsberry, *Bismarck Tribune*, June 28, 1876, p. 2.

[324] "The Black Hills," *Bismarck Tribune*, Jan. 26, 1876, p. 2.

[325] "The Black Hills," *St. Paul Pioneer*, Feb. 8, 1876, p. 4.

[326] "The Black Hills," *St. Paul Pioneer*, p. 4.

[327] Lounsberry, *Early History of North Dakota, 1919*, p. 314.

[328] "The Black Hills," *St. Paul Pioneer*, p. 4.

[329] *Bismarck Tribune*, March 29, 1876, p. 1.

[330] *Bismarck Tribune*, March 15, 1876, p. 8.

[331] The family birth information was provided to the author during an interview in June 1983 with Helen Adele Lounsberry Hennessy, a daughter of Clement Lounsberry's fourth child, Fred, who himself had been born in Minneapolis Dec. 5, 1873.

[332] Interview with Mrs. Hennessy, June 1983.

[333] John S. Gray, *Centennial Campaign*, p. 58.

[334] *Bismarck Tribune*, March 15, 1876, p. 1.

[335] *Bismarck Tribune*, March 15, 1876, p. 1.

[336] *Bismarck Tribune* , March 22, 1876, p. 8.

[337] His 1874 correspondent, Nathan H. Knappen, had, by 1876, returned to Minnesota.

[338] Mark H. Kellogg, "Diary," *North Dakota History*, Vol. 7, July 1950, p. 171.

[339] Elizabeth B. Custer, *Boots and Saddles, or, Life in Dakota with General Custer* (Norman: University of Oklahoma Press, 1980), pp. 209-215.

[340] Oliver Knight, "Mark Kellogg Telegraphed for Custer's Rescue," *State Historical Society of North Dakota Quarterly*, Spring 1960, p. 95-99.

[341] Elizabeth Custer, *Boots and Saddles*, p. 273.

[342] Elizabeth Custer, *Boots and Saddles*, p. 212.

[343] Clement A. Lounsberry, "A Story of 1876," *Fargo Record*, January 1897, p. 2-4.

[344] *Bismarck Tribune*, March 22, 1876, p. 8.

[345] *Bismarck Tribune*, March 22, 1876, p. 8

[346] *Bismarck Tribune*, April 26, 1876, p. 4.

[347] *La Crosse Liberal Democrat*, July 16, 1876, p. 4.

[348] *Bismarck Tribune*, May 3, 1876, p. 1.

[349] *Bismarck Tribune*, May 24, 1876, p. 1.

[350] *Brainerd Tribune*, June 3, 1876, p. 1.

[351] *Brainerd Tribune*, June 10, 1876, p. 1.

[352] *Bismarck Tribune*, May 17, 1876, p. 1.

[353] Mrs. John P. Dunn, Works Project Administration Historical Data Project Records Series 529, Box 18, Pioneer Biography Files, State

Historical Society of North Dakota. She was interviewed about her recollections of pioneer Bismarck in the late 1930s.

[354] Letter to R.P. Johnson from Fannie Dunn Quain, Oct. 6, 1947. Fannie Dunn Quain Collection, State Historical Society of North Dakota.

[355] Christina Dunn Miscellaneous Papers, Fannie Dunn Quain Collection, State Historical Society of North Dakota.

[356] Utley, *Cavalier in Buckskin*, p. 162.

[357] Gray, *Centennial Campaign*, p. 70.

[358] *Bismarck Tribune*, July 19, 1876, p. 4.

[359] Lounsberry, *Fargo Record*, August, 1895, p. 4.

[360] Letter of Clement Lounsberry to Walter Camp, Oct. 16, 1911, Camp Collection, Brigham Young University.

[361] *Bismarck Tribune*, July 19, 1876, p. 4. Brig. Gen. George Crook had a number of correspondents accompanying his Wyoming Column.

[362] Clement A. Lounsberry, *Early History of North Dakota* (Duluth, Minn.: F.H. Lounsberry & Co., 1913) p. X.

[363] Hixon, "Custer's 'Mysterious' Mr. Kellogg," p. 162.

[364] John Ryan, "One of Custer's First Sergeants Tells Story of Reno's Part in Fight on Little Big Horn," *Hardin (Mont.) Tribune*, June 22, 1923, n.p.

[365] *Bismarck Tribune,* May 17, 1876, p. 1.

[366] Knight, *Following the Indian Wars*, p. 199.

[367] Utley, *Cavalier in Buckskin*, p. 167.

[368] *Bismarck Tribune,* July 12, 1876, p. 2.

[369] Letter of Clement Lounsberry to Walter Camp, Oct. 16, 1911, Camp Collection, Brigham Young University.

[370] *Bismarck Tribune*, May 24, p. 1.

[371] Elizabeth A. Custer, *Boots and Saddles*, p. 218.

[372] Gerald G. Newborg and Richard E. Collin, "The Bloodstain Myth of Mark Kellogg's Notebook," *North Dakota History* (Bismarck: State Historical Society of North Dakota, Winter, 1996), pp. 33-35.

[373] *Bismarck Tribune*, June 14, 1876, p. 2.

[374] Utley, *Cavalier in Buckskin*, p. 168.

[375] Kellogg erroneously states in both his letter and in his diary that Sergeant Stempker, Company L, died Aug. 25, 1873. However, the area where he died and was buried is along the 1873 trail, which may have confused Kellogg. Also, several sources say Stempker died Aug. 26,

1874. See "Mark Kellogg's Diary," *North Dakota History* (Bismarck: State Historical Society of North Dakota, 1950), Footnote 11, p. 168.

[376] Two other *Herald* columns attributed to Kellogg by Knight appeared June 19 and June 27, but some experts, including Robert M. Utley and John S. Gray, attribute these two to Custer himself. The more crisp writing style appears to differ from Kellogg's other works, suggesting that Gray, Utley and others are correct.

[377] Utley, *Cavalier in Buckskin*, p. 172.

[378] *New York Herald*, July 11, 1876, p. 3.

[379] *New York Herald*, July 11, 1876, p. 3.

[380] *New York Herald*, July 11, 1876, p. 3.

[381] *Bismarck Tribune*, July 5, 1876, p. 1.

[382] *Fargo Record*, August 1895, p. 4.

[383] *Sturgeon Bay, Wis., Advocate*, Nov. 15, 1890, n.p.

[384] Letters of Clement Lounsberry to Walter Camp, September and October 1911, Camp Collection, Brigham Young University. The author wishes to acknowledge the assistance of C. Lee Noyes, who brought this correspondence to his attention.

[385] *New York Herald*, July 8, 1876, p. 3.

[386] *Sturgeon Bay, Wis., Advocate*, Nov. 15, 1890.

[387] New York Herald, July 8, 1876, p. 3.

[388] Much of the information on the contents of Kellogg's satchel was provided by Mark Halvorson, curator of collections research, SHSND.

[389] Utley, *Cavalier in Buckskin*, p. 177.

[390] Utley, *Cavalier in Buckskin*, p. 178.

[391] Utley, *Cavalier in Buckskin*, p. 178.

[392] Utley, *Cavalier in Buckskin*, p. 179.

[393] Utley, *Cavalier in Buckskin*, p. 180.

[394] Kenneth M. Hammer, ed., *Custer in '76* (Provo, Utah: Brigham Young University Press, 1976), p. 231.

[395] David Humphreys Miller, *Custer's Fall* (Lincoln, Neb.: University of Nebraska Press, Bison Book edition, 1986), p. 69-70.

[396] Utley, *Cavalier in Buckskin*, p. 185.

[397] Alan and Maureen Gaff, eds., *Adventures of the Western Frontier, Major General John Gibbon* (Bloomington: Indiana University Press, 1994), p. 148.

[398] Charles Kuhlman, "Mark Kellogg Elected to Stay With Custer, Believes Montana Man, " *Bismarck Tribune*, Aug. 15, 1939.

[399] Fox, *Archaeology*, p. 31.

[400] Fox, *Archaeology*, p. 32.

[401] Fox, *Archaeology*, p. 180.

[402] Hammer, *Custer in '76*, p. 79.

[403] Richard G. Hardorff, *The Custer Battle Casualties* (El Segundo, Calif.: Upton and Sons, 1989), p. 122.

[404] George W. Glenn Letter to Walter Camp, undated, Camp Collection, Little Bighorn Battlefield National Monument.

[405] Hammer, *Custer in '76*, p. 136.

[406] Moore and Donahue, "Gibbon's Route," *pp.* 22-32.

[407] James M. Bradley, *Helena (Mont.) Daily Herald*, July 25, 1876.

[408] *New York Herald*, July 8, 1876, p. 3.

[409] *Hardin (Mont.) Tribune*, June 22, 1923, n.p.

[410] Hardorff, *The Custer Battle*, p. 121.

[411] E.A. Brininstool, *A Trooper With Custer* (Columbus, Ohio: The Hunter-Trader-Trapper Co., 1926), p. 46. In his lengthy account, Slaper mentions he had read the 1892 account by Gen. E.S. Godfrey. It's possible Slaper's statements about Kellogg's death site aren't completely original.

[412] *New York Herald*, July 10, 1876, p. 3.

[413] Moore and Donahue, "Gibbon's Route," p. 29.

[414] Letter of Douglas Scott to author, Aug. 20, 1993.

[415] Fox, *Archaeology*, p. 176.

[416] Hammer, *Custer in '76*, p. 252.

[417] Hammer, *Custer in '76*, p. 79.

[418] Camp Collection, Little Bighorn Battlefield National Monument.

[419] *Sturgeon Bay, Wis., Advocate*, Nov. 15, 1890, n.p.

[420] "Errors, Deficiencies, Etc., in the marking of the Battlefield of the Little Big Horn," Camp Collection, Little Bighorn Battlefield National Monument, n.p., n.d.

[421] Don Rickey Jr., *History of Custer Battlefield* (Crow Agency, Mont.: Custer Battlefield Historical & Museum Association, 1967), p. 69.

[422] Letters file, E.S. Luce to the *Bismarck Tribune,* Little Bighorn Battlefield National Monument.

[423] Vaughn, "The Mark Kellogg Story," p. 87-88.

[424] Douglas D. Scott, Richard A. Fox, et al, *Archaeological Perspectives on the Battle of the Little Bighorn* (Norman: University of

Oklahoma Press, 1989), p. 255-256.

[425] Hopkins, *The Kellogg*, p. 1028.

[426] *The War of the Rebellion: A Compilation of the Official records of the Union and Confederate Armies, Series I, Vol. XLVI, Part I* (Washington, D.C.: Government Printing Office, 1894), p. 1047-1049.

[427] Vyzralek, *Plains Talk*, p. 2.

[428] *Bismarck Daily Tribune*, July 6, 1894, p. 4.

[429] *Bismarck Tribune*, July 12, 1876, p. 1.

[430] *Bismarck Tribune*, July 12, 1876, p. 2.

[431] *New York Herald*, July 10, 1876, p. 3.

[432] *New York Graphic*, July 10, 1876, p. 56. The term apparently refers to Buncombe, a county of western North Carolina whose congressman in 1820 felt obligated to give a dull speech "for Buncombe."

[433] *New York Herald*, July 10, 1876, p. 3.

[434] *New York Evening Post*, July 11, p. 2.

[435] *Council Bluffs Nonpareil*, July 17, 1876, p. 4.

[436] *Bismarck Tribune*, July 19, 1876, p. 4.

[437] *Bismarck Tribune*, July 19, 1876, p. 4.

[438] Letter from Mrs. Charles Robinson (Kellogg's mother-in-law) to John P. Dunn, March 4, 1877. Contained in Fannie Dunn Quain Collection, State Historical Society of North Dakota.

[439] Christina Dunn Miscellaneous Papers, Fannie Dunn Quain Collection, State Historical Society of North Dakota.

[440] Mrs. Robinson's letter was written on the letterhead of "Lillie J. Robinson, General Superintendent of the Juvenile Temples" in La Crosse. Hannah's other daughter was Eliza Jane Robinson, who apparently was known as Lillie. A CDV of Eliza in the author's collection bears on the reverse the signature "Lillie Robinson."

[441] *Pomeroy's Democrat*, July 15, 1876, p. 4.

[442] *Fargo Record*, August 1895, p. 4.

[443] *Bismarck Tribune*, July 6, 1894, p. 4; Lounsberry, *Early History*, p. 316.

[444] Letters of Clement Lounsberry to Walter Camp, September and October 1911, Camp Collection, Brigham Young University.

[445] Letter of John M. Carnahan to William A. Falconer, File B112, William A. Falconer, 1859-1943.

[446] Undated newspaper clipping, H.R. Porter Scrapbook, State Historical Society of North Dakota.

[447] Newspaper clipping, apparently *Bismarck Tribune* for 1954.

[448] *Bismarck Tribune*, June 15, 1940, p. 1.

[449] *Bismarck Tribune*, July 9, 1921, n.p.

[450] *Bismarck Tribune*, June 24, 1921, n.p.

[451] Vaughn, "Mark H. Kellogg Story," p. 89.

[452] Bridgeport, Conn., City Directory, 1880-1881.

[453] Copy of Record of Death, Commonwealth of Massachusetts, No. 60344.

[454] In September 1981, the author visited the cemetery and located the graves of the two women. In his article, Vaughn erred by saying Mattie died in June 1953 in Lowell, Mass. He was relying on the memory of Lillie Disbrow, identified as a cousin of Mattie's son, Franklin. However, Mattie's Massachusetts' death certificate, obituary notices and cemetery burial records confirm she died June 1, 1917.

[455] Phone interview with Winifred Stewart, Chico, Calif., Feb. 2, 1996.

[456] Letter of Richard Balch, Chico, Calif., to author, July 1983.

[457] Letter of Richard Balch, Chico, Calif., to author, September 1983

SANDY BARNARD

Bibliography

I. MANUSCRIPTS AND RECORDS COLLECTIONS

Camp, Walter M. Collection of papers, Little Big Horn Battlefield National Monument, Crow Agency, Mont.; Lilly Library, Indiana University, Bloomington, Ind.; Brigham Young University, Provo, Utah

Custer, Elizabeth Bacon. Collection of papers, Little Big Horn Battlefield National Monument, Crow Agency, Mont.

Dunn, Mrs. John P., Works Project Administration Historical Data Project Records Series 529, Box 18, Pioneer Biography Files, State Historical Society of North Dakota

Miscellaneous Files, Bridgeport, Conn., Public Library

Miscellaneous Files, La Crosse, Wis., Public Library

Miscellaneous Files, Minnesota Historical Society

Miscellaneous Files, Little Bighorn Battlefield National Monument

Miscellaneous Files, North Dakota Historical Society

Miscellaneous Files, University of Wisconsin Area Research Center at La Crosse

National Archives, Records Group 94, Records of the Adjutant General's Office, 1780s-1917

Quain, Fannie Dunn. Collection, State Historical Society of North Dakota

Slaughter, B.F. Collection, State Historical Society of North Dakota

Vaughn, J.W. Collection, American Heritage Center, University of Wyoming

II. GOVERNMENT PUBLICATIONS

War of the Rebellion: A Compilation of the Official Records of the Union and Confederate Armies. Series I, 128 vols. Washington: Government Printing Office, 1902

III. Books

A. *Bailey's La Crosse Directory for 1866-1867* (La Crosse, Wis.: A. Bailey, Publisher, 1866)

Ambrose, Stephen E., *Crazy Horse and Custer: the Parallel Lives of American Warriors* (Garden City, N.Y.: Doubleday & Company Inc., 1975)

Bird, George F. and Taylor, Edwin J., Jr., Part I, *History of the City of Bismarck, North Dakota, The First 100 Years, 1872-1972* (Bismarck: Bismarck Centennial Association, 1972).

Brady, Cyrus Townsend, *Indian Fights and Fighters* (Lincoln: University of Nebraska Press, 1971)

Brady, Cyrus Townsend, *Northwestern Fights and Fighters* (Williamstown, Mass.: Corner House Publishers, 1974)

Brininstool, E. A., *Troopers With Custer* (Columbus, Ohio: The Hunter-Trader-Trapper Co., 1926)

Carroll, John M., *Charley Reynolds, Soldier, Hunter, Scout and Guide* (Mattituck, N.Y.: J.M. Carroll Co., 1978)

Carroll, John M., ed., *Ten Years With General Custer Among the American Indians (and Other Writings by John Ryan)* (privately published, Bryan, Texas, 1980)

Carroll, John M., ed., *They Rode With Custer* (Mattituck, N. Y.: J. M. Carroll & Company, 1987)

Crocker, Les and Heisler, Caroline B., *The Kellogg House* (unpublished manuscript, University of Wisconsin at La Crosse Area Research Center Files, 1977)

Custer, Elizabeth B., *Boots and Saddles, or, Life in Dakota with General Custer* (Norman: University of Oklahoma Press, 1980)

Custer, George A., *My Life on the Plains* (Lincoln: University of Nebraska Press, 1972)

du Bois, Charles G., *The Custer Mystery* (El Segundo, Calif.: Upton and Sons, 1982)

Fougera, Katherine Gibson, *With Custer's Cavalry* (Lincoln: University of Nebraska Press, 1986)

Fox, Richard Allan, *Archaeology, History, and Custer's Last Battle* (Norman: University of Oklahoma Press, 1993)

Frost, Lawrence A., *General Custer's Libbie* (Seattle: Superior Publishing Co., 1976)

Frost, Lawrence A., *The Court-Martial of General George Armstrong Custer* (Norman: University of Oklahoma Press, 1968)

Gaff, Alan and Maureen, eds., *Adventures of the Western Frontier, Major General John Gibbon* (Bloomington: Indiana University Press, 1994)

Graham, W. A., *The Custer Myth: A Source Book of Custeriana* (New York: Bonanza Books, 1953)

Graham, W. A., *The Story of the Little Big Horn: Custer's Last Fight* (New York: Bonanza Books, 1959)

Gramling, Oliver, *AP, The Story of News* (New York: Farrar and Rinehart Inc., 1940),

Gray, John S., *Centennial Campaign* (Ft. Collins, Colo.: The Old Army Press, 1976)

Gray, John S., *Custer's Last Campaign* (Lincoln: University of Nebraska Press, 1991)

Greene, J.A., *Battles and Skirmishes of the Great Sioux War, 1876-1877* (Norman: University of Oklahoma Press, 1993)

Greene, J. A., *Evidence and the Custer Enigma* (Golden, Colo.: Outbooks, 1986)

Grinnell, George Bird, *The Fighting Cheyennes* (Norman: University of Oklahoma Press, 1983)

Hale, William Harlan, *Horace Greeley, Voice of the People* (New York: Harper & Brothers, Publishers, 1950)

Hammer, Kenneth, ed., *Custer in '76, Walter Camp's Notes on the Custer Fight* (Provo, Utah: Brigham Young University Press, 1976)

Hammer, Kenneth, ed., *Men With Custer: Biographies of the 7th Cavalry* (Hardin, Mont.: Custer Battlefield Historical & Museum Assn., Inc. 1995)

Hardorff, Richard G., *Markers, Artifacts and Indian Testimony: Preliminary Findings on the Custer Battle* (Short Hills, N. J.: Don Horn Publications, 1985)

Hardorff, Richard G., *The Custer Battle Casualties* (El Segundo, Calif.: Upton and Sons, 1989)

Hedren, Paul A., ed., *The Great Sioux War* (Helena: Montana Historical Society Press, 1991)

History of La Crosse County, Wisconsin (La Crosse: La Crosse Area Society for Historic Preservation, 1977)

Hopkins, Timothy, *The Kelloggs in the Old World and the New* (San Francisco: Sunset Press and Photo Engraving Co., 1903)

Hunt, F., and Hunt, R., *I Fought With Custer: The Story of Sergeant Windolph* (New York: Charles Scribner's Sons, 1947)

Hutton, Paul A., *Phil Sheridan and His Army* (Lincoln: University of Nebraska Press, 1985)

Jewell, Marshall H., *Jewell's First Annual Directory of the City of Bismarck*, (Bismarck, 1879)

Karolevitz, Robert F., *Newspapering in the Old West* (Seattle, Wash.: Superior Publishing Co., 1965)

Kraft, Louis, *Custer and the Cheyenne: George Armstrong Custer's Winter Campaign on the Southern Plains* (El Segundo, Calif.: Upton and Sons, 1995)

Knight, Oliver, *Following the Indian Wars: The Story of the Newspaper Correspondents Among the Indian Campaigners* (Norman: University of Oklahoma, 1960)

Kuhlman, Charles, *Legend Into History* (Harrisburg, Pa.: Old Army Press, 1951)

La Crosse County Historical Sketches (La Crosse, Wis.: La Crosse County Historical Society, 1940)

Langellier, J., Cox, K. and Pohanka, B., eds., *Myles Keogh: The Life and Legend of an Irish Dragoon in the Seventh Cavalry* (El Segundo, Calif.: Upton and Sons, 1991)

Leckie, Shirley A., *Elizabeth Bacon Custer and the Making of a Myth* (Norman: University of Oklahoma Press, 1993)

Liddic, Bruce R., ed., *I Buried Custer: The Diary of Pvt. Thomas W. Coleman, 7th U.S. Cavalry* (College Station, Texas: Creative Publishing Co., 1979)

Lounsberry, Clement A., *Early History of North Dakota* (Washington, D.C., Liberty Press, 1919)

MacKaye, Loring, *The Great Scoop* (New York: Thomas Nelson & Sons, 1956)

Miller, David Humphreys, *Custer's Fall* (Lincoln, Neb.: University of Nebraska Press, Bison Book edition, 1986)

Monaghan, Jay, *Custer, the Life of General George Armstrong Custer* (Lincoln: University of Nebraska Press, 1959)

Merington, Marguerite, ed., *The Custer Story: The Life and Intimate Letters of General Custer and His Wife Elizabeth* (New York: Devin-Adair Company, 1950)

Mulford, Ami Frank, *Fighting Indians in the 7th United States Cavalry* (Corning, N. Y.: Paul Lindsay Mulford, 1878)

Nichols, Ronald H., ed., *Reno Court of Inquiry* (Crow Agency, Mont.: Custer Battlefield Historical & Museum Association, 1992)

O'Grady, Donald J., *The Pioneer Press and Dispatch, History at Your Door, 1849-1983* (St. Paul, Minn.: Northwest Publications, 1983)

Overfield, Loyd J., Jr., *Official Documents of the Little Big Horn* (Lincoln: University of Nebraska Press, 1990)

Reedstrom, E. Lisle, *Custer's 7th Cavalry, From Fort Riley to the Little Big Horn* (New York: Sterling Publishing Co. Inc., 1992)

Rickey, Don, Jr., *Forty Miles a Day on Beans and Hay* (Norman: University of Oklahoma Press, 1989)

Rickey, Don, Jr., *History of Custer Battlefield* (Crow Agency, Mont.: Custer Battlefield Historical & Museum Association, 1967)

Riegel, Robert E., *The Story of the Western Railroads* (Lincoln, Neb.: Bison Books, 1964)

Robinson, Elwyn B., *History of North Dakota* (Lincoln, Neb.: University of Nebraska Press, 1982)

Sanford, Albert H. and Hirshheimer, H.J., *A History of La Crosse, Wisconsin 1841-1900* (La Crosse: La Crosse County Historical Society, 1951)

Scott, Douglas D., and Fox, R. A., Jr., *Archaeological Insights into the Custer Battle* (Norman: University of Oklahoma, 1987)

Scott, Douglas D., ed., *Papers on Little Big Horn Battlefield Archaeology: The Equipment Dump, Marker 7, and the Reno Crossing* (Lincoln, Neb.: J&L Reprint Company, 1991)

Scott, Douglas D., et al, *Archeological Perspectives on the Battle of Little Big Horn* (Norman: University of Oklahoma, 1989)

Slotkin, Richard, *The Fatal Environment: the Myth of the Frontier in the Age of Industrialization, 1800-1890* (New York: Atheneum, 1985)

Stewart, Edgar I., *Custer's Luck* (Norman: University of Oklahoma Press, 1955)

Taunton, Francis, B., *Custer's Field: A Scene of Sickening, Ghastly Horror* (London: Johnson-Taunton Military Press, 1986)

Taylor, Joseph Henry, *Frontier and Indian Life and Kaleidoscopic Lives* (Valley City, N.D.: Washburn's 50th Anniversary Committee, 1932)

Urwin, Gregory J. W., *Custer Victorious: The Civil War Battles of General George Armstrong Custer* (Lincoln: University of Nebraska Press, 1990)

Utley, Robert M., *Cavalier in Buckskin* (Norman: University of Oklahoma Press, 1988)

Utley, Robert M., *Custer and the Great Controversy: The Origin and Development of a Legend* (Los Angeles: Westernlore Press, 1962)

Utley, Robert M., *Frontier Regulars: The United States Army and the Indian, 1866-1891* (Lincoln: University of Nebraska Press, 1973)

Utley, Robert M., *The Indian Frontier of the American West, 1846-1890* (Albuquerque: University of New Mexico Press, 1984)

Van de Water, Frederic F., *Glory Hunter, A Life of General Custer* (Lincoln: University of Nebraska Press, 1988)

Wengert, James W., *The Custer Dispatches: The Words of the New York Herald Correspondents in the Little Big Horn Campaign of 1876* (Manhattan, Kan.: Sunflower University Press, 1987)

Willert, James, *Little Big Horn Diary: Chronicles of the 1876 Indian War* (La Mirada, Calif.: James Willert Publisher, 1982)

Willert, James, *March of the Columns: A Chronicle of the 1876 Indian War, June 27-September 16* (El Segundo, Calif.: Upton and Sons, 1994)

Wolfe, J.M., *Council Bluffs Directory for 1869-70* (Council Bluffs, Iowa: Evening Bugle Book and Job Printing House, 1869)

Wood, Charles R., *The Northern Pacific, Main Street of the Northwest* (Seattle, Wash.: Superior Publishing Co., 1968)

Zapffe, Carl, *Seventy-five Years: Aurora Lodge No. 100, Brainerd, Minnesota, 1872-1947* (Brainerd: Aurora Lodge No. 100, 1947)

IV. NEWSPAPERS AND MAGAZINES

Bismarck, D.T., Tribune

Brainerd, Minn. Daily Dispatch

Brainerd, Minn. Tribune

Council Bluffs, Iowa, Democrat

Council Bluffs, Iowa, Nonpareil

Duluth, Minn., Tribune

Fargo, N.D., Record

Hardin (Mont.) Tribune

Helena, Mont., Daily Herald

La Crosse, Wis., Chronicle

La Crosse, Wis., Democrat
La Crosse, Wis., Republican
La Crosse, Wis., Republican-Leader
La Crosse, Wis., Daily Union
La Crosse, Wis., Daily Union and Daily Democrat
La Crosse Tri-Weekly Democrat
La Crosse Tri-Weekly Union and Democrat
New York Evening Graphic
New York Evening Post
New York Herald
Omaha, Neb., Daily Herald
St. Paul, Minn., Pioneer
Sturgeon Bay, Wis., Advocate
Waukegan, Wis., Weekly Gazette

V. PERIODICALS

Brust, James S., "Fouch Photo May Be the First," *Greasy Grass* (May 1991)

Huntzicker, William E., "Historians and the American Frontier Press," *American Journalism* (1988, Vol. 5, No. 1)

Knight, Oliver, "Mark Kellogg Telegraphed for Custer's Rescue," *North Dakota Historical Society Quarterly* (Spring 1960)

Moore, Michael and Donahue, Michael, "Gibbon's Route to Custer Hill," *Greasy Grass* (Hardin, Mont.: Custer Battlefield Historical & Museum Association, 1991)

O'Neal, Bill, "Sixguns on the Diamond," *Old West* (Summer 1983)

Saum, Lewis O., "Colonel Custer's Copperhead: The Mysterious Mark Kellogg," *Montana The Magazine of Western History* (Helena: Montana Historical Society, 1978)

Vaughn, J.W., "The Mark H. Kellogg Story," *The Westerners New York Posse Brand Book*, (New York: The Westerners New York Posse, 1961)

Vyzralek, Frank E., "Clement A. Lounsberry, Journalist & Historian," *Plains Talk* (Summer 1971)

Watson, Elmo Scott, "The 'Custer Campaign Diary' of Mark Kellogg," *The Westerners Brand Book 1945-46* (Chicago: The Westerners, 1947)

VII. UNPUBLISHED MATERIALS AND MISCELLANEOUS

Author's phone interviews with Winifred Stewart, February and March 1996.

Author's interview with Ed Hill, 1981, 1983, 1985, 1988 and 1993

Author's interviews and correspondence with Leonard F. Kellogg, 1981-1990

Author's interview with Helen Adele Lounsberry Hennessy, June 1983

Letters of Richard Balch, Chico, Calif., to author, July and September 1983

Letter to author from Arthur N. McBain Jr., Feb. 14, 1983

Letter to author from Harvey R. Hansen, May 16, 1983

Letter to author from Douglas Scott, Aug. 20, 1993

Henry Mendelson, "A Half Century of Journalism in Council Bluffs from 1849 to 1900," unpublished typescript in Council Bluffs, Iowa, Public Library. Master's thesis, Creighton University, 1935.

Zapffe, Carl, *Charter Members of Aurora Lodge No. 100, A.F 7&A.M.* (Brainerd, Minn.: Aurora Lodge No. 100, 1948)

Kellogg Index

SANDY BARNARD